Palgrave Studies in Professional and Organizational Discourse

Titles include:

Rick Iedema (*editor*)
THE DISCOURSE OF HOSPITAL COMMUNICATION
Tracing Complexities in Contemporary Health Care Organizations

Keith Richards
LANGUAGE AND PROFESSIONAL IDENTITY

H. E. Sales
PROFESSIONAL COMMUNICATION IN ENGINEERING

Forthcoming titles include:

Edward Johnson & Mark Garner
OPERATIONAL COMMUNICATION

Cecilia E. Ford
WOMEN'S TALK IN THE PROFESSIONAL WORKPLACE

Palgrave Studies in Professional and Organizational Discourse
Series Standing Order ISBN 0–230–50648–8
(*outside North America only*)

You can receive future titles in this series as they are published by placing a standing order. Please contact your bookseller or, in case of difficulty, write to us at the address below with your name and address, the title of the series and the ISBN quoted above.

Customer Services Department, Macmillan Distribution Ltd, Houndmills, Basingstoke, Hampshire RG21 6XS, England

Also by Rick Iedema

DISCOURSES OF POST-BUREAUCRATIC ORGANIZATION

The Discourse of Hospital Communication

Tracing Complexities in Contemporary Health Care Organizations

Edited by

Rick Iedema

palgrave
macmillan

First published 2007 by
PALGRAVE MACMILLAN
Houndmills, Basingstoke, Hampshire RG21 6XS and
175 Fifth Avenue, New York, N.Y. 10010
Companies and representatives throughout the world

PALGRAVE MACMILLAN is the global academic imprint of the Palgrave Macmillan division of St. Martin's Press, LLC and of Palgrave Macmillan Ltd. Macmillan® is a registered trademark in the United States, United Kingdom and other countries. Palgrave is a registered trademark in the European Union and other countries.

ISBN-13: 978–1–4039–9848–4 hardback
ISBN-10: 1–4039–9848–5 hardback

This book is printed on paper suitable for recycling and made from fully managed and sustained forest sources.

A catalogue record for this book is available from the British Library.

Library of Congress Cataloging-in-Publication Data
The discourse of hospital communication: tracing complexities in contemporary health care organizations/edited by Rick Iedema.
p. cm. — (Palgrave studies in professional and organizational discourse)
Includes bibliographical references and index.
ISBN 1–4039–9848–5 (cloth)
1. Hospitals—Administration. 2. Health services administration. 3. Health facilities—Administration. I. Iedema, Rick.
RA971.D57 2007
362.11068—dc22 2006049485

10 9 8 7 6 5 4 3 2 1
16 15 14 13 12 11 10 09 08 07

Printed and bound in Great Britain by
Antony Rowe Ltd, Chippenham and Eastbourne

This book is dedicated to all the practitioners we have worked with over the years and who have taught us so much about the complex nature of hospital work.

Contents

List of Figures and Tables

Figures

Tables

Foreword

If any academic work is recognized as a 'good book', by which I mean that it adds to the field it purports to speak about in original ways, it will allow space for the authors' individual approaches to be expressed, but it will nevertheless coalesce around the chosen theme. If it is a really good book, it will deliver a state-of-the-art profile, achieving breakthroughs in analysis and understanding. It will engage its readers, and tantalize them with insights into the intriguing nature of its domain of study. This is such a book.

An academic work that is comprised of the contributions of multiple scholars and practitioners will embody great variety, and its challenge is to create coherence among the interests and concerns of those contributors. Such a work will provide glimpses of an intellectual journey on the part of each of the authors towards a common goal, and it will act as a bellwether of emergent strands thinking as a result. It will tell you a little of where the authors came from, and where they are now as a result of their shared project. The chapters in this volume do this, and it is a fascinating set of journeys and staging points, thanks to the variety of starting points and occupations involved. Read closely and you will discern how this group of researchers has developed penetrating research skills, wide-ranging theoretical understandings and a finely honed appreciation of modern hospitals, clinical practices and health care policy issues. In their own ways, the authors capitalize on their different disciplinary backgrounds, integrating medicine, nursing, anthropology, sociology, discourse analysis and policy analysis in the study of hospital communication and interaction. Together, these perspectives produce an important and innovative set of accounts about the complexity of the contemporary hospital.

As the book explains at a number of points, hospital communication is increasingly at the forefront of the concerns of policy makers, hospital managers, patients and their carers, and clinicians. Because hospital care is becoming more multifaceted thanks to new technologies and treatments, and with patients' trajectories through hospital services becoming more complex as a result, communication is becoming more and more important to the work that people do in hospitals. To this already complicated picture you need to add the rise in social mobility on the part of not just health care workers but also their patients, putting even more pressure on the need to communicate about how to coordinate treatments, professionals and patient trajectories across hospital services. You will not find it surprising in that regard that a recent report issued by a local health authority in Australia states that adequate communication is present less than 50 per cent of the time, the remainder resulting in serious hospital-caused errors of care (Patient Safety and Clinical Quality Programme, 2005).

I have been fortunate to observe the development of this book and the work that it contains. Its authors are driven by a common calling – to wonder about hospital-based clinical practice, reflect on its intricacies, and enquire into how it could work better. The work of these authors provides fascinating accounts of the relationships and communications between clinical professionals, a domain that has thus far not been adequately addressed in the social scientific, clinical professional, and health services literatures. It is for that reason that *The Discourse of Hospital Communication* constitutes an important and timely addition. Many constituent threads of how clinicians organize and negotiate aspects of their work are displayed, discussed, deconstructed, assessed, reviewed and laid bare in ways thus far not publicly recorded. Collectively, these chapters show that communicating hospital work is complex, important, fascinating and extremely rewarding to research and read about.

This volume will likely be one of those that we will read and reread, returning frequently for additional glimpses into the world of hospitals, to learn what happens 'inside the black box' of hospital care. If you are reading it for the first time, however, accept some advice. Set aside several sessions, for you will need them to do the work justice. Then settle down and enjoy the journey. It will prove to be one of the most intellectually rewarding readings you have ever done.

Reference

Patient Safety and Clinical Quality Programme (2005) *Second Report on Incident Management in the NSW Public Health System 2004–2005* (North Sydney: NSW Department of Health).

Jeffrey Braithwaite

Notes on the Contributors

Ellen Barton is a Professor in the Linguistics Programme at Wayne State University (Detroit, USA). Her research interests in medical communication include end-of-life discussions, recruitment to clinical research, the discourse of specialty medical encounters, and, most recently, the emergence of ethical principles and deliberation in situated interactions like those above. Her work appears in the journals *Communication and Medicine, Qualitative Health Research, Discourse Studies, Discourse and Society*, the *Journal of Applied Linguistics, Narrative Inquiry*, the *Journal of Pragmatics* and *TEXT*.

Jeffrey Braithwaite is Associate Professor at the University of New South Wales in Sydney and is a leading health services organizational researcher with expertise in health service restructuring, the culture and structure of acute settings, and leadership, management and change in health sector organizations. He publishes his work in journals such as the *Journal of Health, Organisation and Management, Organisational Studies, Health Services Management Research, Social Science and Medicine*, the *British Medical Journal, The Lancet* and the *Journal of the Royal Society of Medicine*.

B. J. Brown is a Reader in Health Communication at De Montfort University and has published widely on the philosophies of human inquiry, the experience of people in the health care workforce and on social policy in relation to education.

Christopher N. Candlin is Senior Research Professor in Linguistics at Macquarie University, Sydney, and Leverhulme Visiting Research Professor in the Health Communication Research Centre at Cardiff University, UK. His research is in the analysis of professional/institutional discourse, particularly in the domains of health care and law. Recent research includes: the intercultural appraisal of quality of life among HIV+ patients; issues of compliance/concordance in doctor–patient interaction in the context of HIV/AIDS; risk and risk management in health care contexts; and, more generally, the relationship between communicative competence and professional expertise.

A current project with the Royal Australian College of General Practitioners explores expert communication in general practice.

Sally Candlin is an Adjunct Associate Professor at the University of Western Sydney, and Senior Research Fellow in the Department of Linguistics at Macquarie University, Sydney. She is a registered nurse, midwife and health visitor. Her academic qualifications include: BA (Hons) in Linguistics and Psychology, Lancaster University; MSc (Public Health), University of Hawaii; PhD in Linguistics, for her thesis 'Towards Excellence in Nursing: an Analysis of the Discourse of Nurses and Patients in Assessment Situations', from Lancaster University. She has taught in both undergraduate and postgraduate programmes in Nursing and Health in Australia and Hong Kong, as well as in postgraduate programmes in Communication in Professions and Organizations (Linguistics) at Macquarie University, Sydney. Her research and publications are primarily related to issues in health communication.

Paul Crawford is an Associate Professor in Health Language and Communication in Nottingham University's School of Nursing. His interests span communication in health care settings, literature, medicine, and the philosophy of science. In his spare time he enjoys writing fiction and his debut novel *Nothing Purple, Nothing Black* was recently published by The Book Guild.

Anneke Fitzgerald is a Senior Lecturer and Research Studies Programme Coordinator for the College of Business at the University of Western Sydney. After many years as a health manager and educator she pursued an academic career in organization studies. Anneke is currently leading international research into professional identity influences on organizational decision-making comparing triage systems in The Netherlands and NSW, Australia. She also leads a large research project investigating the relationship between working in synch with natural drives and effects on personal well-being.

Dawn Goodwin is ESRC/MRC Post-Doctoral Research Fellow at the Institute for Health Research, Lancaster. Having previously worked as a nurse she undertook her PhD as part of the anaesthetic expertise project described in this chapter and is now developing her interest in Science and Technology Studies to research issues of professional accountability.

Pamela Hobbs is a Lecturer in Communication Studies at the University of California, Los Angeles, where she teaches classes on the First Amendment and language and gender. She received her PhD in Applied Linguistics from the University of California, Los Angeles and her J.D. from the University of Michigan. Her research interests include legal discourse, medical discourse, and language and gender.

Rick Iedema is Professor and Associate Dean (Research) at the University of Technology, Sydney. His research centres on clinical communication in hospitals, focusing on how doctors, nurses, allied health staff, managers and consumers communicate about the organization of hospital work. He publishes his research in journals that include *Organization Studies* and *Social Science & Medicine.*

Christine Jorm has worked as the Lead Medical Clinician for Quality at St George Hospital, Sydney after working for 15 years as full-time anaesthetist. In addition to a doctoral degree in medicine she is now doing a social scientific doctoral research degree into medical cultural identity and how it intersects with clinical quality and safety.

Hannele Kerosuo is a PhD candidate and a researcher at the Centre for Activity Theory and Developmental Work Research, University of Helsinki, Finland. Her doctoral dissertation investigates the boundary dynamics of development, learning and change in multi-organizational fields of health care. She has recently completed projects related to the development of 'negotiated care' and 'knotworking' in health care. Currently, she is doing research on stabilization and diffusion of innovative forms of working and learning in health care projects. Hannele Kerosuo has a professional background in the social and health care administration.

Bonsan Bonne Lee is a spinal injury and rehabilitation medicine specialist, who works as a staff specialist at the Prince of Wales Hospital in Sydney. He has postgraduate masters' degrees in clinical epidemiology and health management, and a graduate certificate in information technology. He has developed innovative approaches to running clinics for his patients devising cross-traditional roles and responsibilities for clinicians, and which have produced successful clinical outcomes. He has an ongoing interest in the sustainability of innovative management interventions, in the changing roles of health care providers, and in the blurring of boundaries which occur while interdisciplinary projects are successfully implemented.

Debbi Long is a medical anthropologist, currently working as a research fellow at the Centre for Clinical Governance Research, University of New South Wales. She has undertaken ethnographic research in a variety of hospital settings, including spinal, intensive care, maternity and pathology laboratory. Her current research involves video ethnography in multidisciplinary clinical teams. She is interested in the use of video as a tool for clinician reflexivity; in developing methodologies for hospital ethnography; and in the application of (video) ethnography for hospital infection control strategies.

Martin Lum is Senior Medical Advisor at the Access and Metropolitan Performance Branch, Metropolitan Health and Aged Care Services, Department of Human Services in Victoria, Australia. Martin has a background in anaesthetics and has special expertise in health organizational change management and clinical practice improvement.

Elizabeth Manias is a registered nurse and pharmacist, and is Associate Professor at the School of Nursing at the University of Melbourne. Her research endeavours include patient safety, interpersonal and organizational communication, and consumer participation. In particular, her work considers different individuals' perspectives and the complexities of the dynamic environment in which communication takes place. Associate Professor Manias has extensive experience and expertise in undertaking hospital ethnographic research in diverse environments, including critical care, post-surgery and emergency care.

Per Måseide is Professor in Sociology at Bodø University College, School of Social Sciences, Norway. He is Director at the Centre of Disability Research, Nordland Research Institute, and teaches sociology of health and illness, social interaction, sociological theory and qualitative methodology. Per Måseide has extensive experience from fieldwork within psychiatric health care systems and somatic hospitals. Per's research interests include doctor–patient interaction, multiprofessional collaboration, the social organization of medical work, medical decision-making and pragmatics.

Maggie Mort is Senior Lecturer in Health Research at the Institute for Health Research, University of Lancaster. Her research expertise is in

Science and Technology Studies and previous work includes studies of telemedicine and telecare; innovation in health science and technology; health policy and politics and health technology and social change.

Catherine Pope is Reader in the School of Nursing and Midwifery, University of Southampton. Her research interests include the evaluation of health services, the organization and delivery of health services, and the sociology of professional practice.

Robin Riley has worked as a clinical nurse for over 25 years. She recently completed her PhD, which involved a discourse analysis of operating room nursing. She has extensive experience in the specialty of operating room nursing, and has worked in public and private hospitals in Australia and internationally. She has published widely in peer-reviewed international journals in the areas of clinical governance and operating room practice. Her research areas of interest include patient safety and risk management.

Andrew Smith is Consultant Anaesthetist at Royal Lancaster Infirmary and Honorary Professor at the Institute for Health Research, Lancaster. His research interests include evidence in clinical practice (he is an Editor in the Cochrane Anaesthesia Review Group), and perceptions of risk and safety in professional practice.

Jo Travaglia is a Research Fellow at the Centre for Clinical Governance Research, the University of New South Wales. Jo has a professional background in social work and a research background in medical sociology, health care services research, diversity and equity issues and adult education. Jo's current expertise is in the area of clinical quality and safety in which she is doing her doctoral research.

1
Communicating Hospital Work

Rick Iedema

Introduction

The focus of this volume is on hospital communication and interaction. Our interest in what goes on in hospitals reflects a general rise in public scrutiny of the enactment and organization of hospital work (Davies and Harrison, 2003; Harrison, 1999). This increase in scrutiny is evident in a number of ways. Over the last decade and a half, we have seen a number of government-level inquiries into highly publicized failures affecting hospitals in the UK, the USA and Australia (Adrian, 2003; Douglas, 2002; Kennedy, 2001; Kohn *et al.*, 1999). Each of these inquiry reports contains the recommendation that the (re)organization of hospital care should be a priority concern for policy makers (UK Department of Health, 1997), health managers (Degeling *et al.*, 2004a) and practitioner clinicians (Berwick and Nolan, 1998). We also know from the public media (Meek, 2001), from policy announcements (UK Department of Health, 2000) and from academic research (McKee and Healey, 2002) that hospitals' organizational profiles and the contours of clinical work are changing rapidly. While many of these changes have been discussed in sociological and organizational theoretical terms (Dent, 1998; Flynn, 1999, 2004; Kitchener, 2000; albeit not to everyone's satisfaction: Davies, 2003), they have only in a very limited way been documented from microsociological, anthropological and discourse analytical perspectives (Iedema, 2003). It is for that reason that the research collected in this volume foregrounds discussions about what is happening in acute care and uses analyses of hospital discourse and interaction. By targeting hospital interactions, the research presented here captures the specifics of how clinicians address the organizational dimensions of care, and how these dimensions are negotiated alongside the patient diagnosis and expert professionalization issues that are more commonly pursued in the literature.

This volume also appears at a time when much large-scale research is being done on how to change and improve health care in the face of social, organizational and technological complexities (Ferlie and Shortell, 2001; Grimshaw and Russell, 1993; Hoff *et al.*, 2004). Central here are concerns about 'barriers to reform', 'reasons for organizational inertia', 'lack of success of change strategies'. These concerns are most frequently addressed in terms of what in clinical terms is seen as 'gold standard' research: a quantification of large numbers of people's views on, and reactions to, reforms. These quantifications become the basis for causal–instrumental claims about 'what works' in influencing clinicians to work differently, more effectively and more efficaciously (Shojania and Grimshaw, 2005). Quantitative research is prevalent in health services research and hospital organizational research, but it runs the risk of obscuring what many of the reforms and proposed improvements mean for clinical professionals 'on the ground' (see Degeling *et al.*, 2004a, b); that is, how these reforms and improvements affect how clinicians enact, informate and communicate about their work. Given the changes that clinicians are facing and the pressures that are being brought to bear on them, describing not just opinions and espoused views but clinical conduct at the level of situated interaction (Greatbatch *et al.*, 2001) may enable policy makers as well as clinicians and clinician-managers to reflect on how professionals manage and organize the interactive details of contemporary health care. In sum, coming to terms with and centring reform debates around how hospital change is realized (or not) in situated interaction is an urgent task.

Perhaps most importantly, the emphasis on 'situated communication and clinical interaction' in this volume derives from the now widely shared acknowledgement that the quality of communications and interactions among clinicians is to a large extent a determiner of the outcomes of their work for patients. The efficacy of what clinicians do for patients – the ultimate protagonists in health care – depends of course in an important way on clinicians' expert-professional acumen. However, it is also increasingly clear that achieving good clinical outcomes for patients is contingent on interprofessional and professional–patient communications about the systematization and dynamic coordination of care processes (Pincock, 2004; Sutcliffe *et al.*, 2004) as well as a 'mindful' negotiation of professionals' mutual expectations and relationships over the substance of care (Weick and Sutcliffe, 2001). These issues are precisely the focus of this book.

Analysing hospital communication and clinical interaction: four aims

Having specified the general orientation of the book, let us now turn to the contribution it seeks to make to the literature. First, the book brings together recent research in the field of hospital communication and interaction done by discourse analysts, communication researchers, activity theorists and workplace studies researchers. In one sense, the book elaborates on work that has been done on clinician–patient communication (Ainsworth-Vaughn, 2003; Fisher and Dundas Todd, 1993; Maynard, 2003), intraprofessional relationships and clinical decision-making (Atkinson, 1995; Labov and Fanshel, 1977; Pettinari, 1988), medical professionalization (Atkinson, 1999; Erickson, 1999; Pomerantz *et al.*, 1995), and the documentational and administrative realities of in-hospital clinical work (Garfinkel, 1967; Rees, 1981), as well as the social dimensions of such clinical information (Cook-Gumperz and Messerman, 1999).

In another sense, the research presented here extends existing work by focusing on in-hospital communication against the background of the increasingly 'crowded clinical space' that is the contemporary hospital, the organizational challenges, clinical complexities and multiple roles that clinicians now have to confront and enact, and the rising levels of public scrutiny targeting what clinicians do and say to each other and to their patients. More specifically, the book acts as a forum for a number of international researchers who are engaged in studying the complex influences that are currently crowding into the clinical space: health policy and hospital reform, ethics guidelines, changing interprofessional positionings, shrinking resources, complex technologies, cross-organizational service agreements, and last but not least, the rising levels of communication work or 'immaterial labour' that characterizes face-to-face interactions among clinicians (Iedema *et al.*, 2006b).

A second contribution of this volume is that it provides a resource for researchers and students in the field of health research more broadly such that they can become acquainted with more detailed analysis of hospital–clinical interaction and communication than is currently available. While the sociology of health and illness has a problematic relationship with health organizational communication (Davies, 2003), applied linguistic and discourse research in health (Candlin and Candlin, 2003) and in hospitals in particular (Iedema, 2005) has at best been intermittent. Applied linguists and discourse researchers have therefore thus far been excluded not just from forums that address the reform of hospital care but also from forums that determine the shape and focus of education about hospital communication. This is all the more unfortunate in light of the contribution that these researchers can make to the growing debate about the structuring of hospital services, and to informing the solutions that are currently being mobilized to deal with these complex issues (Degeling *et al.*, 2004b). As this volume demonstrates, the research methods and analyses presented here are able to throw special light on clinical conducts that are at the interstices between acute care expertise, clinical standards and evidence, hospital ethics, involvement of patients and consumers, and the organization, management and integration of cross-organizational services.

Important too in this regard is that the chapters in this volume are not exclusively the work of discourse analysts, but are also written or co-written by researchers from a range of different and complex backgrounds. Besides discourse analysts with a strong interest in health (Barton, Måseide, C. Candlin), a medical sociologist (Pope) and a medical anthropologist (Long), the book incorporates chapters by social scientists with backgrounds in nursing (Riley, Brown, Fitzgerald, S. Candlin), medicine (Jorm, Lum), allied health (Travaglia), pharmacy/nursing (Manias) and law (Hobbs). This variety of author backgrounds is further evidence of the relevance of discourse research for the exploration of health care and hospital organizational issues not just for the sake of advancing discourse theory, but for the sake of addressing and potentially resolving issues that confront health policy makers, health care practitioners and health managers.

A third contribution is that this volume enriches discourse analysis by testing its methods and approaches in a hitherto little explored site. With some exceptions (Wodak, 1996), discourse research has generally focused on sites that are populated with limited numbers of participants and stakeholders (such as general practitioners' consulting rooms). Replicating medicine's own preferred conception that positions medicine as the essence of hospital work (Colwell, 1995), such focus runs the risk of 'invisibilizing' the extent to which the doctor's work and the patient's treatment trajectory depend on exchanges with others (pathology laboratory scientists, allied health professionals, health administrators and managers, to name but some) in addition to the patient and immediate peers. The chapters brought together in this book bring these more complex facets of clinical work to the fore, showing how hospital work interweaves the contributions of many professionals. But in addressing these complexities, the chapters also come face to face with methodological assumptions that underpin discourse analytical research. Prominent issues here are the shifting boundaries between text and context; between ethnography and language analysis, and between outside observer and inside change agent.

For example, each of the chapters shows that analysts have a lot of intimate sociological and anthropological knowledge of situated medical, nursing, allied health and managerial–administrative practice. This resonates with what Cicourel (1982) noted many years ago:

> Participants of discourse or readers of a text are always engaged in selective use of the information that they can attend to. Limited capacity processing constraints imposed by a complex setting and the participants' knowledge base can sharply reduce the participants' comprehension of what is taking place. The researcher faces similar problems. We normally examine single utterances or connected discourse that run for a few lines, giving careful attention to lexical items, pronominal usage and repetition, the repetition of clauses that give referential prominence to a person, object or event, WH-cleft constructions, IT-cleft constructions, relative clauses, rhetorical questions, and the like; yet we may avoid or be unaware of information that presupposes organizational constraints and complex social relationships that can be obtained only by ethnographic field research. (Cicourel, 1982, p. 53)

The centrality of ethnographic description in the research presented here has important implications for how discourse analysis goes about its business. Because many spheres of social life are becoming more complex, analysis of what goes on inevitably requires more explanation, contextualization and description. At the same time, the emphasis on ethnographic description helps to foreground actors' own concerns and interests, and may lead to a backgrounding of discourse analytical frameworks, technical categories and formal models. Rather than deploying conventional lenses such as hedging, control, power or politeness, this emerging research may instead choose to emphasize the specific problems and logics that are inscribed into sites and their practices. Immersed in ethnography, discourse research is not just a powerful sociological form of analysis, but also a form of enquiry that is of use to practitioners. Of relevance to the present book, this involves using discourse analysis to clarify the problems that clinicians have in coordinating complex services that straddle specialties (see the chapters by Riley and Manias, and by Lum and Fitzgerald); the struggles that result from policy makers seeking to reform hospital organizations and restructure workforce capabilities and rights (see the chapters by Brown and

Crawford, and by Jorm, Travaglia and Iedema), or the organizational–cultural and educational challenges that face health care workers in structuring and integrating their services in ways that benefit the patient (see the chapter by Sally and Chris Candlin).

A fourth contribution of this volume is that it contextualizes clinical–professional discourse with the growing centrality of information and communication in the workplace more generally. As several commentators have emphasized, contemporary workplaces are increasingly being reconfigured into becoming knowledge/information/communication networks (Castells, 1990) that demand not just more knowledge and information, but more *intelligent* and *affective* practices generally: 'today labour and society have to informationalize, become intelligent, become communicative, become affective' (Hardt and Negri, 2004, p. 109). The intelligent and affective dimensions of contemporary work are inherent in it not merely being 'done' but increasingly being 'talked' as well. This means employees have to be able to negotiate difference and dissent among one another, and 'organizationalize' their feelings, relations and selves (Iedema and Scheeres, 2003).

These developments are particularly evident in health care (Iedema *et al.*, 2005) where we are witnessing a particularly strong rise in communication work or 'immaterial labour' (Hardt and Negri, 2004): clinicians are becoming more and more involved not just in 'informationalizing' their work, but also in determining how to act on that information through mutual or self-directed management (Iedema *et al.*, 2006b). In addition to clinicians having to informate their work in increasingly far-reaching ways, the changes in health care organizations confront clinicians with having to renegotiate the bases of their relationships (as recounted in Riley and Manias's chapter); they have to revisit their understandings of what other professionals do (as Kerosuo's and Maseide's chapters show), and they have to carefully balance competing interests and wants (as is evident in Barton's chapter).

Together, communication, the informationalization of care and the devolved management among clinicians serve to create new sites of clinical identification and struggle. They displace old ways of doing and saying and make possible, and *require*, new ones (Rose, 1999). Spending increasing amounts of time on immaterial labour, clinicians are having to invent new rules, genres, rituals and structures with which to govern and 'contain' this immaterial labour (Deetz, 1994). Central here is that clinicians have no choice but to rethink their professional–occupational relationships, their power balances and their self-identities. The hospital policy and health care reform literatures address these matters only tangentially, lacking ways in which to talk about identity, identity change and the performance of identity of clinical employees. It is here in particular that the present volume makes an important contribution.

The contemporary hospital

The hospital is one among the most complex kinds of social organization produced by humankind. This complexity is evident at a number of levels. First, it is inherent in the work that hospitals do, which includes helping mothers to give birth to babies, providing palliative care for people who are dying, with a wealth of medical and surgical interventions in between. These services are provided by a large variety of professionals: doctors who belong to a wide range of specialties, nurses and their various specializations, allied health professionals, clinical and lay managers, medical technologists and pathology laboratory scientists, each of whom is expected to organize their work relationships with each of the others in dynamic and flexible ways in situations where people's lives may be at stake. Second, hospitals are complex environments because the many services just referred to rely on many different mechanical, informational and pharmaceutical technologies. These technologies, moreover, are undergoing constant change, to the point that a clinician who leaves work for a few months will generally need some training upon re-entry. Finally, hospitals' complexity derives from the historical ways in which the clinical professions have negotiated their relationship with the state. Besides a wide variety of clinical certification controls, this relationship encompasses complex funding models, cost hierarchies and resource allocation decision-making. Moreover, these mostly historical arrangements are now coming under challenge from changes in clinical treatment focus, workforce pressures and accountability requirements, with the twenty-first century witnessing growing concerns about how to fund and achieve appropriate levels of clinical quality, safety and service integration.

With people getting older and contracting chronic and co-occurring diseases, and with medicine raising its technological capability with which to take on these diseases, the need to manage this complexity is now acute. Historically, and in most Western nations, the management of hospital processes was built on an uneasy relationship between clinicians and lay administrators. The global economic downturn in the 1970s coupled with rising hospital expenditures motivated governments to target hospitals with more stringent approaches to rationalizing hospital work and to managerialize the clinical work. Policy makers set in train hospital reform processes that encouraged clinicians to assume managerial responsibilities and they began to issue and monitor the deployment of formalized guidelines, procedures and regulations as a means to further closing the gap between clinical practice and policy reform.

While these developments began to be debated in literatures informing medicine, nursing and allied health, as well as in medical sociology and anthropology, they largely left discourse analysis and health communication research untouched. This is all the more surprising given the rising importance of communication and information in the contemporary hospital, and the growing emphasis on these matters in clinical–professional forms of education. Thus, there is a clinical communication research literature that inspects clinicians' interactive processes with patients with the purpose of formulating doctor–patient communication competencies (Hulsman *et al.*, 2005), and a health information management literature that studies options for the storage and handling of clinical information (Hovenga and Lloyd, 2002). The complexities of the communication–information interface have been researched in sociotechnical terms (Berg *et al.*, 2000; Berg and Timmermans, 2000), but less often in interactive terms (Aarts and Peel, 1999; Greatbatch *et al.*, 2001). Research into the interactive dimensions of hospital communication and information practices remains overshadowed by studies that transform the details of situated clinical interaction into a discourse of formal categories, numerical values and causal relationships with the aim of deducing certainty about the effects of particular kinds of behaviour (Lingard *et al.*, 2004).

Complementing this existing body of literature, the present volume addresses the challenges of organizing the contemporary hospital at the level of how hospital employees communicate and interact with one another. In doing so, the book adds to attention thus far accorded by scholars working in discourse analysis to public institutions such as the media and education, and to specific spheres of institutional life such as the courtroom and the GP consultation. At the same time, the book seeks to initiate dialogue with other literatures that have pondered over the challenge of hospital organization and communication for quite some time now, but without the benefit of being able to critically analyse the details of situation interaction or of medical and policy documentation bearing on hospital interaction. To this end, this book presents a range of chapters by scholars from around the world to provide insight into the discourses and practices of the hospital.

An overview of the chapters in this volume

The book's main aim is to illuminate how hospital clinicians coordinate and organize their everyday work. Accordingly, the chapters in the book focus on situated interactions among clinicians, on the ways in which clinicians document their work, and on the discourses that bear on how clinicians do their work. These issues are presented by drawing on empirical data of situated practice, clinical documentation and interview transcripts. These data are analysed to map the tensions that arise from the shifting relationships between clinicians' professional and institutional practices and discourses (Sarangi and Roberts, 1999).

In their own way, the studies collected here illustrate how hospital-based clinical discourse is a 'crowded space'. Rather than just being comprised of expert–clinical talk with peers and patients, this discourse encompasses kinds of talk and writing that reveal and acknowledge the interests and 'the presence' of many other stakeholders, such as policy makers, researchers, professional colleagues, whole patient populations, as well as the public generally. The present studies illustrate the tensions that affect how clinical work is currently done by panning out to take these crowded spaces into account. For example, Hannele Kerosuo's chapter discusses an intervention that showed how complex care can be organized across organizational and service boundaries without information getting lost and patients thereby being put at risk. The challenge taken on here is to institutionalize cross-boundary communications involving GPs, specialists and community carers, and to support these communications with a care management plan that all the parties give their approval to.

In her chapter, Ellen Barton considers how doctors enrol patients in clinical trials without exacerbating the conflict of interest that they already embody in being both doctors that are charged with caring for patients and researchers wanting to experiment on patients. Barton's chapter offers a sensitive description of enrolment discussions, and addresses the ethical constraints that doctors are now answerable to. She carefully delineates the risks of principlism, or the notion that we can impose sweeping normative principles on people's actions without taking account of the specifics of situated practice.

In her chapter, Pamela Hobbs homes in on how various clinicians communicate about the progress of women's pregnancies and deliveries through the obstetrics medical chart. She traces the progress of a pregnant woman from admission to delivery of her baby through a careful reading of how the different clinical professionals write in her chart. Hobbs thereby illustrates how the paper chart is a dynamic device through which clinicians together negotiate and home in on uncertainties and significant developments. Hobbs contextualizes her discussion of this practice with the impending computerization of the medical chart, and offers a view of the issues that an electronic chart confronts in respecting the existing dynamics that link clinical progress and notation.

Robin Riley and Elizabeth Manias's chapter looks at how nurses and surgeons negotiate over the order of patients going into surgery and how they 'manage' their frequently diverging professional priorities and interests in doing so. Riley and Manias reveal 'the list' (the theatre list on which the order of patients going into surgery is documented) as a space of interprofessional contestation and gendered struggle. The nurses are described as being caught in a contradictory position: being responsible for managing the 'domestic' logistics of the operating theatre, they are in a position of relative power that nevertheless turns on their familiarity with, and ability to manoeuvre around, surgeons' personalities and expectations. Riley and Manias conclude the nurses embody a curious 'governmentality': their intimate knowledge of individuals does not automatically translate into power over those individuals, but becomes the basis for their considerable emotional labour to maintain nursing–medicine relationships.

In a companion chapter, Lum and Fitzgerald investigate clinicians' views about how surgery lists are drawn up and changed. Adding to Riley and Manias's perspective from nursing, Lum and Fitzgerald's chapter shines a light on the tensions internal to medicine. In eliciting views on the logic that underpins the surgery list, the authors explore the possibility of referring priority decisions to a shared system of criteria. They find that the grey area that bridges non-urgent cases and highly urgent cases remains permeated with claims and contestations over the perceived importance of some kinds of medical work compared to others. The conclusion that the authors draw from their analysis is that the challenge of uniting clinicians around a common set of criteria with which to manage the surgery list remains.

Looking out towards the impact of health policy on health care work, Brian Brown and Paul Crawford discuss the implications of contemporary UK mental health policies for how health care workers approach their work and their patients. They reveal how UK mental health documentation and related policy and professional guidelines promote a clinical definition of personality disorder as hinging on an unduly 'open-ended self', which contrasts with the reflexive, self-governing and 'ordered' person preferred in contemporary political regimes. At the same time, the mental health care worker's role is increasingly defined and characterized in terms of organizational and occupational flexibility. The contradiction between these two tendencies, they argue, leads to new kinds of uncertainties and contradictions for the individuals who populate the interface between mental health care work and mental disability.

Hannele Kerosuo, drawing on her recent doctoral research, describes clinicians' and patients' involvement in an experiment which she and her colleagues Yrjö and Ritva Engeström devised to enhance the continuity of care across organizational boundaries. This important work devised face-to-face meetings among clinical and community participants in the care process, as well as documentary devices with which to facilitate these interactions and render the information produced there portable. Kerosuo's chapter presents a unique example of how applied social scientific research can extend the communicative and linguistic repertoires of (health) organizational actors.

For their part, Catherine Pope, Maggie Mort, Dawn Goodwin and Andrew Smith describe how anaesthetists coordinate among themselves the application of anaesthetic drugs to their patients while at the same time monitoring the drugs' effect on patients. The seemingly casual talk that anaesthetists engage in with patients is shown to be integral not just to monitoring patient's anaesthetic progress but also to communicating that progress to other members of the anaesthetic team. Safe practice here, far from being a proceduralized and formalized process, is a delicate unfolding of embodied sensitivities and communications that involves the whole anaesthetic team.

Debbi Long, Rick Iedema and Bonne Lee report in their chapter on the complexity of clinicians' corridor interactions, and how these are important for the coordination of their patients' care. The authors show how the talk in one hospital corridor in a spinal pressure sore clinic is different from the talk that takes place in the consulting room, the meeting room and the ward round. Taking place away from the patient and away from formalized organizational spaces, they show that corridor talk is highly dynamic by being oriented towards significant facets in patients' progress and towards specific details of the unfolding care. The space within which the talk occurs makes it possible for clinicians to move dynamically from one to the other without formalized agenda, enabling them to act on what they see as requiring urgent attention or resolution.

Per Måseide investigates the use of X-rays and how radiologists' 'ways of seeing' are heavily interdependent on their 'ways of talking'. Måseide analyses in detail how seeing is dynamically produced from talking, suggesting that the visual object (the X-ray) does not contain 'objective' information in and for itself, but becomes seeable as a result of clinicians' comments, their pointing and questioning, and their intent to draw conclusions from this practice for how to treat their patients.

In their chapter, Christine Jorm, Jo Travaglia and Rick Iedema investigate the construction of personal agency on the part of medical specialists with regard to their relationship with 'the system'. The system represents the organizational context within which these doctors do their medical work, and includes the hospital, the health bureaucracy and the health political stratum. The chapter argues that doctors speak about themselves in ways that construct different kinds of agency, thereby revealing different attitudes towards 'the system'. On one end of the spectrum, doctors see themselves as being able to act, but only in defiance of a system that 'gets in the way'. On the other end, doctors speak about the system in more personalizing terms, using 'we' to suggest they see themselves as integral to 'the system'. These constructions, the authors argue, have crucial implications for how and the extent to which doctors engage with the patient safety agenda, by aligning themselves (or not) with organization-wide initiatives to ensure patients are not harmed while in their clinical care.

Finally, Sally and Chris Candlin reflect on the changes that nursing has undergone over the last three decades. They use the concept of community of practice (CoP) to highlight the complexity of these changes, and in doing so take the opportunity to raise questions about the term 'CoP'. They argue that, given the growing multiplicity of roles inherent in contemporary nursing, the notion of CoP may come up against difficulties. This is because, while in the past nursing was relatively homogeneous in its roles, responsibilities and practices, nursing now encompasses a wide variety of intersecting specializations, such as the nurse practitioner, the community nurse, emergency nursing, intensive care unit nursing, and so forth. The authors also comment on the tensions that have developed between the rising importance of spiritual and emotional labour on the part of nurses to engage with their increasingly older and sicker patients on the one hand, and nurses' growing involvement in technical specializations such as nuclear and neurological medicine on the other, putting considerable pressure on the social and interpersonal dimensions of nursing.

Conclusion

As Davies *et al.* (2000) point out, much health care reform policy is framed within mechanistic and 'Taylorist' approaches to intervening in hospital culture.[1] Prominent in these approaches are 'human factors engineering' (Gosbee and Anderson, 2003) and other techniques such as 'root cause analysis' (Bagian *et al.*, 2002) adopted into health care from the commercial sector (Iedema *et al.*, 2006b). In contrast to these rather mechanistic approaches to understanding and intervening in clinicians' communications and situated interactions, discourse research depicts the formal, non-formal[2] and affective dimensions of communication and interaction (Iedema *et al.*, 2006a). This detail provides not just a better sense of how much goes on between people in their everyday exchanges, but also of the complexity of what they do and say.

Perhaps more importantly, discourse research calls attention to how people's communications and interactions are not just motivated by the 'objective circumstances' they are part of and want to express in language, but also by the personal investments they make into how they speak, who they speak with and what they speak about. Put in these terms, discourse research holds the mirror up to the discursive practices that constitute personal and professional identity as well as – in this case – the complex facets of hospital work. The point is that discourse research seeks not merely to understand and explain how things work. It also engenders reflexivity about how things work that enables actors to reassess the efficacy, appropriateness and convenience (for others) of what they do and say. Reading through the chapters presented in this book, we are alerted to facets of everyday clinical and hospital work that we – even those deeply familiar with hospital practice – previously might not have noticed. Having now been alerted to them, we may be able to engage with them in our own contexts and find ways of revisiting the practices and assumptions that sustain them.

The research presented in this book shows that it is possible to address the imperatives of policy reform and hospital reorganization without lapsing into mechanistic conceptions of how people act and think (Dale, 1997; Davies *et al.*, 2000). It also shows that it is possible to keep the complexity of situated work in focus, while at the same time engaging with the general contours of hospital work. In that sense, the research collected in this volume goes beyond the Taylorist principle popular in health and hospital reform policy and management. In that sense, it adds an important new dimension to the health debates currently occupying most industrialized nations, by acknowledging and engaging with the complexities that hospital staff confront.

Notes

1 F. W. Taylor (1856–1917) was a US engineer who restructured organizations into conveyor belt factories, rendering their production process more efficient but also more mechanistic and depersonalizing.

2 Non-formal here refers to a modality of interaction that is neither informal and personalized, nor formal and proceduralized, but that affords negotiation of organization managerial issues in a dynamic, ad hoc or *heterogeneous* way.

References

Aarts, J. and Peel, V. (1999) 'Using a Descriptive Model of Change when Implying Large Scale Clinical Information Systems to Identify Priorities for Further Research', *International Journal of Medical Informatics*, 56, pp. 43–50.

Adrian, A. (2003) *Investigation Report Campbelltown and Camden Hospitals MacArthur Area Health Service* (Sydney: Health Care Complaints Commission).

Ainsworth-Vaughn, N. (2003) 'The Discourse of Medical Encounters', in D. Schiffrin, D. Tannen and H. E. Hamilton (eds) *The Handbook of Discourse Analysis*, pp. 453–69 (Oxford: Blackwell).

Atkinson, P. (1995) *Medical Talk and Medical Work: the Liturgy of the Clinic* (London: Sage).

Atkinson, P. (1999) 'Medical Discourse, Evidentiality, and the Construction of Professional Responsibility', in S. Sarangi and C. Roberts (eds) *Talk, Work and Institutional Order: Discourse in Medical, Mediation and Management Settings*, pp. 75–108 (Berlin: Mouton de Gruyter).

Bagian, J. P., Gosbee, J., Lee, C. Z., Williams, L., McKnight, S. D. and Mannos, D. M. (2002) 'The Veterans Affairs Root Cause Analysis System in Action', *Journal on Quality Improvement*, 28, pp. 531–45.

Berg, M. and Timmermans, S. (2000) 'Orders and their Others: On the Constitution of Universalities in Medical Work', *Configurations*, 8, pp. 31–61.

Berg, M., Hostman, K., Plass, S. and van Heusen, M. (2000) 'Guidelines, Professionals and the Production of Objectivity: Standardization and the Professionalism of Insurance Medicine', *Sociology of Health and Illness*, 22, pp. 765–91.

Berwick, D. and Nolan, T. W. (1998) 'Physicians as Leaders in Improving Health Care: a New Series of Annals of Internal Medicine', *Annals of Internal Medicine*, 128(4), pp. 289–92.

Candlin, C. and Candlin, S. (2003) 'Health Care Communication: a Problematic Site for Applied Linguistic Research', *Annual Review of Applied Linguistics*, 23, pp. 134–54.

Castells, M. (1990) *The Rise of the Network Society* (The Information Age: Economy, Society and Culture, Vol. 1) (Oxford: Blackwell).

Cicourel, A. (1982) 'Language and Belief in a Medical Setting', in H. Byrnes (ed.) *Contemporary Perceptions of Language: Interdisciplinary Dimensions*, pp. 48–78 (Washington, DC: Georgetown University Press).

Colwell, C. (1995) 'Postmodernism and Medicine: Discourse and the Limits of Practice', in B. E. Babich, D. B. Bergoffen and S. V. Glynn (eds) *Continental and Postmodern Perspectives in the Philosophy of Science*, pp. 153–72 (Aldershot: Avebury).

Cook-Gumperz, J. and Messerman, L. (1999) 'Local Identities and Institutional Practices: Constructing the Record of Professional Collaboration', in S. Sarangi and C. Roberts (eds) *Talk, Work and the Institutional Order: Discourse in Medical, Mediation and Management Settings*, pp. 145–82 (Berlin and New York: Mouton de Gruyter).

Dale, K. (1997) 'Identity in a Culture of Dissection: Body, Self and Knowledge', in K. Hetherington and R. Munro (eds) *Ideas of Difference: Social Spaces and the Labour of Division*, pp. 94–113 (Oxford: Blackwell Publishers/*The Sociological Review*).

Davies, C. (2003) 'Some of our Concepts are Missing: Reflections on the Absence of a Sociology of Organisations in *Sociology of Health and Illness*', *Sociology of Health and Illness*, 25, Silver Anniversary Issue, pp. 172–90.

Davies, H. T. O. and Harrison, S. (2003) 'Trends in Doctor–Manager Relationships', *British Medical Journal*, 326 (22 March), pp. 646–9.

Davies, H. T. O., Nutley, S. M. and Mannion, R. (2000) 'Organisational Culture and Quality of Health Care', *Quality in Health Care*, 9, pp. 111–19.

Deetz, S. (1994) 'The Micro-Politics of Identity Formation in the Workplace: the Case of a Knowledge Intensive Firm', *Human Studies*, 17(1), pp. 23–44.

Degeling, P., Maxwell, S. and Iedema, R. (2004a) 'Restructuring Clinical Governance to Maximize its Development Potential', in A. Gray and S. Harrison (eds) *Governing Medicine: Theory and Practice*, pp. 163–79 (Maidenhead: Open University Press).

Degeling, P., Maxwell, S., Iedema, R. and Hunter, D. (2004b) 'Making Clinical Governance Work', *British Medical Journal*, 329(18) (September 2004), pp. 679–81.

Dent, M. (1998) 'Hospitals and New Ways of Organizing Medical Work in Europe: Standardisation of Medicine in the Public Sector and the Future of Medical Autonomy', in C. Warhurst and P. Thompson (eds) *Workplaces of the Future*, pp. 204–24 (Basingstoke: Macmillan).

Douglas, N. (2002) *Inquiry into Obstetric and Gynaecological Services at King Edward Memorial Hospital 1990–2000* (Perth: Minter-Ellison Lawyers).

Erickson, F. (1999) 'Appropriation of Voice and Presentation of Self as a Fellow Physician: Aspects of a Discourse of Apprenticeship in Medicine', in S. Sarangi and C. Roberts (eds) *Talk, Work and the Institutional Order: Discourse in Medical, Mediation and Management Settings*, pp. 109–44 (Berlin and New York: Mouton de Gruyter).

Ferlie, E. B. and Shortell, S. (2001) 'Improving the Quality of Health Care in the United Kingdom and the United States: a Framework for Change', *The Milbank Quarterly*, 79(2), pp. 281–315.

Fisher, S. and Dundas Todd, A. (eds) (1993) *The Social Organization of Doctor–Patient Communication* (Norwood, NJ: Ablex Publishing).

Flynn, R. (1999) 'Managerialism, Professionalism and Quasi-Markets', in M. Exworthy and S. Halford (eds) *Professionals and the New Managerialism in the Public Sector*, pp. 18–36 (Buckingham: Open University Press).

Flynn, R. (2004) ' "Soft bureaucracy", Governmentality and Clinical Governance: Theoretical Approaches to Emergent Policy', in A. Gray and S. Harrison (eds)

Governing Medicine: Theory and Practice, pp. 11–26 (Maidenhead: Open University Press).
Garfinkel, H. (1967) *Studies in Ethnomethodology* (Englewood Cliffs, NJ: Prentice Hall).
Gosbee, J. and Anderson, T. (2003) 'Human Factors Engineering Design Demonstrations can Enlighten your RCA Team', *Quality and Safety in Health Care*, 12(2), pp. 119–21.
Greatbatch, D., Murphy, E. and Dingwall, R. (2001) 'Evaluating Medical Information Systems: Ethnomethodological and Interactionist Approaches', *Health Services Management Research*, 14, pp. 181–91.
Grimshaw, J. M. and Russell, I. T. (1993) 'Effects of Clinical Guidelines on Medical Practice: a Systematic Review of Rigorous Evaluations', *Lancet*, 342, pp. 1317–22.
Hardt, M. and Negri, A. (2004) *Multitude: War and Democracy in the Age of Empire* (New York: The Penguin Press).
Harrison, S. (1999) 'Clinical Autonomy and Health Policy: Past and Futures', in M. Exworthy and S. Halford (eds) *Professionals and the New Managerialism in the Public Sector*, pp. 50–64 (Buckingham: Open University Press).
Hoff, T., Jameson, L., Hannan, E. and Flink, E. (2004) 'A Review of the Literature Examining Linkages between Organisational Factors, Medical Errors and Patient Safety', *Medical Care Research and Review*, 16(1), pp. 3–37.
Hovenga, E. and Lloyd, S. (2002) 'Working with Information', in M. Harris and associates (eds) *Managing Health Services: Concepts and Practice*, pp. 195–228 (Sydney: MacLennan and Petty).
Hulsman, R., Visser, A. and Makoul, G. (2005) 'Addressing Some of the Key Questions about Communication in Healthcare', *Patient Education and Counseling*, 58(3), pp. 221–4.
Iedema, R. (2003) *Discourses of Post-Bureaucratic Organization* (Amsterdam and Philadelphia: John Benjamins).
Iedema, R. (2005) 'Medicine and Health, Inter and Intra-Professional Communication', in K. Brown (ed.) *Encyclopaedia of Language and Linguistics* (2nd edn), pp. 745–51 (Oxford: Elsevier).
Iedema, R. and Scheeres, H. (2003) 'From Doing Work to Talking Work: Renegotiating Knowing, Doing and Identity', *Applied Linguistics*, 24(3), pp. 316–37.
Iedema, R., Meyerkort, S. and White, L. (2005) 'Emergent Modes of Work and Communities of Practice', *Health Services Management Research*, 18, pp. 13–24.
Iedema, R., Jorm, C. M., Braithwaite, J., Travaglia, J. and Lum, M. (2006a) 'A Root Cause Analysis of Clinical Error: Confronting the Disjunction between Formal Rules and Situated Practice', *Social Science and Medicine*, 63 (2006), pp. 1201–12.
Iedema, R., Rhodes, C. and Scheeres, H. (2006b) 'Surveillance, Resistance, Observance: the Ethics and Aesthetics of Identity (at) Work', *Organization Studies*, 27(8), pp. 1111–30.
Kennedy, I. (2001) *The Bristol Royal Infirmary Inquiry* (London: Department of Health).
Kitchener, M. (2000) 'The "Bureaucratization" of Professional Roles: the Case of Clinical Directors in UK Hospitals', *Organization*, 7(1), pp. 129–54.
Kohn, L. T., Corrigan, J. M. and Donaldson, M. S. (1999) *To Err is Human: Building a Safer Health System* (Washington, DC: National Academy Press).
Labov, W. and Fanshel, D. (1977) *Therapeutic Discourse: Psychotherapy as Conversation* (Orlando, Fla: Academic Press).

Lingard, L., Espin, S., Whyte, W. F., Regher, G., Baker, G. R., Reznick, R., Bohnen, J., Orser, B., Doran, D. and Grober, E. (2004) 'Communication Failures in the Operating Room: an Observational Classification of Recurrent Types and Effects', *Quality and Safety in Health Care*, 13, pp. 330–4.

McKee, M. and Healey, J. (2002) *Hospitals in a Changing Europe* (Buckingham and Philadelphia: Open University Press).

Maynard, D. W. (2003) *Bad News, Good News: Conversational Order in Everyday Talk and Clinical Settings* (Chicago: University of Chicago Press).

Meek, J. (2001) 'Brave New World of Life and Hope', *The Sydney Morning Herald*, 18 October (Sydney: Australia).

Pettinari, C. (1988) *Task, Talk and Text in the Operating Room: a Study in Medical Discourse* (Norwood, NJ: Ablex Publishing Company).

Pincock, S. (2004) 'Poor Communication Lies at the Heart of NHS Complaints', *British Medical Journal*, 328(7430), p. 10.

Pomerantz, A. M., Ende, J. and Erickson, F. (1995) 'Precepting Conversations in a General Medical Clinic', in G. H. Morris and R. J. Chenial (eds) *The Talk of the Clinic: Explorations in the Analysis of Medical and Therapeutic Discourse* (Hillsdale, NJ: Lawrence Erlbaum Associates).

Rees, C. (1981) 'Records and Hospital Routine', in P. Atkinson and C. Heath (eds) *Medical Work: Realities and Routines*, pp. 55–70 (Farnborough: Gower).

Rose, N. (1999) *Powers of Freedom: Reframing Political Thought* (Cambridge: Cambridge University Press).

Sarangi, S. and Roberts, C. (1999) 'Introduction: the Dynamics of Interactional and Institutional Orders in Work-related Settings', in S. Sarangi and C. Roberts (eds) *Talk, Work and the Institutional Order: Discourse in Medical, Mediation and Management Settings*, pp. 1–57 (Berlin and New York: Mouton de Gruyter).

Shojania, K. G. and Grimshaw, J. M. (2005) 'Evidence-based Quality Improvement: the State of the Science', *Health Affairs*, 24(1), pp. 138–51.

Sutcliffe, K. M., Lewton, E. and Rosenthal, M. M. (2004) 'Communication Failures: an Insidious Contributor to Medical Mishaps', *Academic Medicine*, 79(2), pp. 186–94.

UK Department of Health (1997) *The New NHS: Modern, Dependable* (London: The Stationery Office).

UK Department of Health (2000) *Shaping the Future NHS: Long Term Planning for Hospitals and Related Services* (London: Department of Health).

Weick, K. and Sutcliffe, K. M. (2001) *Managing the Unexpected: Assuring High Performance in the Age of Complexity* (San Francisco: Jossey-Bass).

Wodak, R. (1996) *Disorders of Discourse* (London: Longman).

2

Institutional and Professional Orders of Ethics in the Discourse Practices of Research Recruitment in Oncology

Ellen Barton

Introduction: theoretical and methodological frameworks

The focus of this volume is 'the changing relationship between clinical professionals and the organizations they work in... trac[ing] whether and how clinicians deal with increased pressure... from having to coordinate increasingly complex kinds of clinical work' (see Iedema, Chapter 1 in this volume). The focus of this chapter is the recruitment of patients to participate in medical research in the United States, specifically recruitment to clinical trials in cancer research.[1] A clinical trial is defined formally as a protocol for experimental treatment, including chemotherapy in cancer research (www.cancer.gov), and a serious problem in medicine today is that too few patients enrol in clinical trials in cancer research, creating significant obstacles to progress in medical research and patient care (Harris Interactive, 2001; Russo, 1999). The National Cancer Institute (NCI) estimates that fewer than 5 per cent of patients nationwide enter clinical trials, a number that is even lower for minority groups, and many trials are delayed or even discontinued due to low enrolment (www.cancer.gov/clinicaltrials/digestpage/boosting-trial-participation). Research recruitment in oncology is at the nexus of multiple dimensions – patient and family decision-making, sociocultural attitudes about cancer and medical research, economic concerns about costs of serious illness, legal considerations, institutional policies, professional practices, and ethical issues related to participation in research. It is the interplay between institutional policies and professional practices with respect to ethical issues that will be under consideration here.

The analysis of research recruitment in this chapter follows the interdisciplinary approach of joint problematization as proposed by Sarangi and Roberts (1999). Research recruitment is well recognized as an important but problematic communicative event in cancer medicine since, as noted above, relatively few patients actually enter clinical trials. Research recruitment is an interesting communicative event for linguistic discourse analysis, too. In recruitment to research, there is a unique shift in institutional/professional interaction in medicine, from the delivery of what are typically definitive treatment recommendations based on established medical knowledge and clinical judgement to the offer of experimental treatment based on open questions in research and clinical care.

Within the interdisciplinary approach of joint problematization for the analysis of workplace discourses, Sarangi and Roberts (1999) observe that an institutional order is created and reflected in the interactional order of any particular communicative event (see also Drew and Heritage, 1992). As Iedema (Chapter 1, this volume) notes, this interplay between institutional and interactional orders has grown increasingly complex as professionals must manage the multiple dimensions of contemporary health care, which often extend far beyond the traditional model of a doctor and patient engaged in one-on-one decision-making to a contemporary model that incorporates, as Rothman (1991) puts it, *Strangers at the Bedside*, a number of whom are bioethicists. In the case of research recruitment, the institutional order is oriented toward a formal model of regulated accountability with an ethical imperative of voluntary participation in research, which will be described in the Background section. However, this institutional order is often in conflict with the professional order of medicine that remains oriented toward a more informal commitment to clinical accountability with an ethical imperative to offer the best possible treatment to a patient, and it is this professional order that prevails in the interactional order of research recruitment, which will be described in the section 'The interactional order of research recruitment'. These two orders have significantly different views of persuasion within research recruitment, and the way that physicians manage this conflict between competing ethical orders is described in the section 'Managing institutional/professional conflict in research recruitment'.

Background

Although there is no literature in linguistics specifically on research recruitment as far as I am aware, there is an extensive literature in medicine on barriers to enrolment in clinical trials. Previous research in medicine has identified physician–patient communication as a key factor in the decision to accept or decline recruitment to participate in a clinical trial (Fleming *et al.*, 1994; Gotay, 1999; Jenkins and Fallowfield, 2000; Roter and McNeilis, 2003). In these studies, however, the investigation of communication and clinical trial enrolment has generally been retrospective, primarily utilizing surveys, focus groups and interviews. Another literature on barriers to enrolment suggests best practices, most often based on reflection on clinical experience by practitioners (Lerner, 2004; Markman, 2004). Recently, however, there has been a growing interest in empirical studies based on data from actual medical encounters (Albrecht *et al.*, 1999, 2003, 2005; Ruckdeschel *et al.*, 1996; see also Brown *et al.*, 2004, for suggestions toward best practices based on actual encounters).

The findings from the retrospective barriers research suggest that patients enter clinical trials for a variety of reasons, including trust in the physician, a good understanding of the particular study and/or of medical research in general, hope for the best or latest treatments (known as direct benefits in the ethics literature), a treatment protocol with 'manageable' side effects, and a sense of altruism that participation will help other patients in the future or contribute to the progress of medical research. Patients refuse to enter clinical trials for a variety of related reasons: mistrust in the physician or in the institution of medicine generally, a poor understanding of the particular study and/or of medical research in general, an unwillingness to move the control of treatment from the individual physician to the research protocol, a lack of perceived direct benefits, a preference for standard treatment, concerns about randomization and the use of placebos, reluctance to endure significant side effects, and, importantly, concerns about complicated logistics of participation and the fear that it will be a burden, especially to caregivers. The emerging findings from the observational research suggest that strategic communication leading to clinical trial enrolment is both informational and supportive (Albrecht *et al.*, 1999). The informational dimension of such strategic communication includes content about the particular study, defined in terms of the elements of informed consent (see below). The supportive dimension of strategic communication includes patient-centred communication (Roter and Hall, 1992), with specific attention paid not only to the patient's motivation for enrolment (such as hope for direct benefits or altruism) but also to the logistical needs patients may have while participating in a clinical trial (such as alleviating the potential burden for a caregiver).

To a linguist, however, this literature has a significant methodological and analytical gap because very few studies have been based on naturally occurring data, and those studies that do look at observational data usually analyse content and communicative style of the physician alone. But the decision to accept or decline recruitment to enrol in a clinical trial takes place during the physician–patient interaction within the medical encounter, so without studies of the interaction from naturally occurring data, it simply cannot be known how discourse practices of research recruitment actually operate, since retrospective and impressionistic accounts of communication are known to be notoriously unreliable descriptions of the actual interaction itself (Labov, 1984; Silverman, 1993).

If we now turn to the institutional order of medical research in the United States, we note that the participation of patients in medical research has a complicated historical and contemporary context. Historically, research has been a prized value in twentieth-century American medicine, leading to a century of real progress, from early discoveries in germ theory in the late 1800s and early 1900s; through the exponential accumulation of research during the 1940s and 1950s; to the contemporary advances in medical research and treatment, notably including advances in cancer care (Porter, 1997). Rothman (1991, p. 69) calls the American 1940s and 1950s 'The Gilded Age of Research', a time when researchers 'ran their laboratories free of external constraints'. Ethical considerations and concerns within the operation of research were the same as the traditional model of paternalism that prevailed in clinical care at the time: patients were presumed to trust individual physicians who were assumed in turn to be accountable to the standards of the profession of medicine (Starr, 1982). In the case of research, a utilitarian ethics of progress was assumed to justify individual researchers' decisions about who to enrol in research studies and whether to tell them about it:

> The standards for health research on human subjects should recognize the imperative need for testing new procedures, materials and drugs on human subjects as essential to the public interest. . . . [a] public necessity to use people – sick or well – as subjects for health research. (Rothman, 1991, pp. 67–8)

This 'Gilded Age' of research in American medicine, however, allowed all-too-frequent abuses of participants in research, when researchers assumed free and often unethical access to subjects, including exposure of soldiers and citizens to ground zero radiation, which helped set parameters for radiation therapy in cancer; deliberate infection of institutionalized and hospitalized patients to investigate questions of infectious spread and immunological response; and the infamous Tuskegee experiment, where a cohort of rural African-American men were left untreated for syphilis in order to chart the course of the disease, long after penicillin was known to be a cure for this potentially debilitating and fatal condition (Goodman *et al.*, 2003; Reverby, 2000; Rothman, 1991).[2]

In response to ethics scandals in research and in conjunction with ongoing challenges to the paternalistic authority of the profession of medicine (Arney and Bergen, 1984), the contemporary context of research participation is one of regulation. Following the scandal of the Tuskegee experiment, the Belmont Report (1979), after research in philosophy and bioethics, set out three principles for the ethical treatment of human subjects in research – autonomy, beneficence, justice. These principles have been codified in US federal law 45 CFR 46, which mandates review of research using human subjects through the institutional review boards (IRBs) of individual institutions. 45 CFR 46 operationalizes the principle of autonomy through an informed consent process that is designed to safeguard voluntary participation in research studies; informed consent, in turn, is operationalized in the form of a written consent form to be reviewed and signed by participants enrolling in a research study. The principle of beneficence (maximize benefits, minimize harm) is operationalized in the assessment of risks and benefits of participation in research, which is the basis of IRB review. The principle of justice is operationalized in the review of subject selection to ensure that the groups participating in research, such as minority or underprivileged populations, are not selected for convenience, and that the groups participating in research also receive the benefits of research (in other words, the flow of research benefits should not be primarily to already advantaged groups, such as patients in higher socio-economic classes).[3]

This particular context of research regulation has been shaped primarily by the emergence of bioethics as a paradigm for medical research and care, specifically medical decision-making (Rothman, 1991). For the first part of the twentieth century, American medicine operated within a strongly autonomous professional domain. Under this paternalistic model, physicians took virtually complete responsibility not only for medical decision-making but also decisions about medical communication – what, when and how to tell the patient and/or family about diagnosis, treatment and prognosis (Starr, 1982). In the second part of the twentieth century, the profession of American medicine has come to operate within a much more constrained domain of autonomy; in fact, within the bioethics paradigm, strong autonomy has shifted to the patient rather than the professional (the standard text on bioethics is Beauchamp and Childress, 2001; for historical descriptions of the emergence of bioethics, see Fox, 1991; Katz, 1984/2002; Rothman, 1991; for a critique of autonomy, see Schneider, 1998). Autonomy is typically defined as the right of patients to exercise self-determination in medical care, in particular by making their own medical decisions and treatment choices based upon their personal values and beliefs (Beauchamp and Childress, 2001). In the context of research, autonomy is generally defined as the right of a patient to voluntary participation in research, specifically by making a decision to enter a research study based upon information in understandable language about the study's purpose; procedures; risks; possible benefits; confidentiality of records; alternative treatments available; compensation for participation; costs of participation, including the costs for a research-related injury; contact information for the investigator and the IRB; and a full statement of voluntary participation (the elements of informed consent mandated in 45 CFR 46).

Within the bioethics model, both recruitment and consent are intended to be informative, not persuasive, discussions that position potential participants as autonomous decision-makers acting upon the information with respect to their own values and beliefs. The institutional order of American universities and hospitals operationalizes the bioethics model through the process of IRB review, and this institutional order is accountable to the US federal government, which has, over the past 10 years, taken an increasingly active role in enforcing compliance: acting in response to the death of a healthy volunteer enrolled in a gene therapy trial, the Office for Human Research Protection (Department of Health and Human Services) has recently shut down research at a number of prominent universities that were not following regulated practices of review and consent. The institutional order of ethical practices in research has even become the subject of a popular literature in American newspapers and magazines (Lemonick and Goldstein, 2002): a recent *TIME* magazine cover, for instance, showed a patient in a hospital gown crouched in a cage, with the headline reading, 'How Medical Testing Has Turned Millions of Us into Human Guinea Pigs'. This institutional order of research recruitment, however, may not always be in alignment with the professional practices of physician-researchers in the interactional order of recruiting patients to participate in research.

The interactional order of research recruitment

The data for this discourse analysis of research recruitment came from a study in a large, urban, academic medical centre, in its NCI designated comprehensive cancer centre.[4] The data consist of 35 observed and recorded encounters between patients and their medical oncologists at the Midwestern Cancer Institute (MCI). Of these encounters, seven included recruitment to clinical trials: one of these recruitments led to enrolment within the encounter, four recruitments were deferred (in other words, the patients were recruited but not asked for a specific decision about enrolment in this particular encounter), and two recruitments led to refusals within the encounters. The finding that a deferral was the most common result of the research recruitment interaction was not expected, and is the focus of the analysis here.

The discourse analysis of the data was inductive, looking to describe the recurring structural organization of research recruitment as a communicative event as well as the variation in research recruitment across the set of encounters (Barton, 2001; Johnstone, 2000; Sarangi and Roberts, 1999; Schiffrin *et al.*, 2001). The analysis here follows Chafe's (1994, 2001) description of discourse flow, which he argues is organized in terms of topics, which are developed with schemas of subtopics. Chafe's (2001, p. 674) definition of topic includes both content and interaction: a topic

> is a coherent aggregate of thoughts introduced by some participant... developed either by that participant or another or by several participants jointly, and then either explicitly closed or allowed to peter out. Topics typically have clear beginnings... and their endings are sometimes well defined, sometimes not.

The analysis of the full set of encounters found that research recruitment was embedded as an identifiable topic within the treatment discussion of an oncology encounter (for a description of the structural organization of treatment discussions in oncology encounters, see Barton, 2004).

The analysis presented here is a comparison of two encounters where the topic of research recruitment ended with a deferral: one of these interactions (the R family) eventually led to enrolment and the other did not (the H family). Two different physicians conducted the encounters, one American-born, and one born in India and a permanent resident of the United States. The two patients were of different genders and races, and both brought a family member with them to the appointment: Mrs R, Caucasian-American, was accompanied by her son; Mr H, African-American, was accompanied by his wife. Both recruitments were for what is colloquially called the Iressa trial, which was designed to test the use of Iressa as an experimental medication to be taken after the standard treatment for advanced lung cancer (a combined radiation therapy–chemotherapy regimen). After treatment, patients on the trial were randomized to a treatment arm (patients who received Iressa) and a control arm (patients who received a placebo), and patients were to stay on the trial for five years.

The structural organization (or schema of subtopics) of the topic for research recruitment in these two encounters was as follows. First, the standard treatment was summarized as the end of the previous topic in the treatment discussion:

(1a) Dr M: But basically where we start from is that we're going to give chemotherapy and radiation, OK. (H family)

(1b) Dr S: Now I have talked to you about what we would do [standard treatment]. (R family)

Then the topic of participation in research commenced, with the first sentence introducing the topic in terms of an eligibility statement:

(2a) Dr S: There's a possibility that I might be able to enrol you on a clinical trial. (R family)

(2b) Dr M: Now what I'd like to propose for you is that you're eligible for something called a clinical trial that I'd like to tell you about because it may work for you and it's worth considering. (H family)

Both statements introduce the possibility of participation in research using the medical language of eligibility, thereby positioning the patient positively in terms of being able to participate in research. This is a deliberate strategy, at least on the part of some physicians; one of the physicians who participated in this study noted, 'The one thing I did was to stop asking people if they were interested in a trial and start saying "you might be a candidate for a trial". And it works' (Dr L, field notes). The topic introductions above are on a continuum of informative and persuasive. Neither statement is informative only, but (2a) is less persuasive than (2b). Persuasion in (2a) is based upon the single feature of eligibility as a positive positioning. (2b) includes additional features of persuasion: the direct recommendation for participation from the physician ('what I'd like to propose for you'), the mention of direct benefits ('it may work for you'), and the professional evaluation of participation ('it's worth considering').

After the introduction of the topic of participation in a clinical trial via an eligibility statement, the topic was developed with a schema of subtopics, typically in the following order:

- reference to medical research in general
- description of the study
  - (a) identification of experimental drug
  - (b) previous performance of the drug
  - (c) purpose of the study
- description of the procedures of the study
  - (a) standard treatment plus
  - (b) randomization
- mention of the possibility of direct benefits

The one subtopic that varies in placement across the corpus is the reference to medical research in general.

In the two encounters described here, the subtopic of medical research appeared near the end in one encounter [(3a)] but near the beginning in the other [(3b)]:

(3a) Dr M: It's totally voluntary to participate in that, but we're always looking to improve the treatment of lung cancer, and if you're interested in doing that, we'd love to have you sign up. (H family)

(3b) Dr S: As you know, we are a university center. (R family)

These statements vary in the directness of their references to the general purposes and procedures of medical research. In (3a), participation in research is noted to be voluntary, and the goal of research is specified in clinical terms – 'to improve the treatment of lung cancer'. In terms of the typical discourse of a medical encounter, interest in participation is described in off-register terms – 'we'd love to have you sign up'. Rarely in medical discourse is a decision described in terms of such a positive endorsement by the medical community, the invoked 'we' responding with the highly emotional verb 'love'. As in (2b), the physician in this encounter positions the family's participation in research in overtly positive terms. In (3b), the reference to medical research is more opaque, and the physician's reference to the family's knowledge ('as you know') may not, in fact, refer to a good understanding of medical research, thereby implying a background which is not shared.

The next subtopic in recruitment, which is the description of the particular clinical trial at hand, however, receives considerable development. The development of this subtopic is characterized by its length and/or its repetition. For the H family, the description of the study was the lengthiest subtopic within the topic:

(4) Dr M: We give everybody in your situation chemotherapy and radiation. We currently have a clinical trial that's open that involves getting chemotherapy and radiation but that has an extra added twist to it. There is a new drug, kind of experimental drug, but a drug that has a track record that's been given to literally thousands of people. So, we know what it does, but it hasn't yet been approved by the FDA [US Food and Drug Administration]. This is the drug we're considering giving at the end of the treatment because we think that it might improve the odds that the disease won't come back. But because the drug isn't approved by the FDA, and we don't know yet whether it does what we think it would it's part of a clinical trial. (H family)

With some repetition, specifically the fact that the drug has not yet been approved by the FDA, the description of the study includes several elements – the timing of the study as after standard treatment; the identification of the treatment drug as experimental; the previous performance of the drug, which justifies the current trial; and the general purpose of the study, here, to answer the open question of whether Iressa works to improve survival rates in advanced lung cancer.

For the R family, the description of the clinical trial, particularly the open question of the research, was repeated three times:

(5a) Dr S: At the end of the treatment, after all you've gone through, we are looking at whether there is a new medication, a pill called (Iressa), it's still an experimental medication. And it looks like it might have some (effect) in lung cancer. We don't have all the data. (R family)

(5b) Dr S: But we don't know whether it is going to truly help Stage III patients right now. And that's why they're doing this study. (R family)

(5c) Dr S: But that is the only (way) we will know whether one, the pill is beneficial or not, because even though it looks like it might be beneficial, actually there might be a downside to it that we don't know about. And in only by doing the study we can know whether there is any upside to it or a downside to it. (R family)

This development includes most of the elements of the description of the study in (4) – the timing of the study, the identification of the drug as experimental, and the previous performance of the drug (although not the (possibly obstructive) role of the FDA). It presents a more elaborated version of the open question of the study to include the possibility of the experimental drug having a 'downside', perhaps in terms of efficacy, but also in terms of side effects.

After the description of the particular study, with an emphasis on the open question(s) of the research, recruitment continues with a description of the procedures of the study:

(6a) Dr S: After finishing all of this treatment I told you, chemo, radiation, and then some more additional chemotherapy, then, at that point, you would be randomized into two groups. There's a fifty percent that you will get onto those pills or a fifty percent that you won't . . . You might say – you could definitely – some people may say you're not comfortable with this. There's a chance that even if I go on the study that I won't get the pill. (R family)

(6b) Dr M: And basically how it works is this. Everybody gets the standard treatment, chemotherapy, radiation, short rest, more chemotherapy. Everybody gets that. But half of the patients also get this extra added drug. It's called Iressa. But we don't know which half it is because the other people get a pill that's a placebo that looks just like the Iressa. So at the end of the treatment we give the extra added pill which in half the people is actually a drug that may prevent the disease from coming back. Since we didn't know whether it works, the only way to find whether it works is to treat a bunch of people, half with and half without, and see which group does best. (H family)

This description of the procedures of the study foregrounds two elements: the design of the trial as standard treatment followed by experimental treatment, and the double-blind design of the trial with randomization to a treatment arm versus a placebo arm. In terms of the

Iressa trial, these two features are regarded by the physicians as the 'best and worst' of the research design. That patients will first receive standard treatment without any experimental manipulation is considered an advantage since patients will in fact receive the best known treatment for their condition. That the study involves randomization with a placebo arm is considered a disadvantage since patients are thought to be especially suspicious of randomization and placebos (the barriers literature reviewed above regularly finds that a design with randomization and/or placebo is in and of itself a barrier to participation in research). Of trials with randomization, one of the physicians participating in this project noted, 'They're the hardest [to recruit to]. The patients don't want to be randomized' (Dr M, field notes). When asked why not, the physician answered in terms of patients not fully understanding that the question of the research is, in fact, open: 'Certain patients don't believe you when you say you don't know which [treatment] is better' (Dr M, field notes). In sum, in research recruitment, physicians believe that patients respond positively to certainty (receiving the standard treatment as the 'best' treatment) and negatively to uncertainty (not fully accepting that research is based on open questions).

After the study and its procedures are described, the final subtopic in research recruitment is the mention of the possibility of direct benefits from the experimental treatment. In other words, the possibility of being randomized to the treatment arm is presented as an incentive to enrol in the trial:

(7a) Dr M: If you don't decide to take the trial, you're still going to get the same treatment anyway, the chemo, the radiation, and the rest, and the consolidation chemo. Everybody gets that, whether they're on the trial or off. But if you would decide to participate in the trial there's a fifty-fifty chance that you get the other drug at the end as well. (H family)

(7b) Dr S: And the other thing I would say is that if you didn't go on the study there's a one hundred percent chance that you can't get the pill because it's still experimental and it's not available in the market. But by going on the study you have at least a fifty percent chance of getting the pill. (R family)

In this subtopic, the possibility of direct benefits is presented overtly and positively to patients and their families. According to the bioethics model, this is the most problematic aspect of research recruitment in these encounters since it is clearly more persuasive than informative.

The most interesting feature of research recruitment as an interaction is that the topic, which began with an eligibility statement, most often ends not with overt decision-making sequences leading to enrolment or refusal, but with a deferral of enrolment instead. Both encounters described here deferred the decision to enrol or not enrol, and then moved on to initiate the next topic in the treatment discussion, which is making arrangements to start the standard treatment as soon as possible:

(8a) Dr S: Again, I am just mentioning that [the clinical trial]. It is a little bit early because I think we need to repeat her scan, we need to do a brain scan . . . Last here I want to mention is that obviously now that you know that you have lung cancer you want treatment right away. (R family)

(8b) Dr M: But you don't have to decide that [enrolment in the clinical trial] right now . . . The first thing we need to do is ==
Pt: ==start the treatment.
(H family)

As noted above, deferral was the most common way to end research recruitment, which will be discussed below (cf. 'Managing institutional/professional conflict in research recruitment').

The only significant variation across these two encounters was the interaction between the physicians and the patient and family. The H family encounter was a monologue with no uptake on the part of the patient or family: no one asked any questions, offered any positive back-channels, or otherwise contributed to the development of the topic or its subtopics. On the other hand, the R family was partly a recruitment monologue from the physician but also a dialogue with the family. The R family asked questions about the experimental drug and about randomization with the possibility of a placebo:

(9a) Son: Is this the pill form of chemotherapy that they were talking about?
Dr S: It's an experimental drug, that's why it's part of a trial right now. But you can think of it as an oral chemotherapy.
Son: Right.

(9b) Son: OK, do they give just the pill, or do they give one group the pill and the other group a placebo?
Dr S: It's a placebo.
Son: Right, so one has placebo, one has the pill . . .

> Dr S: You will get all the initial treatment. That is not placebo. You get chemotherapy, radiation, and then more chemotherapy.
> Son: So you won't really know whether you're getting the real pill or –
> Dr S: Absolutely.
> Son: OK.

In addition to these question–answer sequences, the R family also indicated uptake with positive back-channels like 'right' or 'OK' throughout the recruitment.

Physicians themselves regard the presence or absence of interactional uptake as predictive of the family's decision to enrol or not enrol in a clinical trial. Dr M, who recruited the H family with no uptake, said as he left the examining room, 'They won't sign', a reference to the informed consent as the official enrolment document of the trial. It is important to note here that the H family exhibited no positive uptake specifically to the topic of the clinical trial; in other parts of the treatment discussion, such as the description of side effects and the logistics of treatment scheduling, the H family asked questions and used positive back-channels. Dr S, who recruited the R family with uptake, seemed to have in place a positive trajectory of alignment that began with recruitment in this encounter and led to enrolment in a subsequent encounter.

Managing institutional/professional conflict in research recruitment

Incorporating the principles of current models of bioethics – autonomy, beneficence, justice – the institutional order of research regulation mandates patient autonomy and specifies that recruitment is to be informational, not persuasive, centred around the process of informed consent (Beauchamp and Childress, 2001). The principlism of this model presumes a rational decision-maker, one who calculates risks and benefits in terms of values and beliefs that are presumed to be known in a form that can guide logical decision-making. However, there is abundant evidence that decision-making in the real world, including medical decision-making, is often not rational and logical. Instead, decisions are typically subjective and sometimes emotional (Hogarth and Kunreuther, 1995; for a recent best-seller, see Gladwell's (2005) *Blink*). In the case of medical decision-making, many patients and families ask specifically for guidance and recommendations about clinical trials, often in personal, even paternalistic, terms:

(10) Ms G: Let me ask you what I consider an important question. Are you married?
Dr T: Yeah.
Ms G: If it were your wife, would you have her do this, if she had my cancer?
Dr T: I'd have her try.
Ms G: What if it was your mother, because I don't know the relationship you have with your wife [*laughter*].
Dr T: I would encourage her to at least try. I would be disappointed if I honestly didn't get the [drug], but that's the other standard. You don't get anything anyways, so there's no losing to me. (G family)

As Schneider (1998, p. 41) concludes in a review of empirical studies on medical decision-making, 'these studies consistently conclude that, while patients largely wish to be informed about their medical circumstances, a substantial number of them do not want to make their own medical decisions'. Further, Schneider (1998, p. 108) argues, '[M]any patients seem to have declined to seize the power of decision bioethics has proffered... [T]hose patients may have legitimate reasons to shun the burdens of medical decisions.'

As constructed by physicians as well as patients and families, the interactional order of research recruitment is in considerable conflict with the bioethics model: particularly on the part of physicians, the discourse practices of research recruitment are much more persuasive than informative. Data from actual recruitment encounters show that physicians are selective in their coverage of the elements of informed consent. While both encounters identified the study as research with voluntary participation and described the purpose and procedures of the trial, the coverage of risks and benefits was notably skewed: benefits were foregrounded, and risks were backgrounded (for example, side effects of Iressa were not mentioned). Further, recruitment incorporated a number of overtly persuasive features in a systematic positioning of participation in research as positive: eligibility statements, direct recommendations, positive evaluations of medical research in general and the specific clinical trial in particular, positive reference to the track record of the experimental treatment, and, most problematically, foregrounded emphasis on the possibility of direct benefits as a result of participating in the research. Finally, research recruitment typically did not even ask for an explicit or autonomous decision; instead, deferring the decision to another encounter separate from the recruitment. Participation in research thus seems to follow less of a decision-making process and more of a trajectory of alignment, sometimes positive (the R family) and sometimes negative (the H family). Schneider (1998, p. 93) calls this 'a drift-process rather than a deliberative decision-process'.

From a bioethics perspective, the interactional order of research recruitment as described above must be seen as prima facie unethical. From another perspective, however, research recruitment may be seen to follow a professional model of ethics in medicine, one that is based on the long-standing standards of the profession rather than the imposed standards of bioethics principlism and its dubious reliance on the assumption of rational decision-making by autonomous agents. In a professional model, strong autonomy is not the centrepiece, but paternalism is not, either. A professional model leans more to physician-recommended care within what could be called an assent model that incorporates physician expertise and experience as well as patient perspectives and preferences (Timothy Buchman, personal communication). In an assent model, the patient has the autonomy to make medical decisions, but the physician has the professional authority to make recommendations and to make them persuasively. An assent model follows a strongly held tenet of the ethics of the profession of medicine, namely that the patient should be provided with the best treatment possible. DelVecchio Good (1995, p. 178) calls this commitment to expertise-based patient care *The Quest for Competence*, noting that 'helping patients make good decisions is the essence of competent care'. DelVecchio Good (1995, p. 203) specifically legitimates expertise-based persuasion as a dimension of medical competence: 'Competence . . . focuses attention on how clinical knowledge is used to select and negotiate a clinical course, at times to persuade patients . . . of the appropriateness of treatment, of a course of action.' In an assent model, patients can refuse particular treatments, but physicians are ethically bound to provide their best recommendations concerning those treatments.

In terms of research, particularly in academic medical centres, clinical trials are often seen as an opportunity to provide cutting-edge treatment, and physicians want to be able to offer the most promising treatment to their patients, especially in oncology with such low survival rates for so many cancers. That clinical trials offer not absolute certainty but reasonable hope that a treatment is promising emerges strongly in research recruitment, where physicians point to the track record of the drug and the hopes for its efficacy. Physicians often talk of clinical trials in these terms: 'That's a good study' (Dr T, field notes) is not an unusual comment both to patients and to colleagues. 'Good' here has multiple meanings, including not only good design but also good preliminary results that warrant not only the trial but also the recommendation that patients enter the trial. Under the ethical imperative to offer the best possible treatment to patients, then, physicians are warranted to shape recruitment as both informative and persuasive, especially when the trial seems to offer promising treatment.

Physicians' informal talk of trials articulates this professional and ethical commitment that legitimates persuasion in research recruitment. Dr M, for example, noted, 'the patient should receive the best treatment possible . . . [and] sometimes this [a trial] is the best we have'. In another case where a patient presented for a second opinion about a trial at another hospital, Dr T noted, '[It's] not a bad protocol. I would actually encourage him to go back out there.' Dr S acknowledges the persuasion incorporated into research recruitment: 'Very honestly, when you pitch a trial to a patient, and I hate to use the word pitch but that is what you're doing. I honestly believe that it's the best option for the patient and when you go through all that and they say no there is a sense of disappointment.' Within a professional model, recommending participation in research is an ethical practice not only to advance research but also to advance treatment and care for the individual patient.

Physicians recognize the conflict between the interactional order and the institutional order, and they manage it by taking advantage of one of the characteristic features of medical communication – its discontinuous and ongoing nature. In effect, physicians separate recruitment and enrolment by recruiting themselves and then deferring enrolment to a later encounter with research staff (most often research nurses) where the informed consent is reviewed and signed. In this way, the actual enrolment takes place within the institutional order, so patients do receive an informational presentation at the time of formal decision-making. With the awareness that enrolment will take place in a context of informed consent to satisfy the ethics of the institutional order, physicians then shape recruitment as more persuasive in response to the profession's ethical commitment to recommend and provide the best treatment possible within the clinical judgement based on their expertise and experience. It is this less formal interactional order, rather than the formal institutional order, that underlies the recruitment to research in oncology encounters. It is true that the professional order privileges itself by retaining control of the interactional order, but it would be too simple to call this order unethical. Rather it seems that there are both professional and institutional orders incorporated into the medical communication concerning research.

Conclusion

Although the findings of this research need further investigation in a larger number of encounters, the preliminary implications of this work suggest that discourse analysis has the potential to make a contribution to the description of what could be called 'ethics in interaction', that is, ethical issues and principles that can be identified as ones of importance evidenced by their emergence in interaction between physicians and patients/families (Barton and Sarangi, 2005). Under this perspective, physicians and patients/families actively construct interactions to raise and address their ethical concerns, which may be quite different from the concerns expected by the principlism of the bioethics model. What the discourse analysis above has shown is that physicians incorporate both the informed consent processes mandated by the bioethics model and the recommendations for best treatment mandated by the professional model. This incorporation takes place within the interactional order of research recruitment, where physicians recruit within the professional order, but defer enrolment to the institutional order. A discourse analysis of the interactional order thus challenges the absolute principlism of the bioethics model, suggesting that the ethics of contemporary medicine take place in a much more complicated context, one that ideally encompasses not only the ethical principles of autonomy and informed consent but also the ethical principles of clinical care within the profession of medicine.

Notes

1 Although a cross-cultural and cross-linguistic discourse analysis of recruitment to research would be fascinating and important, it is beyond the scope of this chapter where I confine myself to American medicine, which was the site of my field research.
2 Because my focus in this chapter is on American medicine, I do not mention the best known case of abuse of research subjects, the Nazi experimentation in wartime Germany, which took place in clinics, institutions and concentration camps. For more on Nazi experimentation and research, see Annas and Grodin (1992), Caplan (1992) and Gallagher (1990).

3 There is a large bioethics literature on informed consent for participation in research, which will not be reviewed systematically here. The reader is referred to Beauchamp and Childress (2001) and other references, including Espago (2003) and Jecker *et al.* (1997).

4 To preserve confidentiality of participants, the site will be called the Midwestern Cancer Institute (MCI). This research was reviewed and approved by the Clinical Trial Office of the MCI, and by the IRB of its university. Participants' confidentiality will be protected by the use of title plus initials for physicians (e.g. Dr X) and title plus initials or family names (for example, Ms G, Wife, Son).

References

45 CFR 46 (1991) *Protection of Human Subjects* (Washington, DC: Department of Health and Human Services). http://ohsr.od.nig.gov/guidelines/belmont/html/ (accessed 27 April 2006).

Albrecht, T., Blanchard, C., Ruckdeschel, J., Coovert, M. and Strongbow, R. (1999) 'Strategic Physician Communication and Oncology Clinical Trials', *Journal of Clinical Oncology*, 17(10), pp. 3324–32.

Albrecht, T., Penner, L. and Ruckdeschel, J. (2003) 'Understanding Patient Decisions about Clinical Trials and the Associated Communication Process: a Preliminary Report', *Journal of Cancer Education*, 18(4), pp. 210–14.

Albrecht, T., Franks, M. and Ruckdeschel, J. (2005) 'Communication and Informed Consent', *Current Opinion in Oncology*, 17(4), pp. 336–9.

Annas, G. and Grodin, M. (eds) (1992) *The Nazi Doctors and the Nuremberg Code: Human Rights in Human Experimentation* (Oxford: Oxford University Press).

Arney, W. and Bergen, B. (1984) *Medicine and the Management of Living* (Chicago: University of Chicago Press).

Barton, E. (2001) 'Design in Observational Research in Medicine: Toward Disciplined Interdisciplinarity', *Journal of Business and Technical Communication*, 15(3), pp. 309–32.

Barton, E. (2004) 'Discourse Methods and Critical Practice in Professional Communication: the Front-stage and Back-stage Discourse of Prognosis in Medicine', *Journal of Business and Technical Communication*, 18(1), pp. 67–111.

Barton, E. and Sarangi, S. (July, 2005) 'Autonomy in Interaction: Decision-Making in Palliative Care', Paper presented at COMET (Communication, Medicine, and Ethics), University of Sydney, Australia.

Beauchamp, T. and Childress, J. (2001) *Principles of Bioethics* (5th edn) (Oxford: Oxford University Press).

Belmont Report (1979) *Ethical Principles and Guidelines for the Protection of Human Subjects of Research* (Washington, DC: National Commission for the Protection of Human Subjects of Biomedical and Behavioral Research). http://ohsr.od.nig.gov/guidelines/belmont/html/ (accessed 27 April 2006).

Brown, R., Butow, P., Butt, D. *et al.* (2004) 'Developing Ethical Strategies to Assist Oncologists in Seeking Informed Consent to Cancer Trials', *Social Science and Medicine*, 58, pp. 379–90.

Caplan, A. (ed.) (1992) *When Medicine Went Mad: Bioethics and the Holocaust* (Totowa, NJ: Humana Press).

Chafe, W. (1994) *Discourse, Consciousness, and Time: the Flow and Displacement of Conscious Experience in Speaking and Writing* (Chicago: University of Chicago Press).

Chafe, W. (2001) 'The Analysis of Discourse Flow', in D. Schiffrin, D. Tannen and H. Hamilton (eds) *Handbook of Discourse Analysis*, pp. 673–87 (Oxford: Blackwell).

DelVecchio Good, M. J. (1995) *American Medicine: the Quest for Competence* (Berkeley: University of California Press).

Drew, P. and Heritage, J. (1992) 'Analyzing Talk at Work: an Introduction', in P. Drew and J. Heritage (eds) *Talk at Work*, pp. 3–65 (Cambridge: Cambridge University Press).

Espago, R. (ed.) (2003) *Biomedical Ethics: Opposing Viewpoints* (San Diego, Calif: Greenhaven).

Fleming, I., Schain, W. and Mansour, E. (1994) 'Barriers to Clinical Trials: Parts I–III', *Cancer*, 74, pp. 2662–75.

Fox, R. (1991) 'The Evolution of American Bioethics: a Sociological Perspective', in G. Weisz (ed.) *Social Science Perspectives on Medical Ethics*, pp. 201–20 (Philadelphia: University of Pennsylvania Press).

Gallagher, H. (1990) *By Trust Betrayed: Patients, Physicians, and the License to Kill in the Third Reich* (New York: Holt).

Gladwell, M. (2005) *Blink: the Power of Thinking without Thinking* (New York: Little, Brown).

Goodman, J., McElligott, A. and Marks, L. (eds) (2003) *Useful Bodies: Humans in the Service of Medical Science in the Twentieth Century* (Baltimore: Johns Hopkins University Press).

Gotay, C. (1999) 'Accrual to Cancer Clinical Trials: Directions from the Research Literature', *Journal of Clinical Oncology*, 17, pp. 3324–32.

Harris Interactive (2001) 'Misconceptions and Lack of Awareness Greatly Reduce Recruitment for Clinical Trials', *Harris Interactive Healthcare News*, 11(3), pp. 1–3. http://www.harrisinteractive.com/news/newsletters/healthnews/HI_HealthCareNews2001Vol11_iss3.pdf/ (accessed 25 April 2006).

Hogarth, R. and Kunreuther, H. (1995) 'Decision-making under Ignorance: Arguing with Yourself', *Journal of Risk and Uncertainty*, 10(1), pp. 15–36.

Jecker, N., Jonson, A. and Perlman, R. (1997) *Bioethics: an Introduction to the History, Methods, and Practice* (Sudbury, Mass: Jones and Bartlett).

Jenkins, V. and Fallowfield, L. (2000) 'Reasons for Accepting or Declining to Participate in Randomized Clinical Trials for Cancer Therapy', *British Journal of Cancer*, 82, pp. 1783–87.

Johnstone, B. (2000) *Qualitative Methods in Sociolinguistics* (Oxford: Oxford University Press).

Katz, J. (2002 [1984]) *The Silent World of Doctor and Patient* (Baltimore: Johns Hopkins University Press).

Labov, W. (1984) 'Field Methods of the Project on Linguistic Change and Variation', in J. Baugh and J. Sherzer (eds) *Language in Use: Readings in Sociolinguistics*, pp. 28–66 (Englewood Cliffs, NJ: Prentice-Hall).

Lemonick, M. and Goldstein, A. (2002) 'At Your Own Risk', *TIME Magazine*, 22 April, pp. 46–56.

Lerner, B. (2004) 'Sins of Omission: Cancer Research without Informed Consent', *New England Journal of Medicine*, 351, pp. 628–30.

Markman, M. (2004) 'Ethical Conflict in Providing Informed Consent for Clinical Trials: Problematic Exams from the Gynecologic Cancer Research Community', *Oncologist*, 9, pp. 3–7.

National Cancer Institute, US National Institutes of Health. http://www.cancer.gov/(accessed 25 April 2006).

National Cancer Institute, US National Institutes of Health, 'Clinical Trial of Gefitinib for Advanced Lung Cancer Closes Early'. http://www.cancer.gov/newscenter/pressreleases/gefitinibNSCLC/ (accessed 25 April 2006).

National Cancer Institute, US National Institutes of Health, 'Lung Cancer'. http://www.nci.nih.gov/cancertopics/types/lung/ (accessed 25 April 2006).

Porter, R. (1997) *The Greatest Benefit to Mankind: a Medical History of Humanity* (New York: Norton).

Reverby, S. (ed.) (2000) *Tuskegee's Truths: Rethinking the Tuskegee Syphilis Study* (Chapel Hill: University of North Carolina Press).

Roter, D. and Hall, J. (1992) *Doctors Talking to Patients/Patients Talking to Doctors: Improving Communication in Medical Visits* (Orlando, Fla: Auburn House/Greenwood).

Roter, D. and McNeilis, K. (2003) 'The Nature of the Therapeutic Relationship and the Assessment of its Discourse in Routine Medical Visits', in T. Thompson, A. Dorsey, K. Miller and R. Parrott (eds) *Handbook of Health Communication*, pp. 121–40 (Mahwah, NJ: Lawrence Erlbaum).

Rothman, D. (1991) *Strangers at the Bedside: a History of How Law and Bioethics Transformed Medical Decision Making* (New York: Basic Books).

Ruckdeschel, J., Albrecht, T., Blanchard, C. and Hemmick, R. (1996) 'Communication, Accrual to Clinical Trials, and the Physician–Patient Relationship: Implications for Training Programs', *Journal of Cancer Education*, 11(2), pp. 73–9.

Russo, F. (1999) 'The Clinical-Trials Bottleneck', *The Atlantic Monthly*, May, pp. 30–6.

Sarangi, S. and Roberts, C. (1999) 'The Dynamics of Interactional and Institutional Orders in Work-related Settings', in S. Sarangi and C. Roberts (eds) *Talk, Work and Institutional Order: Discourse in Medical, Mediation and Management Settings*, pp. 1–60 (Berlin: Mouton de Gruyter).

Schiffrin, D., Tannen, D. and Hamilton, H. (eds) (2001) *Handbook of Discourse Analysis* (Oxford: Blackwell).

Schneider, C. (1998) *The Practice of Autonomy: Patients, Doctors, and Medical Decisions* (Oxford: Oxford University Press).

Silverman, D. (1993) *Interpreting Qualitative Data: Methods for Analyzing Talk, Text, and Interaction* (Thousand Oaks, Calif: Sage).

Starr, P. (1982) *The Social Transformation of American Medicine: the Rise of a Sovereign Profession and the Making of a Vast Industry* (New York: Basic Books).

US National Institutes of Health. http://www.clinicaltrials.gov/ (accessed 25 April 2006).

3

The Communicative Functions of the Hospital Medical Chart

Pamela Hobbs

Introduction

Hospital care is characterized by work in teams, and the effective functioning of clinical teams is critical to the delivery of high-quality patient care. Because the goal of medical teamwork is the diagnosis and treatment of disease, hospital-based medicine is 'fundamentally about action' (Lingard *et al.*, 2003, p. 603). However, the information that forms the basis of this action is derived from a variety of sources, including the patient's report of symptoms, direct observation of clinical signs, and the results of laboratory tests and imaging studies (Hobbs, 2003, p. 451). Moreover, different members of the health care team have differential access to this information, due to differences in training, responsibility and degree of involvement in hands-on patient care; as a result, the sharing of information is essential to optimal case management (Christiansen and Larson, 1993, p. 340). Accordingly, the hospital chart, as a primary vehicle for communication among members of the health care team (ACOG, 1989, p. 45), has significant implications for both the structuring and the quality of patient care (Rees, 1981, p. 55).

Although the physician–patient encounter was long the dominant focus of medical discourse research (see, for example, discussion in Anspach, 1988), more recently scholars in the fields of sociolinguistics and discourse analysis have turned their attention to the collegial communications of medical professionals. These hospital-based studies have examined both the oral case presentations of medical residents and fellows (Anspach, 1988; Atkinson, 1995, 1999, 2004; Erickson, 1999; Hunter, 1991; Lingard *et al.*, 2003) and the rhetorical features of the hospital chart (Cook-Gumperz and Messerman, 1999; Hobbs, 2002, 2003, 2004; Pettinari, 1988; Rees, 1981). However, the majority of these studies focus on individual contributions; thus there is little specific discussion of how communication among team members is managed and coordinated.

This chapter presents an analysis of an obstetrical patient's chart, from hospital admission through to the delivery of her infant, providing a detailed examination of the coordinated interactions by which the patient's progress and condition were monitored and assessed, and treatment decisions were made. By bringing the methods of discourse analysis to the investigation of clinical work, this chapter demonstrates the centrality of communication to the delivery of medical care, and to the functioning of clinical teams.

Background

In the United States, reforms in medical education in the late nineteenth and early twentieth centuries resulted in the development of the teaching hospital as the prime site for the clinical training of medical students and novice physicians (Pecker and Siegler, 2003, p. 46). These hospitals, which often provide advanced specialty and subspecialty training to physicians in a number of different fields (for example internal medicine, obstetrics and gynaecology, oncology, perinataology),[1] are associated with university-based medical schools, and the practice of medicine in this setting is referred to as 'academic medicine'. Academic medicine is widely considered to exemplify the highest standards of medical practice (see Hunter, 1991, p. xxi), and medical discourse research in the hospital setting has focused on teaching hospitals (but see Hobbs, in press). In studying this type of setting, scholars have emphasized the importance of ethnographic observation, in order to gain an understanding of both the cultural domain and the technical content of the medical work that is being done (Atkinson, 1995, p. 18); thus researchers typically gather data during a period of field study ranging from weeks to months (see, for example, Anspach, 1988, pp. 359–60; Atkinson, 1995, p. vii; Cicourel, 1992, p. 299).

My introduction to medical discourse was as a lawyer rather than a scholar. Between March 1993 and December 1995, while employed by a law firm specializing in the defence of medical malpractice cases, I became one of the senior members of a team of lawyers representing an urban teaching hospital which is one of the largest obstetrical centres in the United States. As such, I was expected to acquire a sophisticated understanding of the principles of obstetrics, to be able to read and interpret medical records and fetal monitor strips, and to engage in the critical analysis of clinical management and outcomes. Through the continuous rounds of meetings with physicians, nurses and other health care providers that the preparation of these cases entailed, I learned not only a vocabulary and a set of principles, but a point of view to which I was irresistibly drawn, thus validating Erickson's observation that to internalize a linguistic register is to assume an identity (1999, p. 137). The perspective provided by that experience informs this work.

Progress notes

The hospital chart is the official record of the patient's care and treatment, and serves as the common repository for the observations and impressions of the members of the health care team, thus assuring that all relevant information about the patient will be literally at each treater's fingertips. The chart contains voluminous documentation regarding the patient's identification and insurance status, reason for admission, consent to treatment, physical examination, physicians' orders, laboratory and X-ray reports, treatment protocols and discharge instructions, generated by many departments of the hospital. For ease of reference, however, information about the patient's current physiological status, symptomatology, medications and treatment plan is continuously updated in the patient care notes that are recorded by members of the medical and nursing staff. These notes are typically handwritten on $8\frac{1}{2} \times 11$ inch pages imprinted with the running heading 'PROGRESS NOTES'.

Progress notes function as a running log of the patient's care, each beginning immediately below the preceding entry in order to maximize the amount of information that can be viewed without turning the page. Each note begins with the date and time and ends with the writer's signature, which *may* in the case of physicians, and *must* in the case of non-physicians, include the designation of his or her professional status, that is, 'MD' (medical doctor), 'RN' (registered nurse), 'RNC' (registered nurse-clinician, a nurse with advanced training), or 'LPN' (licensed practical nurse). Medical students are required to include their school and current year of study in their signatures, for example 'M. Smith, CSU III'. In addition, many notes include a heading which identifies the status of the writer, the content of the note, or both, that is, 'Resident's Admit Note', 'Post-Partum Nursing Admission Note', and so on. Each note thus inscribes the division of labour among team members (Atkinson, 1999, p. 99).

A key function of progress notes is communication among team members. The American College of Obstetrics and Gynecology, the credentialing body for the specialty of obstetrics and gynaecology in the United States, states in its practice standards that

> . . . the hospital record serves as a vehicle for communication among all members of the health care team. It should be legible, concise, cogent, and comprehensive. Furthermore, it should permit an easy assessment of the care provided and should reflect the patient's current status. (ACOG, 1989, p. 45)

However, the communication of this information is not an end in itself: its purpose is not passive reception, but ongoing active evaluation. Progress notes 'represent the dynamic assessment of the patient's problems and response to management' (Easton, 1974, p. 76), the goals of which are diagnosis and treatment. Diagnostic skill is the ability to match clinical symptoms and signs to existing descriptions of disease; it is an inductive process in which the physician must sort through the available data, looking for patterns that link observed physiologic manifestations to their cause, in order to produce a coherent medical story (Hobbs, 2003, p. 456; Hunter, 1991, pp. xviii–xix). Thus a team member reviewing a patient's chart 'does not take each entry on its own, but searches the record looking for a "grand design", which will explain the patient's condition' (Rees, 1981, p. 66); that is, the reader consults the aggregated information, searching for clues which may have emerged in the interval between the current reading and his or her own prior assessment. Moreover, in evaluating the information thus assembled, physicians also evaluate the opinions of their colleagues; there is thus 'a dual process of clinical investigation – of the patient and of other physicians' (Atkinson, 2004, p. 13, see also Hobbs, 2003).

The conventions of medical notation

Medical discourse is a professional speech register that is largely inaccessible to the lay public, due to the technical nature of its subject matter. However, its content is not solely a function of specialized disciplinary knowledge, but reflects a distinctive way of approaching and analysing medical problems which results from education and training designed to instil a clinical orientation that will enable the student to 'think like a doctor' (Lingard *et al.*, 2003, p. 607).

Clinical medicine is an investigative process in which information is assembled and analysed. By sifting the evidence gleaned from the patient's report of symptoms, the physical examination and laboratory test results, and by measuring them against competing possibilities and probing to discover missing information, the physician creates a recognizable clinical picture that matches the patient's condition to a known disease. The mode of analysis and presentation is strictly ordered by a set of conventions designed to ensure that the intended meaning is conveyed; the effect of these conventions is such that even physicians who are unfamiliar with the patient, the hospital and the writer can accurately interpret progress notes pertaining to their field of specialty. These conventions include an extensive and highly developed system of abbreviations which are used not only in chart entries but to a lesser but still significant extent in collegial conversations as well (see Erickson, 1999, pp. 116–19; Hobbs, 2003, pp. 476–8), the systematic use of evidential markers to specify the source and reliability of information (Atkinson, 1999; Hobbs, 2003), and pervasive reliance on background knowledge (Hobbs, 2002; Rees, 1981, pp. 66–8). The use of these conventions may be illustrated by the following excerpt from the data examined here:

30 She presented today c/o ® sided headache, epigastric discomfort c̄
31 nausea/emesis as well as swelling of face, hands, feet. While in
32 the LRC during her evaluation a deceleration was noted from
33 a baseline of 140 down to 115 × 2 minutes. The deceleration
34 was noted to be in response to a contraction and late in nature.
35 FHR tracing otherwise reassuring with accels to 165

This writer uses a number of common medical abbreviations, including 'c/o' for 'complaining of'; '®' for 'right'; 'c̄' for the Latin *cum*, meaning 'with'; 'LRC' for 'labour reception centre', the obstetrical emergency room; 'x' meaning 'times', indicating duration; and 'accels' for 'accelerations', the brief periodic increases in the fetal heart rate that signal fetal well-being. The writer also uses the passive voice to describe the episode of slowing of the fetal heart rate: 'While in the LRC during her evaluation a deceleration was noted . . . The deceleration was noted to be in response to a contraction . . . '. In medical notation, the passive voice is used to record the observations of other team members, thus acting as an 'attribution shield' which marks the information recorded for both *source* (another treater) and *mode of knowing* (hearsay), while the writer's own observations are recorded as facts (for example 'Vital signs stable') (Hobbs, 2003, pp. 465–7, citing Prince *et al.*, 1982, p. 91).

The writer's description of the deceleration in the fetal heart rate is limited to factual information and omits an explicit evaluation of the information recorded, stating only that there was a decrease from '140 down to 115 × 2 minutes' which was 'in response to a contraction and late in nature'. This description imputes to the reader knowledge of the fact that such late decelerations are cause for concern as a potential signal of fetal distress. Moreover, such knowledge is necessary to permit the reader to make the connection between this information and the evaluative statement that the fetal heart rate tracing was 'otherwise reassuring', and is thus a factor in producing the text's coherence (Giltrow, 1994, p. 155). Giltrow notes that while such shared 'background knowledge' is 'not exactly a discourse feature' because it is 'what is left unstated by the text', it nevertheless plays an important role in producing the text's intended meaning (Giltrow, 1994, p. 157). Rees (1981) discusses the role of such shared knowledge in the reading and interpretation of patient care notes:

> There has to be a common link between reader and writer for documentary information to produce their intended meaning. Specifically, there has to be a number of circumstances held in common which will allow the reader to 'read into' the statements more than the writer has actually placed on the page. In other words, there has to be a certain amount of 'reading between the lines' which can only be done by someone who shares similar experiences and expectations with the writer. In this way, a writer can 'take for granted' that much of the account can remain unsaid: that the reader will be able to add for himself the details which are not written on the page.
>
> Here we are referring to the 'indexicality' of accounts whereby the reader's knowledge of the typical circumstances of construction and of the typical biography of writers is crucial to making sense of the record. (Rees, 1981, p. 66)

It can thus be seen that the use of abbreviations, evidential markers and reliance on background knowledge shapes not only the form, but also the meaning, of patient care notes.

Data

This chapter presents an analysis of the progress notes of an obstetrical patient, Cheryl Landers, who presented to Fairview Hospital on 4 April 1994.[2] She was nine months pregnant and complained of headache, dizziness, nausea and vomiting, and swelling of the hands and feet, symptoms that are associated with pre-eclampsia. Although this condition poses a significant risk to both the pregnant woman and her fetus (Cunningham *et al.*, 1997, pp. 702–13, 716), pre-eclampsia is 'cured' by delivery (p. 714). Accordingly, where the patient is at term and pre-eclampsia is confirmed, immediate delivery is warranted.

In this case, the patient's symptoms were equivocal: while the combination of headache, dizziness, epigastric disturbances and oedema are classic symptoms of pre-eclampsia (Cunningham *et al.*, 1997, pp. 694–5), and while testing revealed trace protein in the urine that is also supportive of this diagnosis (p. 694), a key indicator of pre-eclampsia was absent. Pre-eclampsia results from pregnancy-induced or pregnancy-aggravated elevation of the maternal blood pressure, and this patient's blood pressure was well within normal range. However, while the patient and her fetus were being evaluated, there was a 25-beat-per-minute drop in the fetus's heart rate, from a normal 140 beats per minute to 115,[3] that lasted for two minutes. These 'prolonged decelerations' represented an additional equivocal symptom, since they may at times signal fetal compromise, but may also occur in labours resulting in normal births (Cunningham *et al.*, 1997, pp. 361–3). Given the presence of two indicia of potential concern in a patient who was at term, the decision was made to proceed with an immediate delivery. Since the patient had previously had three Caesarean section deliveries, a repeat Caesarean section delivery was ordered, to be followed by a tubal ligation at the patient's request.[4] At the stroke of midnight on 5 April 1994, Chantelle Landers, a healthy seven-pound female infant, was born.

The data examined here consist of the progress notes recorded in Cheryl Landers's chart, from the obstetrical nurse's initial entry to the time of delivery. The originally handwritten notes are reproduced here in typewritten form, and line numbers have been inserted; in all other respects, however, the original formatting (abbreviations, line breaks, spacing) has been retained. For the purposes of this analysis, the notes, which total 83 lines, will be divided into six segments, according to the chronological order of their progression: (1) the obstetrical nurse's initial entries documenting the processes of the patient's admission to the obstetrical floor; (2) the obstetrical resident's initial evaluation and the nurse's routine follow-up; (3) the resident's preoperative note containing a comprehensive analysis of the case; (4) the nurse's notes recording the routine preparation for a Caesarean section delivery; (5) the resident's note documenting that informed consent was obtained; and (6) the operative note written by the resident who assisted at delivery.

Analysis

Nurses' notes 1700–1925 (5:00–7:25 pm)

1 4-4-94
2 1700 – Rec pt to LRC #2 c/o swelling
3 in feet and legs. FM. CCMS obtained
4 trace protein. ⊕ H/A, ⊕ dizziness. Denies
5 seeing spots. ⊕ swelling in feet.
6 1720 – 110/51 RLP c̄ leg cuff. Tylenol PO given
7 for H/A. ______________________ G. Hall, RN
8 1815 – Consent signed and witnessed. Clothes
9 bagged and tagged. ⊕ variable noted c̄
10 slow recovery. To L&D for 23° Obs. – G. Hall, RN
11 1900 – closed/30%\fltg per Dr Connor. U/S then
12 to 4CR ______________________ G. Hall, RN
13 1925 – Ext. F.M. applied, FHT's – 140–150's. S. Stern, RN

Although it is nurses who provide the majority of hands-on patient care, the specific role of the obstetrical nurse varies across practice settings (James *et al.*, 2003, p. 814; Sauls, 2002, p. 739). In community-hospital settings where the physician is not normally present at the hospital until called to attend a delivery, nurses play a major role in patient management (Sauls, 2002, pp. 814–15). However, in a teaching hospital, the presence of residents shifts the decision-making responsibilities from obstetrical nurses to the training physicians. As a result, in teaching hospitals, the focus of nursing is patient monitoring and comfort.

Nurses' charting is characterized by the amount of detail that it provides, and reflects nursing's orientation to the documentation and reporting of observations and actions. Moreover, because nurses are not qualified to make medical diagnoses, their entries are framed as information rather than evaluation. However, despite the absence of explicit evaluation, those reviewing these entries, by 'reading between the lines' (Rees, 1981, p. 66), will be able to infer the nurse's implicit evaluations and conclusions.

This is aptly illustrated by the segment reproduced above, which comprises four successive entries by the original admitting nurse, Gina Hall, and a fifth note by a second nurse, Sarah Stern. Nurse Hall's entries display a common feature of the notes of nurses who are often in direct contact with the patient over long or intermittent periods of time during their 12-hour shifts, and this is the separation of information that could theoretically be contained in one continuous entry into segments indicating both the timing and chronology of the nurse's actions and observations. This attention to timing and chronology is one aspect of a universally recognized assumption which controls the style of chart entries: that information will be recorded in a certain order or sequence, the logic of which is governed by the inductive processes involved in medical diagnosis (see Hunter, 1991, pp. 53–6). Thus Easton notes that 'style, order, and sequence in data recording are important. Randomness is to be abhorred' (1974, p. ix). The communicative function of this canonical ordering of information may be demonstrated by an examination of Nurse Hall's initial entries:

4-4-94
1700 – Rec pt to LRC #2 c/o swelling
in feet and legs. FM. CCMS obtained
trace protein. $\oplus$ H/A, $\oplus$ dizziness. Denies
seeing spots. $\oplus$ swelling in feet.
1720 – 110/51 RLP c̄ leg cuff. Tylenol PO given
for H/A. ________________ G. Hall, RN

The note would be interpreted to read as follows:

> 5:00 pm Received patient to Labour Reception Centre Room 2, complaining of swelling in feet and legs. There was no fetal movement. Clear-catch micturation sample [that is, urine sample] obtained; testing showed trace protein. The patient complains of headache and dizziness but denies seeing spots. She has swelling in her feet.
>
> 5:20 pm Blood pressure was 110/51 when taken with leg cuff with patient lying on her right side. She was given Tylenol for her headache.

Here the interruption of the patient's list of symptoms to record the facts that no fetal movement was noted and that a urine sample was obtained appear to violate the rule that patient information should be recorded in its logical sequence. However, to the physician reader, these apparent changes in direction index information that is not recorded (Rees, 1981, pp. 66–7), allowing the reader to infer the nurse's unrecorded evaluation and analysis.

As noted, oedema (swelling) is a symptom associated with pre-eclampsia, a serious complication of pregnancy; however, oedema is very common in pregnant women, including those who are not pre-eclampsic (Cunningham *et al.*, 1997, p. 694), and the presence of oedema thus warrants further investigation. The diagnosis of pre-eclampsia is confirmed by hypertension (elevated blood pressure) plus proteinuria (the presence of protein in the urine), generalized overt oedema, or both (Cunningham *et al.*, 1997). In this case, the nurse, responding to the presenting complaint of oedema, immediately obtained and processed a urine sample, which showed trace protein, a finding associated with mild pregnancy-induced hypertension (Cunningham *et al.*, 1997, p. 695). As the sequencing of her note indicates, at that point she followed up by questioning the patient regarding additional symptoms of pregnancy-induced hypertension; the fact that this information was elicited in response to the nurse's questions is evidenced by the entry 'Denies seeing spots', since a person unfamiliar with the symptoms of pregnancy-induced hypertension would not make this statement spontaneously. The note also records the nurse's observation of the patient's swollen feet.

However, the following note (1720), timed 20 minutes after the first entry, shows that the patient's blood pressure, when taken, was 110/51, which is well within normal range. Thus, the patient was not hypertensive and, since the presence of hypertension is necessary to support a diagnosis of pre-eclampsia, this finding would appear to eliminate the possibility that the patient was pre-eclamptic. As a result, the nurse responded to her symptoms by giving her Tylenol for her headache.

1815 – Consent signed and witnessed. Clothes
bagged and tagged. ⊕ variable noted c̄
slow recovery. To L&D for 23° Obs. – G. Hall, RN
1900 – closed/30%\fltg per Dr Connor. U/S then
to 4CR ______________________ G. Hall, RN
1925 – Ext. F.M. applied, FHT's – 140-150's. S. Stern, RN

The next note (1815), timed at approximately one hour later, documents that the routine bureaucratic procedures of the admission process have been performed: the patient has signed the consent for admission, and her street clothing and other belongings have been bagged and tagged for safe keeping. Following these routine procedures, the patient, having donned her hospital gown, would have been settled in her bed and the external fetal monitor – a device that monitors the fetal heart rate – applied. Here the nurse documents, not the application of the fetal monitor, but the result: a variable deceleration (slowing of the fetal heart rate) with slow recovery was observed. Such decelerations may signal fetal jeopardy and are thus cause for concern. However, the nurse's note contains no evaluation, but simply reports that the patient will be taken to the labour and delivery floor for observation.

The 1900 note indicates that the patient was seen by the resident, who performed a vaginal examination which confirmed that she was in the latent (early) phase of labour.[5] The note records the resident's order to obtain an ultrasound of the fetus and then transfer the patient to the obstetrical unit ('4 Center'). The 1925 note records the reapplication of the fetal monitor following transfer, and documents fetal heart tones in the 140's and 150's, which is within the normal range.

Resident's note 2050 (8:50 pm)

14 2050 Pt c/o ® sided headache. Swelling of hands and feet has resolved on
15 bedrest. ⊕ nausea/gastric upset. Last emesis today in LRC. Still c̄
16 puffiness around eyes. ∅ visual changes.
17 FHTs – Baseline 130 c̄ accels to 150. Ø decels. Good variability.
18 Toco – ∅ contractions. SVE – Deferred.
19 A/P ① IUP @ 39-0/7 weeks. LMP, 22 week sono.
20 ② R/O PIH BPs stable (WNL). ¦PIH labs.
21 ③ Prev C/S × 3 – for repeat C/S if delivered tonight.
23 Continue close monitoring on L&D. P. Raymond, M.D.

In teaching hospitals, resident physicians, as a component of their specialty training, are present at the hospital on a 24-hour basis and are primarily responsible for the management of patients. Physicians must internalize vast amounts of information about human anatomy, physiology and disease pathology; however, memorization is not enough, for they must also be able to manipulate the concepts that medical analysis comprehends (Hobbs, 2004, p. 1600). Residency thus incorporates pedagogical exercises that are designed to develop this ability by making explicit the reasoning and analysis that inhere in the work that is being performed.

Following admission, the resident's initial examination of the patient represents the continuation of a process that begins in medical school, when third-year medical students are initiated into the realities of clinical practice by 'working up' patients, that is, taking a history, performing a physical examination, and analysing the information obtained to formulate a diagnostic assessment (Weinholtz, 1991, p. 156). The resident's mastery of the analytic processes involved in medical diagnosis is fostered by spoken and written genres that require him or her to demonstrate that analysis both orally and in writing to the supervising attending physician.

The oral 'case presentation', which takes place during morning rounds, is a summary and analysis of the facts relevant to the diagnosis and treatment of the patient's condition (Hobbs, 2004, p. 1582). As a 'command performance' on the part of the resident, the case presentation is both a display of specialty knowledge and a vehicle of professional socialization, 'of learning how to be a particular type of doctor within the medical hierarchy' (Sarangi and Roberts, 1999, p. 37). Closely related to the case presentation is the resident's 'admit note', which records the initial examination of the patient and is ordinarily the opening entry in the progress notes (Hobbs, 2004, pp. 1582–3).

Residents' notes are readily identifiable by their length, amount of detail, and by the copybook clarity that distinguishes them from the hurried scribbles of experienced attendings, and betrays the fact that these painstaking analyses are not extemporaneous jottings, but the results of searching analysis. The form of residents' notes is based on Weed's (1969) concept of the problem-oriented medical record as a training tool for physicians, and is referred to as the 'SOAP method', an acronym for Subjective, Objective, Assessment and Plan (Easton, 1974; Hobbs, 2003, p. 454; Waters and Murphy, 1979, p. 74). These categories and their sequence, which formalize the logic of differential diagnosis, act as a mental checklist that guides the resident's performance (Erickson, 1999, p. 112; Weed, 1969, p. 11), and are designed to both develop and demonstrate the resident's acquisition of the ability to construct professional objectivity (Iedema and Wodak, 1999, p. 12; Lingard *et al.*, 2003, p. 604), what Atkinson (1995, p. 5) calls 'the clinical gaze'.

14 2050 Pt c/o ® sided headache. Swelling of hands and feet has resolved on
15 bedrest. ⊕ nausea/gastric upset. Last emesis today in LRC. Still c̄
16 puffiness around eyes. ∅ visual changes.
17 FHTs – Baseline 130 c̄ accels to 150.∅ decels. Good variability.
18 Toco – ∅ contractions. SVE – Deferred.

The initial note written by the resident, Dr Patricia Raymond, follows this formula, beginning with the patient's reported symptoms and the physical examination, the 'subjective' and 'objective' components of the SOAP method of notation. The distinction that is marked by these terms indexes the physician's relationship to the information recorded.

Thus, information regarding a symptom that cannot be assessed by examination, because it involves an internal sensation (headache, gastric upset) or is no longer present (swelling that has resolved), is classified as 'subjective', while information that is directly observable (by physical examination) or independently verifiable (by blood tests, X-rays and so on) is classified as 'objective' (Hobbs, 2003, p. 460). This distinction is medically significant because, while a physician should consider all relevant information in evaluating a patient, the weight to be assigned to a particular piece of information may vary in accordance with the physician's ability to evaluate it (Hobbs, 2003).

In this case, Dr Raymond's notes record the patient's complaints of headache, nausea and gastric upset with vomiting as recently as shortly after her arrival at the hospital, and swelling of the hands and feet that had dissipated and was no longer present, although she was still puffy around the eyes. The probable meaning of these symptoms is not readily accessible to the lay observer; however, taken together, to an obstetrician or obstetrical nurse they are highly suggestive of pregnancy-induced hypertension and/or pre-eclampsia. Because these conditions pose a risk to the fetus, the objective portion of Dr Raymond's note records her evaluation of the fetus' condition.

Fetal status is assessed via the fetal heart rate monitor or tocodynamometer, which provides simultaneous readings of the fetal heart rate and maternal uterine contractions. These appear on a monitor screen mounted on the machine and are also recorded on a continuously printed readout (the fetal monitor strip) which allows retrospective review of the information recorded. Dr Raymond's note indicates a normal heart rate with accelerations, good variability and no decelerations, all of which are positive signs. The readout also reveals the absence of any contractions, indicating that the patient is not in active labour; consequently, vaginal examination of the patient, the purpose of which is to assess the progress of labour, is postponed.

19 A/P ① IUP @ 39-0/7 weeks. LMP, 22 week sono.
20 ② R/O PIH BPs stable (WNL). ↑PIH labs.
21 ③ Prev C/S × 3 - for repeat C/S if delivered tonight.
23 Continue close monitoring on LandD. P. Raymond, M.D.

The assessment and plan (labelled here as 'A/P') summarizes Dr Raymond's evaluation and findings and lists the action to be taken. The assessment indicates a normally implanted pregnancy ('IUP' = intrauterine pregnancy, that is, not ectopic) at term ('39-0/7 weeks', where term is 38–42 weeks), according to calculations based on date of last menstrual period and ultrasound performed at 22 weeks' gestation. The plan is to order blood tests to rule out pregnancy-induced hypertension ('PIH labs'), to schedule a repeat Caesarean section delivery if immediate delivery is warranted, and to closely monitor the patient's condition while awaiting the results of the tests. To the medically trained eye, the contents of this note are symmetrical and balanced, reflecting one of the cardinal rules of construction of progress notes, that the writer records only such information as is medically relevant (cf. Pettinari, 1988, p. 87). Moreover, relevancy is a function of the context in which the information is presented (Atkinson, 1995, p. 97). Thus Rees (1981) notes that

> [t]here should be... a clear relationship between the information recorded as part of the history and examination and the diagnosis which is documented. The House Officer [resident] has to attend to those facts in the written account which point to the condition he has identified. In this way the requirement to produce a diagnosis produces a certain reflexivity in the process of recording the facts of the case. (Rees, 1981, p. 56)

In recording the actions to be taken, Dr Raymond notes that the patient's blood pressure is stable and within normal limits ('WNL'), a finding that is inconsistent with a diagnosis of pregnancy-induced hypertension. Yet the patient's reported symptoms, as recorded in the subjective findings, suggest a contrary conclusion, thus requiring further investigation. Moreover, the uncertainty regarding the significance of the patient's symptoms is matched by uncertainty regarding the fetus' gestational age, as indicated in the objective findings. Information regarding the accuracy of the fetus' estimated gestational age is relevant to the determination of whether immediate delivery is warranted because, if the estimate is inaccurate and the fetus is in fact immature, there are additional risk factors to be considered. In this case, the note indicates that the calculation of gestational age is based on the patient's last menstrual period and a second-trimester ultrasound; what the physician reviewing this note would bring to the text is the knowledge that both menstrual dating and dating by second-trimester ultrasound are subject to a margin of error of plus or minus two weeks.

24 2055 blood labs drawn per orders. D. Peyton, RN.
25 2205 IV started ® hand 18 g $\frac{1}{4}$ jelco
26 1000 cc LR↑ via travenal @ 100 cc/m pt
27 tolerated procedure well. __________ D. Peyton, RN

The nursing notes indicate that the nurse, Donna Peyton, drew the blood for laboratory testing at 8:55 pm, pursuant to Dr Raymond's order, and subsequently began the intravenous infusion of a saline solution, a standard procedure in labouring patients.

Resident's note 2210 (10:10 pm)

28 4/4/94 LandD Note – Pre-Op:
29 2210 38 y.o. G_7 P_{2133} @ 38-1/7 weeks by LMP, 22 week sono
30 She presented today c/o ® sided headache, epigastric discomfort c̄
31 nausea/emesis as well as swelling of face, hands, feet. While in
32 the LRC during her evaluation a deceleration was noted from
33 a baseline of 140 down to 115 × 2 minutes. The deceleration
34 was noted to be in response to a contraction and late in nature.
35 FHR tracing otherwise reassuring with accels to 165. A second
36 late deceleration occurred while undergoing prolonged monitoring on
37 LandD again lasting ~ 2 minutes with good recovery to baseline
38 and good variability noted. PIH labs WNL: {uric acid 4.7 SGOT −17
39 ⊕ History of C-Section ×3 with scheduled repeat{Cr−0.7 SGPT – 21
40 section set for 4/11/94. BPs WNL (110/50).
41 As D/W Dr Vickers, in light of recurrent late decelerations
42 in a pregnancy at term, will proceed with C-Section delivery
43 tonight.
44 A/P ① IUP @ 38-1/7 weeks LMP, 22 week sono
45 ② late decels ⑥Rubella nonimmune – vaccinate
46 ③Hx of PIH in first pregnancy postpartum
47 ④Prev C-Section ×3 For repeat C-Section
48 ⑤Desires PPTL Consent on chart

49 T&C'd for 2UPRBCs: Consent for C-Section on chart.
P. Raymond, MD
50 Agree. Vickers

Dr Raymond's initial assessment can be compared and contrasted with her comprehensive labour and delivery note recording her follow-up evaluation and the decision to perform a Caesarean section delivery. The note incorporates and expands upon the analysis that was developed in the admit note, examining both the maternal and fetal signs and analysing them in light of the gestational age of the fetus and the patient's prior history and risk factors. The purpose of this detail is to both rehearse and display the resident's grasp of the clinical situation (Atkinson, 2004, p. 18; Hobbs, 2002, p. 268). By providing a detailed account which permits the reader 'to identify and reconstruct the most salient findings and to follow the course of management' (Atkinson, 1995, p. 97), the resident demonstrates an ability to analyse the clinical issues that the case presents (Erickson, 1999, p. 112).

Dr Raymond's note begins: '[The patient is a] 38-year-old gravida 7, para 2, 1, 3, 3, at 38-1/7 week by last menstrual period and 22-week sonogram.'[6] This compact summary of the patient's clinical presentation marks the opening move of residents' oral case presentations (Atkinson, 1999, p. 86; Hobbs, 2004, p. 1582) and, ordinarily, of their admit notes as well. Here Dr Raymond's relatively brief admit note omitted this canonical feature, and it is thus included in this subsequent note. The information included provides a framework for analysis by categorizing the patient as an obstetrical patient at term and by specifying her age and parity, factors which are relevant to pregnancy outcome.[7]

The note reviews the history of the patient's presenting complaints – headache, upset stomach with nausea and vomiting and swelling of the hands and feet – and then begins a lengthy and detailed review of the fetal signs, which provides new information in addition to what was described in the admit note. Dr Raymond now notes that, while the patient was being evaluated in the Labour Reception Centre during the admission process, there was a slowing of the fetal heart rate 'from a baseline of 140 down to 115 × [for] two minutes', and that this episode was 'in response to a contraction and late in nature'. Because the same deceleration was described as 'variable' rather than 'late' by the nurse, Gina Hall, who documented it in her 1815 (6:15 pm) note, this entry reveals that the resident has reviewed both the chart and the fetal monitor strips.

Variable decelerations are observed during the majority of labours, and generally are not cause for alarm where they are not repeated or 'significant' (that is, deep) (Cunningham *et al.*, 1997, pp. 359–61). However, 'late' decelerations (those that begin at or after the peak of a contraction) may signal fetal hypoxia (deprivation of oxygen) and thus warrant heightened surveillance, especially where, as here, they are prolonged (Cunningham *et al.*, 1997, pp. 357–8, 362). Dr Raymond's notation that the pattern displayed on the strip was '*otherwise* reassuring with accels to 165' (emphasis added) displays her understanding of the contradictory meanings of these signs: decelerations provide equivocal evidence of fetal jeopardy, while accelerations are strongly correlated with fetal well-being (Cunningham *et al.*, 1997, p. 357). These meanings, which are available to the reader in the form of background knowledge, explain the (implied) decision to take no action at the time that the signs were observed. The additional information that is now available is that a second deceleration occurred after the patient was admitted to the floor; this deceleration was also prolonged, lasting approximately two minutes, followed by a 'good recovery to baseline and good variability', the latter being positive indicators.

After describing the fetal decelerations, Dr Raymond completes her analysis with the following information: the patient's laboratory results have been returned with no abnormal readings; her blood pressure is normal, thus failing to confirm pregnancy-induced hypertension; and, having previously undergone three Caesarean section deliveries, she had been scheduled to undergo a repeat Caesarean section delivery the following week (11 April 1994). The weighing of these factors is revealed in the conclusion, 'As D/W [discussed with] Dr Vickers, in light of recurrent late decelerations in a pregnancy at term, will proceed with C-Section delivery tonight.' The considerations that guided this decision are then summarized in outline form in the assessment/plan: (1) intrauterine pregnancy at term, (2) late decelerations, (3) history of pregnancy-induced hypertension in first pregnancy, (4) three previous Caesarean sections. In addition, the plan notes that the patient desires a post-delivery tubal ligation and has signed a consent authorizing the same, that she will be vaccinated for rubella following delivery, that she has been typed and crossmatched for two units of packed red blood cells, and that the consent form authorizing the Caesarean delivery is on the chart. The note is countersigned by the attending, Dr Vickers, who indicates his concurrence with the word 'Agree'.

There is little explicit evaluation of the information recorded prior to the description of the decision to deliver the patient immediately 'in light of recurrent late decelerations in a pregnancy at term'. However, when this descriptive rationale is reviewed in connection with the symptoms previously detailed, the following analysis may be inferred:

1 Both the maternal and fetal signs are equivocal, in that they are suggestive of potentially serious problems but provide no clear evidence that those problems are in fact present;
2 These signs thus provide no clear grounds for intervention;
3 However, the patient is at term, which is the optimal time for delivery;
4 Moreover, she had been scheduled for a Caesarean section delivery the following week, due to the fact that her previous deliveries were by Caesarean section;
5 Consequently, since the patient is at term, and since it had already been determined that she would be delivered by Caesarean section, an immediate Caesarean section delivery will not pose any additional risk to the patient or her fetus, and will avoid the potential risks that may result from continuing the pregnancy in light of the maternal and fetal signs.

Dr Raymond's note thus displays her medical judgement by allowing the reader to retrace the steps by which her analysis and decision-making were carried out.

Nurses' notes 2240–2305 (10:40–11:05 pm)

51 2240 Indwelling foley catheter placed pt
52 tolerated procedure well – 150 cc clear dark
53 yellow urine emptied from bladder. ________ D. Peyton, RN
54 2250 Abd prep done pt ready for CS per orders. ___ D. Peyton, RN
55 2305 Rec'd pt in RLP. IV ® hand, site clear and
56 intact, LR↑. FM → FHT's 140's. No reg ctx noted.
57 Pt awaiting C/S. Reflexes 1-2+. J. Bly, RN.
58 2330 FM d/c'd. Pt trf to stretcher, to CR 6 for

The 10:40–11:05 pm nurses' notes record the routine preparations for a Caesarean section (that is, operative) delivery: the patient is catheterized and her bladder is drained, the area of the incision is cleaned and sterilized, and she continues to undergo monitoring while awaiting transfer to the operating suite. During this period, her condition is stable, as reflected by notations indicating that she is lying in bed ('in RLP' = in right lateral position) with her intravenous line attached and infusing, that the fetal heart tones are in the 140s (a normal rate), and that no regular contractions are noted. The 11:30 pm note indicates that fetal monitoring has been discontinued and the patient transferred to a stretcher and taken to the operating suite for a Caesarean section delivery. The note is unusual in that it ends in mid-sentence ('Pt trf to stretcher, to CR 6 for') and is not signed, suggesting that the nurse was interrupted and did not remember to return and complete her entry. However, there is no loss of information, for the missing phrase ('Caesarean section delivery') is readily inferable from the context.

Resident's addendum

4/4/94	Addendum –
2325	Discussed with patient that with her dating being
	based on her LMP and a 22 week sono, she may be
	36+ weeks rather than 38+ weeks (/2\ ultrasound may
	be 2 weeks off). Patient understands that there is a
	slight chance for RDS in her infant requiring special
	attention immediately after delivery (i.e. O_2, ventilation).
	All questions concerning repeat Cesarean Section delivery
	answered.
	P. Raymond, MD
	Agree. Vickers

The concept of informed consent embodies the physician's ethical and legal obligation to discuss the plan of treatment with the patient, to ascertain that the patient understands both the treatment to be undertaken and its attendant risks, and to obtain the patient's consent to proceed (Fauci *et al.*, 1998, p. 4). In this addendum to her preoperative note, Dr Raymond documents her discussion with the patient advising her of the potential risks of an immediate Caesarean section delivery. Because dating by last menstrual period and/or second-trimester ultrasound is accurate only to within two weeks (Berkow, 1992, p. 1851), the fetus may be less mature than estimated, resulting in the birth of a premature infant. A common complication of preterm delivery is hyaline membrane disease or respiratory distress syndrome ('RDS'), which in the most severe cases may be fatal (Cunningham *et al.*, 1997, pp. 967–9). Respiratory distress syndrome may require mechanical ventilation and surfactant therapy (p. 968).

Dr Raymond's note displays her understanding of the importance of ascertaining gestational age when expedited delivery is contemplated, of the limitations on the accuracy of dating by last menstrual period and second-trimester ultrasound, and of the risk that preterm delivery will result in the development of respiratory distress syndrome caused by fetal lung immaturity. The countersignature of the attending, Dr Vickers, indicates his agreement that the information provided to the patient was appropriate.

Resident's operative note

70 4/5/94
71 0030 Pre-Op Dx – ® C/S, Bilat. partial
72 Salpin.
73 nonreassuring FHT
74 Postop Dx – same
75 Proced ® C/S
76 Bilat partial salpin
77 Surg Dr Vickers
78 Asst Dr Harper
79 Dr West
80 EBL 500 cc
81 Fin nl tube and ovary
82 VFI c Apgars 9, 9
83 A. West, MD

Surgery is an invasive procedure that has the potential to affect the very life of the patient; accordingly, long-standing tradition requires a formal operative report which presents a precisely detailed description of the procedures and techniques that were used. The operative report is dictated after the surgery, and is then typed, signed and placed in the patient's chart. Operative reports are not part of the progress notes, but are a separate and distinct category within the medical record. Accordingly, pending the preparation of the operative report, an operative note is entered in the progress notes to document the procedure that has been performed. The form of the note is a list rather than a narrative account, and the standard categories include preoperative diagnosis, postoperative diagnosis, procedure, surgeon, assistant(s), anaesthesia, estimated blood loss, and findings. This strict ordering produces remarkably uniform results, as may be illustrated by the following examples from two additional hospitals:

Example A
4-2-95 Pre Op Dx: Fetal distress, 27 weeks, cord presentation
Post Op Dx: Same + placental abruption
Procedure: 1° LTCS
Surgeon: Dr Dewey
Assist: Haines Laura Gomez, CSUIII
Anes: general

EBL: 800 cc
Cord blood gas 7.31/33/56.9 %/51/25.3
Abd x-ray: (No Count) Negative
James Haggerty

Example B

0640 Pre OP Dx: NR FHT
poss. abruption
preg. at 36+ wks
previous C/S
Post Op Dx: The same + ♀ infant wt
and apgar
Procedure: Repeat LTCS
Surgeon: Dr Eden
Asst: Dr Adams
Anesth: Spinal
Compl: None
EBL = 500
IV = 2200
VO = 100
Dictated A. Adams

In the data being examined, the operative note was written by Dr Alan West, one of two residents who assisted at the delivery, which was performed by the attending physician, Dr Vickers. The preoperative diagnosis is 'repeat cesarean section, bilateral partial salpingectomy [tubal ligation]; nonreassuring fetal heart tones'; the postoperative diagnosis is the same. The estimated blood loss, 500 cc, is well within the normal range, and the operative findings ('Fin') are listed as 'normal tube and ovary; viable female infant with Apgars of 9 and 9'.[8]

Discussion

In the modern hospital, patient care responsibilities are distributed among individuals with differing qualifications, training and experience who normally are not co-present with one another, due to the complex structuring of hospital routines. Thus although they are a team in the sense of their joint contribution to the patient's care, their interaction with one another is limited. In this setting, the medical chart plays a critical role in facilitating communication between team members, in order to ensure that all relevant information is taken into account in determining the course of the patient's ongoing management (Christiansen and Larson, 1993, p. 339). In particular, progress notes, as a vehicle of medical action, serve a number of related functions which emphasize the centrality of communication to medical work, and which demonstrate that the communication of health care professionals is not simply communication 'about' medical work; rather the work is enacted through their oral and written communications (Atkinson, 1995, p. 93).

Recording observations and actions

An important function of progress notes is to record observations and actions. Medical treatment is a dynamic process, involving the ongoing evaluation of symptoms and signs and the patient's response to management. The continuous monitoring of the patient's condition is thus essential to the provision of appropriate care. In a teaching hospital, the responsibility for patient monitoring is shared by the nurses and the resident staff. In this setting, the residents are primarily responsible for the management of the patient's labour; accordingly, the focus of nursing is custodial care. Much of a nurse's time is consumed in mundane but essential tasks, including assisting the patient into bed, securing her clothing and other valuables, obtaining blood and urine sample, and routine preparation for surgery; and the recording of these activities serves the bureaucratic function of providing evidence of their performance. However, the nurse is more than a mere 'babysitter'; as the caregiver with the most direct patient contact, her job critically involves monitoring the patient's condition, and recording and reporting any concerning signs. This can be seen in the data in Nurse Hall's recording of what she interpreted as a variable deceleration during the admission process.

Residents also record their observations and actions. However, while nurses' notes are generally framed as log entries which do not evaluate the recorded events, residents' notes are explicitly evaluative, recording both monitoring and decision-making. Residents' notes thus display the resident's exercise of the physician role.

Reporting ongoing assessment

The goals of medical care are diagnosis and treatment. However, where the patient's symptoms are equivocal, or do not suggest a specific aetiology, the process may require a period of observation. In such cases, ongoing assessment of the patient's condition, in order to identify the problem and to implement an appropriate plan of management, is critical to the investigative process. In this case, the patient presented with headache, oedema and dizziness, all suggestive of pregnancy-induced hypertension; yet her blood pressure was normal, a fact that would seem to rule out the diagnosis, while leaving the signs and symptoms unexplained.

The clinical picture was further complicated by a fetal heart rate deceleration that was noted during her initial evaluation. Such decelerations are inherently equivocal, since they may be associated with adverse pregnancy outcome, but are also ordinarily present during the second stage of labour, and thus precede most deliveries of normal healthy infants as well (Cunningham *et al.*, 1997, pp. 363–4). Moreover, although decelerations are classified as 'early', 'variable' or 'late', and also on the basis of whether or not they are 'prolonged' (pp. 357–62), the assignment of a tracing to one of these categories is subject to differing interpretations. In such cases, decision-making is frequently dependent upon the observations and assessments of a number of individuals, which, recorded in the chart, produce a pattern that emerges over a period of hours or of days. This occurred in the present case, where recurrent decelerations in a patient who was at term motivated the decision to proceed with an immediate Caesarean section delivery.

Displaying knowledge, expertise and judgement

Cook-Gumperz and Messerman note that '[n]ot only do medical records provide the history of a course of treatment within a particular setting... but they also establish the documentary evidence of professional competence on the part of all medical personnel attending the case' (1999, p. 145). Progress notes display the professional competence of the writer because the selection of information to be included implies professional knowledge and constitutes an exercise of professional judgement. Moreover, the descriptions that the notes contain are evaluated from the standpoint of both their content and their source: 'Not only do physicians evaluate the information they have about the patient; they also evaluate the work and opinions of their professional students and colleagues' (Atkinson, 2004, p. 13).

For residents, progress notes provide an opportunity to rehearse and display the reasoning and analysis involved in clinical decision-making (Hobbs, 2002, p. 268). Through the repeated production of these records, residents learn to 'systematize their clinical experience' (Weed, 1969, p. 6). As a result, during the successive years of residency, their notes become, in the words of one of Pettinari's informants, 'more [appropriately] detailed, briefer, and more likely to be in proper order' (1988, p. 87). Thus residents' notes, which serve both patient-care and pedagogical goals, record the progress of both the patient and the resident.

Constructing the case

Medical education involves the acquisition of a body of knowledge about human anatomy, physiology and disease pathology that is transmitted primarily through language; and while physicians must learn to translate this knowledge into action (Atkinson, 1995, pp. 100–1), the centrality of language to medical practice is clear. Medical knowledge is narratively constructed (Hunter, 1991, p. xiii), and medical work is enacted through rhetorical forms (Atkinson, 1995, p. x), chief among which is the case itself. The case is the concept that structures medical analysis, and the chart records the discursive processes by which it is constructed, revealing 'how the account is constructed out of embedded accounts, descriptions and opinions' (Atkinson, 1999, p. 98). Yet the chart is more than a mere record of these processes, and is itself an integral part of the processes by which the case is constructed.

However, advances in computer technology over the past several decades have led some to question the chart's continuing efficacy, given its claimed imperfections (that is, illegibility, inaccuracy, availability limited to one person at a time) and the existence of modalities permitting the electronic recording and storage of medical information (see, for example, Hannan, 1996). Yet the 'low-tech' paper-based chart has undeniable advantages: 'Paper is portable and requires no specific workspace configurations; no power source, equipment or network is required; no training is involved in implementing its use; access to data is direct; and rapid scanning of information is facilitated by paper's manipulability' (Coiera 1997: 62). Thus paper has an 'ecological dexterity' that computers cannot match (Luff and Heath, 1998, p. 307).

As the common repository of case-relevant information, the chart provides access to the observations and impressions of all members of the health care team, and this pooling of information is essential in a setting where the management of a case may involve several services, and where each team member's direct knowledge of the patient's condition is limited. The crucial role of the chart in medical diagnosis and treatment is to enable the resident or attending physician to review the entries, particularly the progress notes, in order to search for the cues that will trigger recognition of the patterns implicit in the signs and symptoms presented (Rees, 1981, p. 66): In the space of a few pages, the chart digests hours or days of observations and evaluations constituting the collective knowledge, experience and judgement of numerous nurses and physicians, thus allowing the physician to access the clinical picture that is emerging. The aggregation of information that the chart provides is a formidable tool in the diagnosis of disease.

Conclusion

The hospital chart and the communicative functions that it performs play a vital role in the functioning of medical teams. As the central mechanism for the collection of patient information, the chart serves a number of related communicative functions that are critical to the provision of high-quality patient care: it records observations and analysis, provides information relevant to the ongoing assessment of the patient's condition, and, by integrating information gathered from diverse sources, provides a solid foundation for medical diagnosis and treatment. In teaching hospitals, in addition to these patient-care functions, the chart also serves as a pedagogical tool for the training of medical residents, allowing them to rehearse the analytic processes of case construction and to display their knowledge, expertise and clinical judgement. The chart thus organizes the processes of information exchange and evaluation by which medical work is carried out.

To date, the sociolinguistic study of medical discourse in the hospital setting has focused on physicians' communications (but see Hobbs, in press). However, hospital-based physicians do not perform their work in isolation; rather, hospital teams are composed of physicians, nurses and other allied health care professionals. Accordingly, a thorough understanding of hospital communication requires an examination of the interactions of all members of the health care team. This chapter has examined the role of the hospital chart in coordinating team-oriented care. Through an analysis of the progress notes written by obstetrical residents and nurses in a patient's chart from the time of her admission to the hospital through the delivery of her infant, this chapter has shown how the clinical picture of a case emerges through the coordinated communications of team members. By tracing the interactive processes by which the patient's signs and symptoms were evaluated and analysed, this chapter thus demonstrates the centrality of communication to the delivery of medical care.

Notes

1 Specialty training programmes (such as internal medicine and the combined specialty of obstetrics and gynaecology) are known as 'residencies' and the physician-trainees are known as 'residents'. Subspecialty training programmes (such as oncology, a subspecialty of internal medicine, and perinatology, a subspecialty of obstetrics and gynaecology) are known as 'fellowships', and the physician-trainees are known as 'fellows'. The fully qualified specialists and subspecialists who supervise the training physicians are known as 'attending physicians' or 'attendings'.

2 All personal and institutional names have been changed.

3 The normal baseline fetal heart rate is 120–160 beats per minute (Cunningham *et al.*, 1997, p. 351).

4 The patient was 38 years of age and had three other children.

5 The purpose of the examination is to monitor the condition of the cervix, the orifice through which the infant emerges. It is located at the back of the vagina, and ordinarily remains tightly closed. However, during labour, the cervix undergoes progressive dilatation (opening) and effacement (thinning and flattening) until it has expanded sufficiently to permit passage of the fetus. In the normal course of events, as this is occurring, the fetus moves into position and becomes 'engaged' in the birth canal. Here the note indicates that the cervix is closed and 30 per cent effaced, and that the fetus is 'floating', that is, not yet engaged.

6 The term 'gravida' refers to the total number of pregnancies a woman has had, including the current pregnancy; the term 'para' refers to pregnancy outcome. Here the notations indicate that the patient is in her seventh pregnancy and has previously had two deliveries at term, one premature delivery, three miscarriages or abortions (term is non-specific), and has three living children (see Cunningham *et al.*, 1997, p. 229).

7 Pregnancy in women over the age of 35 is associated with increases in the risk of maternal, fetal and newborn complications (Cunningham *et al.*, 1997, pp. 572–7), as is grand parity (five or more pregnancies) (Aliyu *et al.*, 2005).

8 The Apgar scoring system is a widely used means of evaluating the condition of newborn infants in order to assess their need for immediate resuscitation. The score consists of five measures: heart rate, respiratory rate, muscle tone, reflex irritability and colour, each of which is given a score of 0, 1 or 2, yielding a maximum possible score of 10. Infants are evaluated at one minute of age and again at five minutes of age (Cunningham *et al.*, 1997, pp. 400–1). In this case, the infant's Apgar scores of 9 at both one and five minutes of age were consistent with a normal, healthy infant.

References

ACOG (American College of Obstetrics and Gynecology) (1989) *Standards for Obstetric-Gynecologic Services* (7th edn) (Washington, DC: American College of Obstetrics and Gynecology).

Aliyu, M. H., Jolly, P. E., Ehiru, J. E. and Salihu, H. M. (2005) 'High Parity and Adverse Birth Outcomes: Exploring the Maze', *Birth*, 32(1), pp. 45–59.

Anspach, R. R. (1988) 'Notes on the Sociology of Medical Discourse: the Language of Case Presentation', *Journal of Health and Social Behavior*, 29, pp. 357–75.

Atkinson, P. (1995) *Medical Talk and Medical Work: the Liturgy of the Clinic* (London: Thousand Oaks and New Dehli: Sage Publications).

Atkinson, P. (1999) 'Medical Discourse, Evidentiality and the Construction of Professional Responsibility', in S. Sarangi and C. Roberts (eds) *Talk, Work, and Institutional Order: Discourse in Medical, Mediation and Management Settings*, pp. 75–107 (Berlin and New York: Mouton de Gruyter).

Atkinson, P. (2004) 'The Discursive Construction of Competence and Responsibility in Medical Collegial Talk', *Communication and Medicine*, 1, pp. 13–23.

Berkow, R. (ed.) (1992) *The Merck Manual of Diagnosis and Therapy* (16th edn) (Radway, NJ: Merck Research Laboratories).

Christiansen, C. and Larson, J. R., Jr (1993) 'Collaborative Medical Decision Making', *Medical Decision Making*, 13, pp. 339–46.

Cicourel, A. V. (1992) 'The Interpenetration of Communicative Contexts: Examples from Medical Encounters', in A. Duranti and C. Goodwin (eds) *Rethinking Context: Language as an Interactive Phenomenon*, pp. 291–310 (Cambridge: Cambridge University Press).

Coiera, E. (1997) *Guide to Medical Informatics, the Internet and Telemedicine* (London: Chapman and Hall Medical).

Cook-Gumperz, J. and Messerman, L. (1999) 'Local Identities and Institutional Practices: Constructing the Record of Professional Collaboration', in S. Sarangi and C. Roberts (eds) *Talk, Work, and Institutional Order: Discourse in Medical, Mediation and Management Settings*, pp. 145–81 (Berlin and New York: Mouton de Gruyter).

Cunningham, F. G., MacDonald, P. C., Grant, N. F., Leveno, K. J., Gilstrap, L. C., Hankins, G. D. V. and Clark, S. L. (1997) *Williams Obstetrics* (20th edn) (Stanford, CT: Appleton and Lange).

Easton, R. E. (1974) *Problem-Oriented Medical Record Concepts* (New York: Appleton-Century-Crofts).

Erickson, F. (1999) 'Appropriation of Voice and Presentation of Self as a Fellow Physician: Aspects of a Discourse of Apprenticeship in Medicine', in S. Sarangi and C. Roberts (eds) *Talk, Work, and Institutional Order: Discourse in Medical, Mediation and Management Settings*, pp. 109–43 (Berlin and New York: Mouton de Gruyter).

Fauci, A. S., Braunwald, E., Isselbacher, K. J., Wilson, J.D., Martin, J. B., Kasper, D. L., Hauser, S. L. and Longo, D. L. (1998) 'The Practice of Medicine', in A. S. Fauci, E. Braunwald, K. J. Isselbacher, J. D. Wilson, J. B. Martin, D. L. Kasper, S. L. Hauser and D. L. Longo (eds) *Harrison's Principles of Internal Medicine*, pp. 1–6 (New York: McGraw-Hill).

Giltrow, J. (1994) 'Genre and the Pragmatic Concept of Background Knowledge', in A. Freedman and P. Medway (eds) *Genre and the New Rhetoric*, pp. 155–78 (London: Taylor and Francis Ltd).

Hannan, T. J. (1996) 'Electronic Medical Records', in E. Hovenga, M. Kidd and B. Cesnik (eds) *Health Informatics: an Overview*, pp. 133–48 (Melbourne: Churchill Livingstone).

Hobbs, P. (2002) 'Islands in a String: the Use of Background Knowledge in an Obstetrical Resident's Notes', *Journal of Sociolinguistics*, 6, pp. 267–74.

Hobbs, P. (2003) 'The Use of Evidentiality in Physicians' Progress Notes', *Discourse Studies*, 5, pp. 451–78.

Hobbs, P. (2004) 'The Role of Progress Notes in the Professional Socialization of Medical Residents', *Journal of Pragmatics*, 36, pp. 1579–607.

Hobbs, P. (in press) 'Managing the Division of Labor: the Discursive Construction of Treatment in Two Hospital Obstetrical Units', *Journal of Applied Linguistics.*

Hunter, K. M. (1991) *Doctors' Stories: the Narrative Structure of Medical Knowledge* (Princeton, NJ: Princeton University Press).

Iedema, R. and Wodak, R. (1999) 'Introduction: Organizational Discourses and Practices', *Discourse and Society*, 10, pp. 5–19.

James, D. C., Simpson, K. R. and Knox, G. E. (2003) 'How Do Expert Labor Nurses View Their Role?', *Journal of Obstetric, Gynecologic, and Neonatal Nursing*, 32, pp. 814–23.

Lingard, L., Garwood, K., Schryer, C. F. and Spafford, M. M. (2003) 'A Certain Art of Uncertainty: Case Presentation and the Development of Professional Identity', *Social Science and Medicine*, 56, pp. 603–16.

Luff, P. and Heath, C. (1998) 'Mobility in Collaboration', in S. Poltrock and J. Grudin (eds) *Proceedings of the 1998 ACM Conference on Computer Supported Cooperative Work*, pp. 305–14 (New York: ACM Press).

Pecker, M. S. and Siegler, E. L. (2003) 'Training Physicians in the Hospital', in E. L. Siegler, S. Mirafzali and J. B. Foust (eds) *An Introduction to Hospital and Inpatient Care*, pp. 44–53 (New York: Springer Publishing Company).

Pettinari, C. J. (1988) *Task, Talk and Text in the Operating Room: a Study in Medical Discourse* (Norwood, NJ: Ablex Publishing Company).

Prince, E. F., Frader, J. and Bosk, C. (1982) 'On Hedging in Physician–Physician Discourse', in J. R. Di Pietro (ed.) *Linguistics and the Professions: Proceedings of the Second Annual Delaware Symposium on Language Studies*, pp. 83–97 (Norwood, NJ: Ablex Publishing Corporation).

Rees, C. (1981) 'Records and Hospital Routine', in P. Atkinson and C. Heath (eds) *Medical Work: Realities and Routines*, pp. 55–70 (Westmead, England: Gower Publishing Company Limited).

Sarangi, S. and Roberts, C. (1999) 'The Dynamics of Interactional and Institutional Orders in Work-related Settings', in S. Sarangi and C. Roberts (eds) *Talk, Work, and Institutional Order: Discourse in Medical, Mediation and Management Settings*, pp. 1–57 (Berlin and New York: Mouton de Gruyter).

Sauls, D. J. (2002) 'Effects of Labor Support on Mothers, Babies, and Birth Outcomes', *Journal of Obstetric, Gynecologic, and Neonatal Nursing*, 31, pp. 733–41.

Waters, K. A. and Murphy, G. F. (1979) *Medical Records in Health Information* (Germantown, MD and London: Aspen Systems Corporation).

Weed, L. L. (1969) *Medical Records, Medical Education, and Patient Care: the Problem-Oriented Record as a Basic Tool* (Cleveland: The Press of Case Western Reserve University).

Weinholtz, D. (1991) 'The Socialization of Physicians during Attending Rounds: a Study of Team Learning among Medical Students', *Qualitative Health Research*, 1, pp. 152–77.

4
Governing the Operating Room List

Robin Riley and Elizabeth Manias

Introduction

This chapter focuses on the power relationships in communication between nurses and surgeons as they struggle to structure work activities around the operating room list; that is, the schedule of surgical procedures to be performed each day in operating rooms. Drawing upon data from a larger ethnographic study that explored communication in operating rooms (Riley and Manias, 2001, 2003, 2004, 2005, 2006a, b), in this chapter we deconstruct the discursive communication practices that surround the operating list using the Foucauldian (1977, 1978, 1979, 1980, 1982) tools of discourse, power, knowledge and subjectivity. It is argued that nurses are positioned between competing organizational discourses that privilege time and efficiency and the hierarchical dominance of surgeons. However, despite this complex positioning, nurses challenge surgeons' traditional and hierarchical right to determine the order of the operating list, and position themselves as active subjects in ways that challenge the traditional, handmaiden image of nurses who work in this setting.

We begin our exploration by briefly outlining the traditional positioning of operation room nurses. We then provide some details about the theoretical approach and the methodology used in the study. Extracts of data, in the form of discursive practices evident in nurses' communication, are broken down and discussed to support our argument, namely, that operating room nurses are active in the shaping and governance of clinical practice. In the discussion we focus on two characteristic forms of knowledge and nursing governance: logistic knowledge and discourses of knowing the surgeons.

A traditional view of operating room nursing

The identity of operating room nurses is ambiguous. On one hand operating room nursing is perceived as glamorous and attractive because of the close association nurses have with surgeons, the appeal of teamwork and the highly technical work (Happell, 2000). On the other hand, operating room nursing is devalued by, and alienated from, the wider nursing profession because of nurses' perceived subservience to surgeons: operating room nurses are often conceptualized as handmaidens (Gruendemann, 1970, p. 349) and not 'true' nurses (Sandelowski, 2000).

Originally, the handmaiden image of operating room nursing was considered a sign of prestige and was one that applied across the profession as a whole. Being closely associated with surgeons was regarded as a privilege, a sign of status and a position to be envied (McGee, 1991; see also Chapter 12 in this volume). Nurses derived power from their close association with doctors (Melosh, 1982). In more recent years the handmaiden image of nursing has been seen as derogative and patriarchal, linked with disrepute (Gruendemann, 1970; Sandelowski, 2000). References to it are easily identified in the contemporary nursing literature (Berg, 1996; Brown and Crawford, 2003; Lupton, 1995; Sigurosson, 2001; Sweet and Norman, 1995). However, while it has been proposed that nursing in general outgrew the handmaiden image in the 1970s, it has continued to be used to characterize operating room nursing (Sigurosson, 2001). Several implications can be drawn from this handmaiden image, centring mostly on the idea that nurses' bodies and knowledge are the site for discursive control by others.

First, the handmaiden image emphasizes manual work and the handing of instruments to surgeons during surgery where nursing skills are centred mostly on bodily, task-orientated skills and manual dexterity. This notion seems to imply that there are limitations about the type of knowledge that nurses have access to and use in their practice and that manual work and body knowledge are insufficient to be of real worth in nursing practice. Second, operating room nurses are depicted as having a unidimensional subjectivity, where subject positions other than that of the handmaiden are made invisible or downplayed in comparison to the dominant image. Third, the handmaiden image implies that the body of the operating room nurse is the site of discursive control by others, in which nurses cater to the idiosyncratic needs of surgeons and are accountable to and respond to their command in clinical practice, rather than to their nursing colleagues and managers. Here, the work of nurses is belittled and devalued by displacing nurses' own priorities. To throw alternative light on these matters and assumptions, and drawing on related research that reports on the complexity of theatre nursing (Riley and Manias, 2006a), we explore the question: How is the operating room list constructed and governed in the clinical setting?

Methodology

Taking as a starting point the idea that the operating room nurses' body has been a site for control by others, we undertook a postmodern ethnographic investigation informed by the work of Michel Foucault (1977, 1978, 1982) to deconstruct the communication that surrounded everyday nursing practice, including management of the operating room list.

Foucault (1982) believed that there was an interrelationship between communication and power that shapes the social world, but also recognized that power relations, communication and objective capacities should not be confused and are not reducible to one another. Power relations, communication and the material objects and events coexist and use each other mutually, and as Burkitt recognized, 'giving the place of the individual a meaning within the group and adding to the development of the person's self-identity' (Burkitt, 1999). Thus, in using material communication events as a means of exploring and deconstructing operating room nursing, we can analyse how power positions nurses within social and organizational situations and the effect of power on everyday practice generally.

The tools for this deconstruction were the Foucauldian concepts of power, knowledge and subjectivity (1977, 1978, 1982), which collectively inform the concept of governmentality (Dean, 1999). Foucault promoted an understanding of government beyond the official capacities of the state to that of the professional and their relationship with the lay individual. He used the term 'governmentality' to combine ideas about 'government', or the power to direct conduct, with the concept of 'mentality', or how governing is achieved through the professionalization of everyday issues, which rhetoric is then mentally inculcated in the general population (Allen, 1998). Governmentality is thus concerned not only with the tactics and practices of the state or the individual, but also with practices of the self that shape and mould the individual through directing choices, desires, aspirations and needs (Gordon, 1991; Rose and Miller, 1992).

The data we discuss originate from a study of three operating room departments in metropolitan Melbourne, Australia: a large metropolitan not-for-profit hospital, an outer suburban public hospital and an inner-city specialist public hospital. Participants comprised 11 registered nurses, purposefully selected to act as informants about their cultural groups. They represented a broad cross-section of nursing experience and roles. The data were generated through observational fieldwork, individual and group interviews and the maintenance of a personal diary by the first author, who was working as a clinician during the course of the study. Over 230 hours of observational fieldwork were conducted between 2001 and 2003 and involved sequential data collection from the different institutional settings. Eleven individual interviews and four group interviews were conducted, using the technique of photovoice (Riley and Manias, 2003). The strength of photovoice was that it provided a way of addressing the power imbalance between the participants and the researchers because it allowed the nurses to direct the topics for discussion at interview. The visual snapshots, together with the textual snapshots, provided data and subsequent insight into the behind-the-scenes work and communication of operating room nurses.

As far as analytical strategy is concerned, initially our focus was on identifying the discursive themes in the communication that surround the operating room list. We understood discursive practices to involve the political conditions entertained with language; the social, historical and political conditions of discourse formations (Howarth, 2000). To add another layer of analysis, we formulated questions around the Foucauldian concepts of power-knowledge and subjectivity, such as: 'what forms of knowledge are utilized in nursing interactions?'; 'what subject positions do nurses speak from?'; and 'what characteristic ways of forming the self do nurses engage in?' Thus, in using this methodological and analytical approach, we sought to challenge the very meaning on which the assumptions about operating rooms nursing are based and arrive at a less conventional and more productive understanding. Pseudonyms have been used to protect the identity of participants.

Making the list

Lists were a dominant and pervasive means of communication in operating rooms. Nurses used a multitude of lists, such as surgeons' preference cards, checking lists for trays of surgical instruments, lists for restocking of equipment trolleys, for the recording and organization of work routines that structured their practice. However, one list was more prominent than others: the operating room list. It structured the communication processes among nurses and between nurses and surgeons.

The operating room list is the official record of surgical procedures scheduled for each day. It communicates the surgical procedures undertaken in each operating room and the subsequent nursing actions that supported it. All work in operating rooms revolves around the written operating room list. Borrowing an analogy developed by Berg (1996), the operating room list maintains the 'material infrastructure' (p. 513) of theatre practice. Furthermore, signifying its hierarchical importance, the operating room list is referred to as 'the list' by nurses and surgeons, giving it a privileged place in comparison to other lists in the departments.

In all three departments the list was presented in a typed, word-processed, format. Information was arranged to correspond to the numbered operating rooms, beginning with all the morning sessions, followed by all the afternoon sessions. Details on the list usually included the number of the operating room, patient name and identification number, age, sex, operation details, surgeon and anaesthetist. Most procedures on the lists were elective operations,[1] sometimes booked weeks in advance, or semi-elective procedures[2] that needed to be done within a few hours. In the following sections we discuss the discursive practices in the communication that surrounded the list, including taking bookings, coping with emergencies, changing the order, cancelling cases and managing time.

Taking bookings

Administrative clerks dealt with elective bookings. While they were expected to have knowledge of medical terminology, they had no medical or nurse training. Responsibility for accepting semi-elective bookings usually lay with the nursing coordinator on the shift.

Saying 'yes' or 'no' to bookings: hierarchical nursing power

The exchange below details the process of taking a booking for a semi-elective surgical procedure.

> Louise (nurse coordinator) was standing outside theatre five and Molly (administrative clerk) approached her, having walked from the office to give her a message.

Molly: Louise, I have Mr W's [urologist] rooms on the phone. They want to know if he can do a Holium Laser[3] on Wednesday night.

Louise: In the evening – no!

Molly: What about Wednesday a.m.?

Louise: I'll have to have a look at the staffing and see if there are any urology people [nurses].

And they started to walk to the office. After having a look at the list for Wednesday and the staffing, Louise said:

Louise: Mr P [another urologist] has a list that morning.

Molly: Can we move him?

Louise: No – that's his theatre and it's a booked session. I'm not going to move him. The urology staff will be busy in there, so, no, Mr W will have to find another time.

With that Molly went back to the phone, as the (surgeon's) rooms were waiting for an answer, and she said:

Molly: Hello . . . we have no time on Wednesday.

The administrative clerk was acting as a go-between, conveying messages on behalf of the nurse coordinator and the surgeon. It was not her responsibility to judge the urgency of a case. However, it was evident that she used a certain amount of judgement to screen calls and had learned to distinguish between urgent and non-urgent cases, even though her clinical knowledge was not officially recognized or authorized by the bestowing of a medical or nursing title.

The Holium Laser procedure required nursing staff that had undergone specialist training in its use and an operating room equipped with a special power supply and safety devices. Organizational discourses of safety and law meant that Louise could not allocate staff that had not been trained in its use. Initially Louise, as the timekeeper in the department, refused the surgeon's request, later saying that the procedure would be too labour-intensive and time-consuming for the limited number of nurses on evening shift in the department. She knew the Holium Laser case was not urgent and was catering for the contingency that a more urgent case may arise – a haemorrhaging patient or a mother requiring a Caesarean section. If nursing staff were occupied with a Holium Laser procedure for several hours, the arrival of an emergency case could be life threatening if nurses could not be redeployed.

After this initial decision, Louise and Molly referred to the surgery scheduled for the next day, and Louise once again refused the booking. The nurses trained in laser surgery were already allocated to work with another urologist who was assigned to the only operating room equipped for laser surgery. In this department, and in others, the staff roster was completed weeks in advance. Nurses with specialist skills, such as urology, were rostered to work on the shifts when the urology sessions were scheduled. Developing familiarity between nurses and medical staff, getting to know their technical likes, dislikes and idiosyncratic practices, was important for the smooth running of the operating sessions. Familiarity was achieved through the meticulous scheduling of nurses in the rostering system.

Additionally, surgeons with scheduled elective operating lists worked in the same operating room at the same time each week and they resisted being moved from their familiar environment. They complained to the nurses and the coordinator if their environment or nursing staff changed. Even though surgeons were transitory visitors to the departments, they were constructed as legitimate owners of the space and time for their scheduled elective session by the partitioning and timetabling of the booking system. Disrupting a surgeon's regular session by movement to a different operating room was to be avoided where possible. Nurses also arranged the resources and supplies in and around each operating room to cater for the particular type of surgery being conducted in each room. They constructed logistic efficiencies though the organization of surgical supplies and changing an operating room would mean temporarily rearranging equipment and supplies, and was time-consuming.

In deciding whether to accept the booking, Louise screened and assessed the feasibility and legitimacy of the surgeon's request. She used her experiential knowledge of the individual nurses' skills, her surgical knowledge about the urgency of the procedure and her knowledge of the technical requirements for the procedure – the laser equipment and the discourses of safety that surrounded it. She balanced this technical knowledge with her professional ethics in the form of a responsibility to the surgeon with the scheduled list. There was no negotiation. Using her hierarchical power as the nurse in charge of the department, as the gatekeeper and coordinator of time and space, a barrier through which/whom surgeons had to pass, she refused the surgeon's request. She moved beyond the traditional subservient role of the nurse to one where the surgeon was positioned as subordinate to the concerns of the department and the organization. However, this was an exception.

Questioning nursing judgement

Surgeons contested nurses' decisions about the scheduling of out-of-hours semi-elective cases, as one nurse related when she spoke about a telephone conversation with a surgeon:

> He [the surgeon] just rang to give the details of the second patient – the pacemakers that he had booked from last night, and I [the nurse] was told that it was not a definite time of 1900 hrs. He was adamant that it was going to be. I then progressed to tell him that it may not necessarily be at 1900 hrs and that if we get something else in that he might be bumped. He then told me that 'how do we make the decision of what's more important than a pacemaker, the patient could die. The patient . . . da, da, da', and he kept going on. And then he told me I 'needed to be fair on how we made our decision of what's more important than that'. But I guess if a woman is in labour, and she needs a caesar, and the patient . . . the baby's at risk, then what is more important . . . he was not happy and told me he had originally been booked in at 1330 hours and was moved to 1900 hours.
>
> I sort of said to him, 'look I'm not saying that yours isn't important but this is what I've come onto, this is the list that we are just working through, and if you think you need to do it now you can speak with whoever has the next case'.

This surgeon questioned the nurse's right to determine urgency of his cases. He appealed to a discourse of safety and implied that medical knowledge was superior to nursing knowledge in this regard. While the surgeon had intimate biomedical 'case knowledge' (Liaschenko and Fisher, 1999, p. 29), or generalizable knowledge of a patient's pathophysiology, the nurse did not. Being confined to the operating room department meant that the nurse knew the patient only by the name of the booked procedure. However, she clearly articulated a priority of cases based on this knowledge: a pacemaker was not as urgent as an emergency Caesarean section. Her knowledge of urgency was gained through experience and by being exposed to similar situations.

Furthermore, the surgeon's decision-making rationale remained confined to his medical judgement about the patient, whereas the nurses' decision involved consideration of organizational discourses of efficiency and efficacy. Only a limited number of nursing staff was available on a shift and they had to be used to maximum effectiveness. The nurse in this situation was cognizant of her limited capacity to shape decision-making and she realized that she had little influence over the rostering of staff. It frustrated her when the surgeon appealed to discourses of management that were outside her immediate control. As a result of this move, she became caught between the competing positions of a clinical nurse and the departmental manager.

The nurse related how the surgeon seemed irritated by the organizational restrictions placed on his use of time. She recounted how the surgeon had said, 'it's not fair that surgeons have to sit around all day', and how he implied a professional injustice because his interests were subjugated to the concerns of the organization. Medical time was of great value and importance and should not be wasted. Later, when a more experienced nurse coordinator presented for the afternoon shift, the matter was referred to her. The surgeon was subsequently offered an earlier time but refused, electing to use the time that was originally arranged.

Among themselves, clinical nurses questioned surgeons' designations of urgency. They differentiated between a 'social Caesar', where they deemed it to be done to fit in with surgeons' daily timetable, and a clinically urgent Caesarean section where there was an immediate threat to life. As one participant said at interview, 'I'm sure they put it over us at times because of convenience... How can we call it when we don't know the patient? We would not like to say "no, you can't do it".' This nurse was aware of her limited access to patients' biomedical 'case knowledge' (Liaschenko and Fisher, 1999, p. 29) and realized how this lack of access affected her ability to judge urgency. Although it seemed at times that some cases were not as urgent as surgeons related, she felt that nurses were not in a position to override their scientifically framed judgement.

Coping with emergencies

In none of the three hospitals was there a dedicated operating room for emergency surgery. Sometimes luck would have it that an operating room was vacant and staff were able to be redeployed, but often decisions had to be made about which elective operating session to stop. In extreme emergencies nurse coordinators in the private hospital often made this decision in isolation, while in the public hospital it was sometimes made in conjunction with a staff anaesthetist (see Chapter 5 in this volume).

In one such incident, notification was received by the nurse coordinator that a patient in a cardiac catheter laboratory had suffered a perforated coronary artery and needed immediate, life-saving surgery. The nurse coordinator of the operating room department instantly recognized the extreme urgency of the situation and judged the surgeon's designation of the case as valid. Being able to quickly determine the urgency of specific cases positioned operating room nurses as competent and expert practitioners. It was a skill learned through experience.

At the time of notification all operating rooms were occupied with scheduled elective procedures. Nevertheless, the extremeness of the situation necessitated interrupting one of the elective operating sessions. The nature of the emergency meant that the first available operating room needed to be used. In this incident, it was serendipitous that one surgeon was in-between cases on his elective list and the coordinator requisitioned the room. Her decision was not questioned and the surgeon accepted her clinical judgement and decision. There was no negotiating.

However, such compliance to the exercise of power by nurse coordinators was not always the case. Paradoxically, in less urgent situations, when time was not as important to the life of a patient, surgeons questioned the coordinator's choice of whose list to interrupt. As one coordinator explained at interview, 'some [surgeons] can be quite accepting of it and others can be quite nasty and feel someone else should stand aside'. Knowing this, the idiosyncrasies of different surgeons and the power that they were potentially able to exercise, nurses sometimes chose to 'take the path of least resistance' when making a decision about which elective operating list to stop.

Taking the path of least resistance

At interview, one participant, a nurse coordinator, explained how the discursive practice of taking the path of least resistance worked. She said:

> Delaying the professor, he's not the easiest person to approach about these delays... I know it shouldn't always be that the ones [surgeons] that scream and rant... you try and avoid confrontation with them.
>
> ...but you still have to balance it. Sometimes you just have to delay the ones that jump up and down. You try to get a balance, sometimes if the surgeon has got a big long list and by delaying him, the one that you should delay, you feel well, they're going to be finished late if we do delay them, you tend to look around and see if someone has got a shorter list, even though there's two [cases] to go in that theatre. But if they've just got a little list, then you

> can delay them without upsetting them too much, or delaying the patient.

This nurse coordinator explained how surgeons were able to directly and indirectly exercise power to resist by having their elective operating list interrupted for emergency cases. The hierarchical status of some surgeons, such as professors, and others who had become known as 'difficult', made them hard to approach as their demeanour and presence conveyed authority. Nurses had personal knowledge of individual surgeons that provided insight about such idiosyncrasies, which they used to inform management of the department. The nurse in the episode above disliked and sometimes avoided confronting difficult surgeons, even though she knew that it should not be so. There was a risk of personal humiliation involved in confronting dominating surgeons and this nurse explained how she experienced an inner battle, actively contemplated her decision, to balance her own personal concerns with organizational discourses of efficiency. She explained how delaying or interrupting an elective session, when she was loath to approach a difficult surgeon, was for the greater good of the department and patients.

The power exercised by nurse coordinators in governing the operating room list was derived not from an arbitrary command or order, but, in part, from their legitimate organizational authority as the department's controller of space and time. As well, through their knowledge of the 'flock' (Foucault, 1981, p. 227) of surgeons and their preparedness to put aside their own personal feelings for the collective good and welfare of the department, coordinators drew upon a personal inner strength in order to master their role in the face of hierarchical medical power. In doing so, the nurse coordinators constructed themselves as ethical and competent controllers of time and space in which partiality and favouritism for particular surgeons were avoided.

Changing the order

Surgeons decided the order of their elective operating room list at the time of booking. However, to improve workflow nurses regularly negotiated with surgeons to change the order of patients on the list, or occasionally authorized changes themselves, as described in the following episode.

> There was a clash of equipment – one piece of equipment was needed for two patients, so Mary (nurse) determined. One solution seemed to be to alter the order of one of the lists. Mary and the nurse in the other theatre agreed that it was more appropriate for her [Mary's] surgeon's

> list to change, because he was more approachable, and the order of the other list was complicated. However, she was very ambivalent about changing the order as she was not sure if she had the authority to do this without the surgeon's permission – he had not arrived in the theatre complex for her to consult. Nevertheless, she sent for the next patient on the list, and the second patient would be done first. Mary informed the surgeon when he arrived – speaking with him one-on-one. He was appreciative of the initiative. Mary later confided that she felt much relieved as she was scared that the surgeon would 'blast' her for the unauthorized change.

In this instance, Mary, positioned as the team leader for an orthopaedic operating session, scanned the operating list to get a global perspective of the procedures being performed. She identified another orthopaedic list that required the same piece of equipment and estimated that their needs would coincide. This meant that one session would be delayed while waiting for the other to finish. The two nurses used their personal knowledge of the orthopaedic surgeons to gauge how they would react to a change in the order of their lists, to reach a decision about whose list it was appropriate to change. Recognizing that it was her list that was best changed, Mary felt reluctant to independently authorize the initiative without approval from the surgeon. She was hesitant to act autonomously, reluctant to overstep the traditional lines of hierarchical authority. Nurses could be intimidated by surgeons. Even though nurses possessed organizing knowledge about equipment use, which was logistic knowledge that the surgeon did not have, they feared the consequences of being disciplined by the surgeon – the thought of being 'blasted'. However, waiting for the surgeon to arrive in the department to seek his approval would also cause a delay. Mary was caught in a double bind and reluctantly initiated the change in order of patients.

Most changes to the order of the list were negotiated and discussed with surgeons and anaesthetists. Sometimes, though, as in the case above, nurses made the decision without consultation. Usually these cases were very simple procedures, such as a gastroscopy, arthroscopy or removal of skin lesions. The more complicated the case, the less likely nurses felt able to independently authorize a change. In complex surgery, nurses felt that they lacked access to biomedical case knowledge about patients, and information relating to patients' pathway through the hospital system. Nevertheless, experienced nurses demonstrated judgement, sometimes reluctantly, about the extent to which they could overstep the hierarchical tradition of establishing the order of the list, to independently effect a change.

Deferring the decision: subjugating knowledge

To avoid hierarchical power relations with surgeons, nurses sometimes engaged in the discursive practice of deferring the responsibility for decision-making about the order of the list to surgeons. During an interview, Linda talked about how the practice of deferring decisions worked:

> If you've got an orthopaedic case, a plastics case, ortho case, plastic case, ortho case, it makes more sense to use your resources straight out. Do one surgeon first, then the next surgeon. But we just put that back onto them [surgeons] to negotiate amongst themselves. What was happening is that nurses were very much the meat in the sandwich for providing theatre time with these surgeons. You've heard it yourself where a surgeon will be quite demanding, 'I need a theatre and I need it now.' Then you'll say, 'you need to contact . . . ', and they're actually quite angry at you that you're saying 'no we've actually got other cases booked, but feel free to contact the other surgeon'. Then you hear them on the phone, 'good-day mate, how's it going. Sorry to bother you, don't want to be any trouble, but . . . '. Pleasant as pie.

Linda was concerned about organizing the department to avoid wasting time and effort, so that surgeons were not idle while waiting for another to finish, and so that nurses did not have to rearrange equipment and supplies between cases. Changing the order of the list so that the different types of surgery, such as orthopaedic or plastics surgery, were grouped together would maximize efficiencies – there would be an economy of effort. However, similar to the episode in the previous section 'Changing the order', she indicated that nurses were reluctant to independently authorize such changes. Instead, nurses would make a suggestion to a surgeon: 'There's plastic case before and after you. Do you want to speak with Mr B to see if you can do your cases together?'

In adopting the strategy of deferring the decision about the order of the list to surgeons, nurses suggested a course of action whereby they did not directly challenge surgeons' positions of dominance. Deferring decisions about the order of the list was a game (Stein, 1967) in which nurses avoided assuming hierarchical control. Furthermore, Linda intimated that when dealing with nurses, surgeons adopted a different, superior, subject position to the one they adopted when dealing with their own colleagues, whom they perceive to be of equal professional status. By playing the game of deferring the decision, nurses withdrew themselves from direct decision-making, and avoided being positioned as the go-between and becoming involved in disputes. However, in doing so, they subjugated their scientific knowledge about urgency and case designation as well as their own logistic knowledge about how best to organize the work of surgery.

Negotiating the use of time

Nurses had insight into the surgeon's habits of time, which they used to manage the list. This characteristic form of knowledge is evident in the following conversation between a nurse coordinator and a clinical nurse allocated to work in a plastic surgery operating room. The conversation was recorded during fieldwork:

Louise: What's happening here?

Nurse: [Surgeon's first name] hasn't arrived. The anaesthetist is here but [surgeon's name] has not shown up yet. He's been quite good lately and has been here on time, but he hasn't done well today.

Louise: Do I need to stress about the p.m. list yet?

Nurse: I don't know. He's getting sneaky lately – he knows that we're on to him. He has booked the short case first and long case second so that we can't cancel the second one. He'll be late though – he needs to be told.

Louise: We can beat him at that game, we can change the order.

Nurse: Can we do that now or is it too late?

Louise: I think it's too late now. Anyhow, the patient's probably here now. We'll watch that for next time.

In this episode the nurse who worked with the surgeon on a regular basis knew him as 'always late'. Other surgeons were known as 'always early' or 'always on time'. The nurse in the episode above went on to explain how this surgeon was known to her for arranging the order of his lists so that the short cases were performed first, leaving the more complicated, longer, procedures until last to avoid cancellation. Surgery could not be cancelled halfway through a procedure even if time was exceeded. She implied that he was playing a game to manipulate and control the order of his list so as to maximize the use of time.

The two nurses discussed their ability to change the order of the list before the surgeon arrived, with the coordinator suggesting that it was within her power and authority to do so as the organization's timekeeper in the department. The surgeon's hierarchical, medical, power conflicted with the nurse coordinator's organizational authority. The clinical nurse, however, questioned the appropriateness of changing the order, from both an organizational and ethical perspective. She questioned the nurse coordinator's organizational authority and whether this would override the surgeon's traditional hierarchical authority. She also questioned the ethics of changing the order and the effect for the patient. The first patient had already arrived in the department and it would cause stress and anxiety to be sent back to the ward. In this case, concern for the patient was prioritized over organizational issues of time. However, the coordinator suggested that she would subject this surgeon to increased surveillance in the future, and in doing so, in front of the clinical nurse, she reinforced her position of authority in the department through insight into the politics and logics of operating room practice.

Nursing governance of 'the list'

Although nurses officially positioned surgeons as retaining the legitimate right to determine the urgency of cases and order of the list, it became evident that the list became a site of contested control. In the communication between nurses and doctors it was apparent that they engaged in negotiating the order (Svensson, 1996) of the operating list, based on nurses' territorial knowledge about logistics, or the movement of stock and how best to secure efficiencies for maximizing the use of available time. As well, nurses and doctors engaged in a non-negotiated blurring of the boundaries (Allen, 1997) where the legitimate right of the surgeon to determine the order of the operating room list was transcended by nurse coordinators as an accepted part of everyday practice. This non-negotiated blurring of the boundaries between nurses and doctors occurred most commonly in emergency situations where time was of the essence for optimum outcomes for patients.

Unofficially, nurses used experiential clinical judgement to screen the urgency of cases and determine the legitimacy of surgeons' case designation. As well, evident in their communication were characteristic forms of knowledge, which nurses used as a means of governance to control clinical practice. One strategy of governance was their knowledge of individual surgeons, while another centred on discursive practices of logistics, a discussion of which we now move on to.

Knowledge of individual surgeons

To borrow a term used by Liaschenko and Fisher (1999), operating room nurses built a 'biography' (p. 38) of surgeons that impacted on how the clinical environment functioned. Nurses knew surgeons by having technical knowledge of their needs for surgery, by inscribing them in discourses of time and through having 'deep' knowledge of their souls (Foucault, 1977, p. 237; Rose, 1989). When nursing as a whole has been driven by the need for autonomy and professionalism, achieved through distancing itself from the male-dominated, scientifically based profession of medicine, operating room nurses derive a source of power from being close to the medical profession. Let us break this down and explain it in more detail.

In this study nurses knew surgeons' requirements for surgery and nursing routines and practice were constructed around this technical knowledge. Nurse coordinators accepted or refused elective and semi-elective bookings or cancelled cases based on their knowledge of what equipment was available or in use. In these instances, nurse coordinators exercised hierarchical power to position themselves as organizational gatekeepers, through whom all requests for time and space by surgeons were screened. Clinical nurses, too, knew individual surgeons' requirements for surgery and they initiated efficiencies based on this knowledge. This technical knowledge was evident in minute aspects of practice; how many blades a surgeon liked on a chest retractor, which way to load a needle on a needle holder or how big to cut a hole in a perfusion cannulae (Riley, 2005).

As well as knowing surgeons' technical requirements for surgery, clinical nurses knew surgeons' habits of time (Riley and Manias, 2006a). Through surveillance, nurses knew surgeons as fast or slow, as punctual or as someone who is always late. They also examined and judged the length of time individual surgeons took for particular procedures, and compared and contrasted surgeons against each other to arrive at normalized standards. Inscribing surgeons in discourses of time provided nurses with a means of measuring the latitude and degree of flexibility they had to organize their work activities in operating rooms, to determine when the next case could be scheduled to follow, to decide who would be best placed to work in the role of instrument and circulating nurse before it was time to go off duty, when to take meal breaks, when to commence the instrument set-up, and when to send for the next patient. Nurses inscribed surgeons in discourses of time and used this knowledge as a form of governance to control clinical practice.

Furthermore, in making a decision about whose list to interrupt for an emergency, nurse coordinators were informed by their knowledge of the psyche of surgeons; which surgeons were approachable and likely to conform and who was more likely to resist. Nurses had insight into surgeons' disposition, knowing them as someone who gets stressed, or as someone who is relaxed, someone who is approachable during surgery or someone to be avoided, someone who likes flirting, and as someone who is pedantic or, alternatively, slack. Operating room nurses had 'deep' (Rose, 1989) knowledge that extended to the 'soul' (Foucault, 1977, p. 30) of the surgeon which involved knowing their habits, their vulnerabilities, capacities and inner being.

These 'calculable traces of individuality' (Rose, 1989, p. 7) of surgeons, their technical requirements, as beings inscribed in time, and deep knowledge of their soul, allowed nurses to take actions to coordinate and organize their work routines: they are techniques of governmentality through which nurses exercised power to shape and control practice. That is, through having knowledge of individual surgeons, operating room nurses were active social agents in governing their practice, occasioned by their gendered communication skills and practices.

Others before us have suggested differences in how females and males communicate (Arnold and Boggs, 2003; Coeling and Wilcox, 1994; Gilligan and Pollak, 1989; Kress, 1989), with men and women clustering around constructs of separation and attachment. While making generalizations in this area is difficult (Tannen, 1993), researchers have argued that whereas men emphasize objective factual information and tend to direct conversations and perceive danger from close personal relationships, women put emphasis on the importance of improving relationships and view communication as a form of connectedness (Tannen, 2001). With this in mind, we propose that these peculiarly female ways of communicating, concerned with connectedness, attachment and relationship building, are at the heart of nurses' knowledge of individual surgeons. It is through these gendered understandings of how women communicate that nurses build their relationship with surgeons and from which their power-knowledge is derived. Rather than stressing distance from surgeons, operating rooms nurses' governance is built on their close surveillance and communication with surgeons. But nurses' capacity for governance extended beyond their knowledge of individual surgeons and involved logistic knowledge.

Logistic knowledge

The discourses surrounding nursing practice in the operating room focused on the coordination of surgical procedures. The knowledge used by nurses was practical knowledge, individualized know-how about how to get things done, involving planning, the control, and synchronization of time and space for the flow of goods and services in and around the operating room. Operating room nurses governed clinical practice through discourses of logistics. Their logistic knowledge was integral to the overall functioning of departments and management of the list.

Discourses of logistics were evident in verbal communication and the mundane, everyday discursive practices of operating room nurses at all levels. For nurse coordinators, logistic knowledge involved being aware of the constraints on the availability of resources, the allocation of equipment and staff, the restrictions on the types of cases that could be conducted at the same time, accepting bookings for extra cases, cancelling cases and the making of plans to deal with list overrun. For clinical nurses, logistic knowledge incorporated knowing where equipment and supplies were located in the department and being aware of the type of supplies that were available or out of stock, coordinating who was acting in which nursing role in the operating room, or negotiating a change in the order of a list to minimize wasted time and ensure efficiency.

Surgeons were receptive to changes in the order of the list based on nurses' logistic and organizational knowledge. Nurses were familiar with equipment and whether it was in use, the number and type of instrument trays available and exactly where they were in the process of being processed and recycled for use. They were also familiar with the organizational routines and timetables of other departments in the hospitals: how to contact people, the opening hours of particular departments, phone numbers and on-call rosters. As institutional employees, nurses were in a position to inform surgeons of such knowledge. They assumed the position of organizers and initiated changes to the order of the list, either independently or by raising it for discussion, based on their logistic knowledge of the available resources. Such organizing capability, it has been suggested (Miers, 2000), is a female ability, probably because of the implicit social skill of communication involved. More can be said about this.

One interpretation of these organizing capacities of operating room nurses, the discursive practices of logistic and contingency, could be that nurses' work is an unauthenticated substitute that mirrors traditional domestic housework. The performance of household tasks has long been associated with nursing, albeit often subsumed under the guise of hygiene and not without debates about demarcation and whose responsibility it should be (Gamarnikow, 1978). Feminists and sociologists have also highlighted the sexual division of labour and how the transfer of women's domestic routines to the workplace setting has been seen as a process by which nursing work has been devalued (Miers, 2000; Wicks, 1999). Indeed, some time ago Gamarnikow (1978) suggested that the removal of household tasks, like hygiene, from the sphere of nursing practice, more closely subordinated nursing to medicine though an increased focus on a domain of practice that was under medical control.

Therefore, drawing attention to the logistic discourses in operating room nurses' work could be seen as reinforcing historically derived hierarchical relationships of power and gender differences between nurses and doctors that perpetuate the subservient handmaiden image of operation room nurses. As Allen (1996) has argued, 'Whenever one uses a social category that is also employed as a mechanism of social justice, one is in danger of reproducing the conditions that perpetuate injustice' (p. 99) as they structure opportunity and privilege. However, rather than denigrate their knowledge and tactics, we argue for a more productive conceptualization of nurses' operating room practices, and for a different take on the historically derived understandings of the gendered organizing functions that have been constructed as lowly valued domestic work.

In this study nurses were buffered and supported by their position as institutional employees (Melosh, 1982), and these organizing and logistic forms of knowledge provide them with increased social purchase and constituted a relatively autonomous sphere of practice that distanced and divided nursing practice from medical work. In operating rooms medical staff had no interest in logistic knowledge as long as their needs of surgery were met. Accordingly, rather than realizing devalued 'household tasks', nurses' organizing capacities can be seen as a resource, as a form of power-knowledge that offers possibilities for exercising control and shifting the balance of power in traditional nurse–doctor relationships. Being able to rearrange the operating room schedule to accommodate the sickest patients, organize extra equipment and supplies, maximize the use of time, or just control resources, operating room nurses play an active part in the government and management of operating rooms and surgery.

Conclusion

This chapter took as its starting point the idea that the body of the operating room nurse and their knowledge has been a site for discursive control by others. It has concentrated on demonstrating how power is exercised in communication interactions between nurses and surgeons as they struggle to shape practice through the almost iconic communication mechanism of 'the list'. Far from being passive handmaidens to surgeons, operating room nurses engage in self-authorizing, self-surveillance and self-mastery to actively shape their subjectivity. The undifferentiated handmaiden image has been shown to be a narrow view of operating room nursing that belies the complexity of nurses' subjectivity. We have provided a more productive understanding of operating room nursing by showing how nurses use characteristic forms of knowledge to control and govern practice.

Operating room nurses not only negotiated the competing discourses of medicine and management, but within these discourses their positioning was complex. For nurses, management involved moving back and forward between logistic work that was empowering, because it distanced them from the medical and scientific discourses of surgeons, but it was at the same time disempowering and devalued because it could be perceived as gendered, 'household' work. Hence, nurses' positioning in the discourses of these logistics was profoundly paradoxical.

Through their close association with surgeons, operating room nurses elicited, attributed and ascribed certain qualities to surgeons, often engaging in a highly emotional, intensive form of labour (James, 1989). Nurses knew surgeons so well, that they knew when to coax them, flatter them or leave them alone. They fostered and circulated 'biographies' about individual surgeon's technical needs for surgery, their habits of time and intimate knowledge of their personalities – their 'needs and deeds, and the contents of the soul' (Dean, 1999, p. 75), to promote practices and programmes of control. In exercising this control the onus was on nurses to come to know surgeons so as to be able to direct and manage the work in operating rooms.

Thinking about management in operating rooms in this way, it can be said that operating room nurses exercised a regime of governmentality that moves beyond traditional ideas of what it means to govern, not simply through the exercise of authority and mandated, unidirectional power. Here, governmentality involved a subtle way of directing and intervening that paralleled gendered ways of thinking and behaving by nurses, subtly influencing the conduct and work of surgery by means of a complex exercise of paradoxical knowledge and power.

Notes

1 Surgery that is not life threatening.
2 Surgery that is not life threatening but needs to be done within a reasonable period of time to avoid becoming an emergency.
3 A type of laser used for removal of the prostate.

References

Allen, B. (1998) 'Foucault and Modern Political Philosophy', in J. Moss (ed.) *The Later Foucault*, pp. 164–98 (London: Sage Publications).

Allen, D. (1996) 'Knowledge, Politics, Culture, and Gender: a Discourse Perspective', *Canadian Journal of Nursing Research*, 28(1), pp. 95–102.

Allen, D. (1997) 'The Nursing–Medical Boundary: a Negotiated Order?', *Sociology of Health and Illness*, 19(4), pp. 498–520.

Arnold, E. and Boggs, K. (2003) *Interpersonal Relationships: Professional Communication Skills for Nurses* (4th edn) (St Louis: Saunders).

Berg, M. (1996) 'Practices of Reading and Writing: the Constitutive Role of the Patient Record in Medical Work', *Sociology of Health and Illness*, 18(4), pp. 499–524.

Brown, B. and Crawford, P. (2003) 'The Clinical Governance of the Soul: "Deep Management" and the Self-regulating Subject in Integrated Community Mental Health Teams', *Social Science & Medicine*, 56(1), pp. 67–81.

Burkitt, I. (1999) *Bodies of Thought: Embodiment, Identity and Modernity* (London: Sage Publications).

Coeling, H. and Wilcox, J. (1994) 'Steps to Collaboration', *Nursing Administration Quarterly*, 18(4), pp. 44–55.

Dean, M. (1999) *Governmentality: Power and Rule in Modern Society* (London: Sage Publications).

Foucault, M. (1977) *Discipline and Punish: the Birth of the Prison* (London: Penguin).

Foucault, M. (1978) *The Will to Knowledge: the History of Sexuality* (Vol. 1) (London: Penguin Books).

Foucault, M. (1979) 'Governmentality', *Ideology and Consciousness*, 6, pp. 5–21.

Foucault, M. (1980) 'Two Lectures', in C. Gordon (ed.) *Power/Knowledge: Selected Interviews and Other Writings 1972–1977*, pp. 78–108 (New York: Prentice Hall).

Foucault, M. (1981) 'Omnes et singulatim', in M. McMurrin (ed.) *The Tanner Lectures on Human Values* (Vol. 11), pp. 224–54 (Salt Lake City: University of Utah Press).

Foucault, M. (1982) 'The Subject and Power', in H. L. Dreyfus and P. Rabinow (eds) *Michel Foucault: Beyond Structuralism and Hermeneutics*, pp. 208–26 (Chicago: The University of Chicago Press).

Gamarnikow, E. (1978) 'Sexual Division of Labour: the Case of Nursing', in A. Kuhn and A. Wolpe (eds) *Feminism and Materialism: Women and Modes of Production*, pp. 96–123 (London: Routledge and Kegan Paul).

Gilligan, C. and Pollak, S. (1989) 'The Vulnerable and Invulnerable Physician', in C. Gilligan, J. Ward, J. Taylor and B. Bardige (eds) *Mapping the Moral Domain*, pp. 245–62 (Cambridge: Harvard University Press).

Gordon, C. (1991) 'Governmental Rationality: an Introduction', in G. Burchell, C. Gordon and P. Miller (eds) *The Foucault Effect: Studies in Governmentality*, pp. 1–51 (London: Harvester Wheatsheaf).

Gruendemann, B. (1970) 'Analysis of the Role of the Professional Staff Nurse in the Operating Room', *Nursing Research*, 19(4), pp. 349–53.

Happell, B. (2000) 'Student Interest in Perioperative Nursing Practice as a Career', *AORN Journal*, 71(3), pp. 600–5.

Howarth, D. (2000) *Discourse* (Buckingham: Open University Press).

James, N. (1989) 'Emotional Labour: Skill and Work in the Social Regulation of Feelings', *The Sociological Review*, 37(1), pp. 15–42.

Kress, G. (ed.) (1989) *Communication and Culture* (Maryborough: New South Wales University Press).

Liaschenko, J. and Fisher, A. (1999) 'Theorising the Knowledge that Nurses Use in the Conduct of their Work', *Scholarly Inquiry for Nursing Practice: an International Journal*, 13(1), pp. 29–41.

Lupton, D. (1995) 'Perspectives on Power, Communication and the Medical Encounter: Implications for Nursing Theory and Practice', *Nursing Inquiry*, 2(3), pp. 157–63.

McGee, P. (1991) 'Perioperative Nursing: a Review of the Literature', *British Journal of Theatre Nursing*, October, pp. 12–17.

Melosh, B. (1982) *The Physician's Hand: Work Culture and Conflict in American Nursing* (Philadelphia: Temple University Press).

Miers, M. (2000) *Gender Issues and Nursing Practice* (London: Macmillan Press Limited).

Riley, R. (2005) 'Snap-shots of Live Theatre: Rethinking the Governance of Operating Room Nursing through a Discourse Analysis of Communication Processes', unpublished PhD (Melbourne, Australia: The University of Melbourne).

Riley, R. and Manias, E. (2001) 'Foucault Could Have Been an Operating Room Nurse', *Journal of Advanced Nursing*, 39(4), pp. 316–24.

Riley, R. and Manias, E. (2003) 'Snap-shots of Live Theatre: the Use of Photography to Research Governance in Operating Room Nursing', *Nursing Inquiry*, 10(2), pp. 81–90.

Riley, R. and Manias, E. (2004) 'The Uses of Photography in Clinical Nursing Practice and Research: a Literature Review', *Journal of Advanced Nursing*, 48(4), pp. 397–405.

Riley, R. and Manias, E. (2005) 'Rethinking Theatre in Modern Operating Rooms', *Nursing Inquiry*, 12(1), pp. 2–9.

Riley, R. and Manias, E. (2006a) 'Governance in Operating Room Nursing: Nurses' Knowledge of Individual Surgeons', *Social Science & Medicine*, 62(6), March, pp. 1541–51.

Riley, R. and Manias, E. (2006b) 'Governing Time in Operating Room Nursing', *Journal of Clinical Nursing*, 15, pp. 546–53.

Rose, N. (1989) *Governing the Soul: the Shaping of the Private Self* (London and New York: Routledge).

Rose, N. and Miller, P. (1992) 'Political Power beyond the State: Problematics and Government', *British Journal of Sociology*, 42(2), pp. 173–205.

Sandelowski, M. (2000) *Devices and Desires* (Chapel Hill and London: The University of North Carolina).

Sigurosson, H. (2001) 'The Meaning of Being a Perioperative Nurse', *AORN Journal*, 74(2), pp. 202–17.

Stein, L. (1967) 'The Doctor–Nurse Game', *Archives of General Psychiatry*, 16, pp. 699–703.

Svensson, R. (1996) 'The Interplay between Doctors and Nurses: a Negotiated Order Perspective', *Sociology of Health and Illness*, 18(3), pp. 379–98.

Sweet, S. and Norman, I. (1995) 'The Nurse–Doctor Relationship: a Selective Literature Review', *Journal of Advanced Nursing*, 22(1), pp. 165–70.

Tannen, D. (1993) 'The Relativity of Linguistic Strategies: Rethinking Power and Solidarity in Gender and Dominance' in D. Tannen (ed.) *Gender and Conversational Interaction*, pp. 165–88 (New York: Oxford University Press).

Tannen, D. (2001) *Talking from 9 to 5: Women and Men at Work: Language, Sex and Power* (London: Virago Press).

Wicks, D. (1999) *Nurses and Doctors at Work: Rethinking Professional Boundaries* (St Leonards: Allen and Unwin).

5

Dialogues for Negotiating Priorities in Unplanned Emergency Surgical Queues

Martin Lum and Anneke Fitzgerald

Introduction

More than 4 million Australians are treated annually in emergency departments, with many needing surgical treatment in hospital operating theatres (AIHW, 2005). Despite this, empirical research on the scheduling of emergency surgery is limited and this dearth of knowledge is somewhat reflected in the ad hoc practices found in many operating theatres (Fitzgerald *et al.*, 2004). An *emergency* is commonly understood to be an unforeseen combination of circumstances that demands immediate action, or an urgent need for assistance or relief. In the medical setting, it implies an injury or illness that poses an immediate threat to a person's health or life. In the clinical context, however, determining the immediacy and urgency of interventions becomes the ground for tense negotiation between health care providers within the hospital setting.

Arguably, the existence of an emergency is to a large extent determined by doctors who exercise their medical prowess and insist on priority intervention (Hall, 1954). However, operating suites are comprised of various staff members including surgeons, anaesthetists, nurses and managers. Each has a different role, qualifications and experiences, and each contributes to the decision-making process – whether this be explicitly or implicitly (Ashmos *et al.*, 2000). Each stakeholder also offers different understandings of the term 'emergency'. They utilize additional terms to describe this category of surgery. This includes *urgent* and *acute* surgery, where the notions of immediacy and urgency represent a spectrum of perspectives spawning poorly defined intermediate states, with the *semi-urgent*, the *semi-acute* and the *semi-elective* classifications introducing additional ambiguity.

Given the multidisciplinary setting, the management of emergency surgery can therefore be a politically charged matter, with different hospital staff members vying to assert their *professional opinion*. Freidson (1988) provides a lucid illustration of this point:

> the physician is able to intervene in many places in the hospital and justify his [*sic*] intervention on the basis of a 'medical emergency' – a situation in which the well-being of a patient is said to be seriously in jeopardy and in which it is the physician alone who knows what is best done . . . We are all familiar with the dominant symbolic image: the interruption of orderly routine by a violent convulsion, heart failure, a hemorrhage; the suspension of ordinary relationships and their reorganization around the masterful physician who, by his [*sic*] intervention, saves a life. While this no doubt happens on occasion, far more common in the hospital is the labeling of ambiguous events as emergencies by the doctor so as to gain the aid or resources he [*sic*] believes he [*sic*] needs. (Freidson, 1988, p. 118)

Hospital staff's habitual choice of *emergency surgery* in juxtaposition to planned *elective surgery* brings to the dialogue in the operating theatre an emotional and implied ethical connotation, the array of definitions offered in the literature about how to distinguish levels of emergency notwithstanding.

Thus, the American Hospital Association defines a bona fide emergency as any condition clinically deemed to require immediate medical care (American Hospital Association, 1992). The Audit Commission in the United Kingdom defines an emergency case as 'a patient whose operation was unexpected and could not be planned well in advance' (Audit Commission, 2003, p. 37). Emergency surgery is required by a patient whose poor health requires urgent attention; this is most evident when there is risk to life, limb or organ (Gabel *et al.*, 1999). Despite the terms *emergency, unplanned* and *unscheduled* surgery being commonly interchanged in the literature, for the purposes of our chapter the term 'unplanned surgery' provides a relatively neutral description of the clinical context. Accordingly, unplanned surgery is here defined as surgery that is unscheduled, unexpected and inscribed with varying degrees of urgency.

In this chapter, we present an analysis of data derived from interviews with clinicians involved in surgery list decision-making. In the interviews we explore the scheduling of emergency surgery with an eye to eliciting clinicians' views on the relative priorities between cases. The chapter begins with providing some background about attempts that have been made to rationalize the planning of emergency surgery, and then moves on to presenting the research method and data collection process. In the section that follows, the chapter presents the interview data arranged according to perceived priority: extreme clinical urgency, clinical urgency, non-clinical factors, and professional and interpersonal dynamics. The chapter then moves on to consider the possibility of the anaesthetist enacting an intermediary and coordinating role.

Background: managing unplanned surgery

Despite its apparent criticality, a lack of standardized descriptors for unplanned surgery is evident in the literature, relative to the operating theatre management of elective surgery (Doolan, 1997; Lennox, 1997; Lindgaard Laursen *et al.*, 2003; Wadhwa *et al.*, 1997). The American literature suggests unplanned surgery is stratified by time frame for surgical intervention. In the United States, 'many OR [Operating Room] suites, emergency and urgent cases are classified by their relative urgency. Typically, they are divided into three levels, corresponding to cases that should be attended to immediately, within 4–6 hours, and within 24 hours' (Gabel *et al.*, 1999, p. 111).The Western Canada Waiting List Project reports, however, that use of explicit prioritization methods were poorly accepted (Western Canada Waiting List Project, 2001):

> a transparent and explicit process for developing priority setting criteria may still not be embraced by priority setting decision-makers, in this case front-line clinicians, who have their own traditional implicit procedures. In other words, even well-developed substantiative criteria must still be institutionalized, or used within the context of a priority setting process. (Martin and Singer, 2003, p. 47)

In the United Kingdom, Hadley and Forster (1993) found that operating theatre lists are typically compiled in an unplanned manner, and the negotiations and modifications that follow are also extemporized. In light of such inconsistencies, the National Health Service (NHS) Executive circulated a national directive to guide good practice (Churchill, 1994). Even when theatre lists are established, they are seldom observed, often because of the need to accommodate patients who require unplanned surgery giving rise to extended delays in surgery (Ferrera *et al.*, 2001). Britain's Audit Commission (2003) review of operating theatres identified that data collected for the review on emergency cases cover a range of degrees of urgency, from 'patients needing an operation within an hour through to others needing one within 24 hours' (p. 24).

Norway has also sought to make up for its lack of a standardized approach to manage operating theatre lists. Despite existing policies to guide the management of theatre lists, research there indicates that the clinicians and nurses found the regulations limiting, and thus preferred to follow professional norms (Lian and Kristiansen, 1998). The outcome of this in Norway has been the recent policy of *ring fencing* elective and emergency surgery into separate production lines in an attempt to minimize the interrelated coupling effects on scheduling (Kjekshus and Hagen, 2005; Midttun and Martinussen, 2005).

In Australia, investigations of public hospitals in New South Wales revealed:

> There was significant variation in how . . . operating theatres were managed . . . Differences in practice in forecasting of utilization and management of waiting lists, sessions, non-elective surgery, discharge and post hospital care indicate the need for continuous improvement. (NSW Health, 2002, p. 2)

There is national concord with the Australasian College of Emergency Medicine around the need for a systematic priority system to guide the classification of patients in Emergency Departments (Department of Health and Ageing, 2005). However, there is no similarly agreed upon category system in the operating theatre domain. In 1985, definitions for *types* of emergency surgery were published in the United Kingdom (National Confidential Enquiry into Patient Outcome and Death, 2004); however, these were applied inconsistently across Health Trusts (Audit Commission, 2003), prompting a revision in 2004. No equivalent set has been defined in Australia.

Unplanned surgery presents health care providers with a complex individual and organizational challenge, particularly when multiple patients requiring such surgery are queued. Prioritization requires clinical assessment and a process for deciding on the case order between different patients and competing clinical teams. Ownership of this process and the negotiations surrounding these clinical decisions are inherently problematic. It is apparent then, that when multiple emergency cases are present contemporaneously, the imprecise and variable language surrounding unplanned surgery combines with the clinical jurisdictions of the players to create a challenging context for interprofessional dialogue.

Despite the dominance of the medical profession, and given the problems outlined in the previous paragraphs, members of the medical profession cannot work in isolation (Freidson, 1988; Matchar and Samsa, 2000). Within the hospital setting, decision-making processes are typically influenced by players from multiple disciplines. Within the operating theatre, this can include surgeons, anaesthetists, nurses, registrars (medical specialist trainees), managers and administrators. Barriers to effective decisions about unplanned surgery include a lack of, or inappropriate, communication, differing perceptions of the same event by staff members, and unclear roles within the event (Gaba *et al.*, 1994; Mackenzie *et al.*, 1994). Collectively, these pose a problem, not only among staff members of different disciplines, but also among those within the *same* discipline. Communication difficulties are exacerbated when there is a lack of a clear command structure within the operating theatre. In a recent review of two Sydney hospitals, this was particularly the case between surgeons and anaesthetists (King *et al.*, 2004). As Bogner (1997) explains:

> Surgeons often feel that the patient is their responsibility, hence they are in command. Anesthesiologists also feel the patient is their responsibility and that they are in command. This often is a source of problems in decision-making. When a crisis occurs, there is a question as to the locus of command. Patient care can be and sometimes is briefly subordinated to resolving that question. (Bogner, 1997, p. 66)

Other authors paint a more volatile picture of the operating theatre, suggesting that staff members can become quite territorial, if not malevolent (Mayer, 2001, p. 87). Interactions observed between surgical personnel have yielded descriptions of a chain of command, where nurses were subordinate to surgeons (Riley and Manias, 2005). Riley and Manias (see Chapter 4 in this volume) also identified the OR whiteboard as the communication battleground where strategies were employed to negotiate this hierarchy and pursue particular interests. These communication difficulties demonstrate the challenges for decision-making processes around unplanned surgery. In this context, our research explores the ambiguity around what constitutes an emergency, the descriptors for stratifying unplanned surgery, the multidisciplinary operating theatre environment, and the dialogue of clinicians who negotiate the patient order of unplanned surgical queues.

Researching unplanned surgery

This chapter is based on data derived from a mixed method triangulation study in Australia. The overall study was conducted using two surveys, semi-structured interviews and focus groups from which both quantitative and qualitative data sets were collected and analysed. The two surveys included a *Hospital Survey* that elicited current decision-making practices and protocols around unplanned surgery in New South Wales (NSW) public hospitals, and a more comprehensive survey – the *Emergency Surgery Survey*, which sought to establish clinician attitudes and beliefs among hospital personnel involved with the scheduling of surgical cases. Factor analysis of responses yielded three levels of urgency for surgery (urgency 1, urgency 2 and urgency 3), representing conditions of *extreme urgency, intermediate urgency* and *lesser urgency*. Within each level, specific clinical diagnoses or physiological states were identified, and these were associated with different time frames for surgical treatment. These data were used to inform the development of a prototype triage tool (see Appendix), whose formal taxonomy facilitated discussions with clinicians in the qualitative phase of fieldwork reported on here.

The qualitative phase was designed to explore the factors influencing the scheduling of unplanned surgery, and to test the practical value of the prototype triage tool. Hospital personnel involved in the scheduling of unplanned surgery were interviewed using a semi-structured, open-ended interview schedule that guided discussion around current practices in the scheduling of unplanned surgery; the influence of clinical and time determinants; the influence of logistical or operational determinants; the role of interpersonal and interprofessional dynamics when scheduling unplanned surgery; methods to improve decision-making practices around the scheduling of unplanned surgery, and thoughts about the prototype triage tool. A total of 38 respondents were consulted from eight NSW public hospitals (four metropolitan and four rural locations). This included surgeons (41 per cent), anaesthetists (23 per cent), nurses (30 per cent) and administrators (2.5 per cent). Analysis of interview transcripts provided qualitative data which further served to calibrate the quantitative results (Fitzgerald *et al.*, 2005).

Conceptualizing urgency

This section of the chapter sets out the comments that clinicians made during the interviews in connection with the different degrees of surgical urgency. We begin with their views of what constitutes extreme urgency.

Extreme urgency requiring immediate surgery

The data suggest that there is a considerable agreement about the criteria for establishing urgency of clinical states of patients requiring immediate surgery. When presented with the prototype triage tool, clinicians spoke about 'total agreement' among their colleagues (extract 1), 'decision-making processes that go through our minds anyway' (extract 2), 'we don't argue with that' (extract 3), and 'these processes are what the trained clinician does anyway' (extract 4):

Extract 1

Surgeon: The things that matter most are the urgency one and no one need a protocol to work out what's an urgency one . . . I have never seen an argument about that; everyone's in total agreement about its uniformity.

Extract 2

Anaesthetist: Yes, I think really what you're probably doing is putting into graphical or written terms the sorts of decision-making processing that go through our minds when we are booking cases anyway.

Extract 3

Surgeon: The first thing is clinical urgency; that's the first thing . . . Clinical judgement will always come first . . . If you've got any compromise to neurological or vascular function with a fracture particular in this area, then that just goes straight in; no mucking around in that. Likewise, if a D and C (Dilation and Curettage procedure) comes in and the surgeon says, 'Look, she's bleeding a fair bit. I've got to clean this up', we don't argue with that. That just jumps the queue.

Extract 4

Obstetrician: I think these processes are what the trained clinician does anyway. I think you're putting what happens in writing.

In the next extract (extract 5), a surgeon specifically lists the kinds of conditions s/he associates with high-level urgency:

Extract 5

Surgeon: Our emergencies are listed as Urgency One – caesarean sections and blood loss, and things such as ectopic pregnancies that are really bleeding.

The frequency of these kinds of responses in our data might be seen as suggesting that there is a common perspective on what are urgency one cases. However, when attempting to exemplify conditions of extreme urgency, 'caesarean sections' were singled out frequently by respondents as a way of capturing undue excitement and angst among hospital theatre personnel:

Extract 6

Surgeon: The idea of a caesarean section, to me, carries a quite a heavy emotive sort of overtone and it seems to me... that as soon as there is the briefest whisper or mention that a caesarean section might be on, then everything suddenly goes into a, I don't know, stunned sort of inert-type of situation. Now, if you actually look at the time between the mention of the Caesar and the procedure actually happening, it can sometimes be an hour, an hour plus. And there have been situations where the theatre staff might call the maternity wing or the obstetric wing, only to be told that the patient is having their Betadine bath or something like that.

Comments like this were common, and suggested that the urgency of Caesarean sections expressed by different obstetricians is often inconsistent and unreliable. This variability in Caesarean urgency may thus result in perceptions of exaggeration or understatement of urgency. Reminiscent of the 'social caesar' (Riley and Manias, 2005) and Freidson's (1988) *emergency* evocation, the prioritization of Caesarean sections is archetypal of the politics of medical urgency.

Extract 7

Surgeon: The point that I'm making is that's particularly handy for our obstetric colleagues, because they know that as soon as the Caesar is mentioned, everything sort goes on hold almost; and that, I suppose, gives them, in a way, a bit of a preferential route to the theatre.

Extract 8

Anaesthetist: Physicians lie. The classic one is Caesarean sections; they are always urgent, and when you send for the patient, the patient is not ready to come to theatre, and we are left waiting. That's a worldwide problem. Obstetricians are the worst, everybody will tell you that.

The number and nature of comments made about Caesarean sections indicate that this kind of unplanned surgery is viewed very differently from other unplanned surgeries. Respondents were most vocal about the influence of personal predisposition and private norms on clinical decision-making around this particular procedure. In the context of the politics of constructing *urgency*, the cultural–social capital of birth, babies and mothers enables some specialists to elevate this clinical problem above others. In contrast, special treatment of others, such as old people, the famous, friends and family was not evident.

Non-extremely urgent surgery

The picture becomes more troubled still as soon as we venture outside of the domain of extreme urgency, and specialties take the opportunity to articulate competing claims over temporal and spatial resources necessary for the practice of surgery. It is evident from the interview data that for categories other than *extreme urgency*, interviewees mobilize intuition and tacit knowledge as the prime means to decide the order of cases and associated times of surgery (extract 9).

Extract 9

Surgeon: We got to feel it... how things are likely to flow and give them our best guess.

Although the three urgency levels that were derived from our formal surveys can be quantitatively or statistically distinguished, variations in acceptable surgery response times produce overlaps and a degree of blurring between the levels. Respondents agree that the overlaps and urgency ambiguities create a 'grey zone' (extract 10).

Extract 10

Nurse: When you've got two cases that are very close, they probably would all come within more than one of these types of the categories.

The ambiguity expressed in these descriptions demonstrates that specific kinds of health care decisions are made on the basis of seemingly *irrational* factors, such as emotion and intuition (Kahneman and Tversky, 1979, p. 157; Redelmeier *et al.*, 1993, p. 158). To some extent, and leaving the emotional issues affecting Caesarean sections aside, the clinicians identify and agree on technical factors that can be brought to bear on the operating theatre scheduling. It is clear from their responses, however, that decision-making discourse extends well beyond these characteristics to include non-medical sources of contestation.

Non-medical factors

Several logistical or operational determinants were seen to influence the scheduling of unplanned surgery, giving rise to contestation of others' claims to preferential treatment in the surgery list. These issues cluster around resource allocation; namely, the accessibility of theatre *space and time*, and the *availability of staff*. Thus, it became clear from what respondents said that theatre space (a vacant operating room) and theatre time (a staffed operating team) are difficult to juggle in the case of unplanned surgery. In extract 11, a surgeon comments on the limited availability of theatre space and what this means for the planning of surgery:

Extract 11

Surgeon: The main issue comes about when competing teams are trying to get access to the operating theatre, because it's late at night, they want to get home, and they want to get the cases out of the way and done; and so . . . we have competing desires for the operating theatre . . . If you look at those places that do have problems with prioritization, the common theme is that they have difficulty in getting access to the operating theatres after hours because they have an insufficient number of operating theatres dedicated for that purpose to meet the needs of the hospital. So that's where the problem is; it's a resource problem.

In extract 12, the surgeon interviewed links theatre availability to limits placed on staff availability:

Extract 12

Surgeon: I'd say there's a huge amount of inefficiencies in the theatre; huge amount. Just by the fact that you need a certain number [of staff] to run a second theatre. So if you need four nurses to run a separate theatre, and you've got three, then there's three sitting in a tearoom, and you can't open a second theatre . . . Then we are going to be here until seven o'clock tonight, because we can't operate in the second theatre, and we got staff who are doing nothing, and we haven't got enough of them . . . and that's the real frustration. If you want to know about theatre utilization, I think 65 per cent is probably generous!

These comments suggest that workforce availability and theatre shortages are construed to be a significant influence on unplanned surgery and occupy an important logistical factor in negotiating the operating list. If clinical condition provides a moderately self-evident picture of what is urgent and what is not, the limits placed on resources needed for surgery exacerbate clinicians' disagreements over clinical priority.

(Inter)personal dynamics between professionals

It is clear from the foregoing that the role of (inter)personal dynamics in the scheduling of unplanned surgery is considerable. From interviewees' responses it became clear that these dynamics are often regarded as on a par with struggles over clinical diagnosis and logistical resources.

Extract 13

Obstetrician: I think those other factors that can't be actually put down and can't be put in red, orange and green are very important factors.

The obstetrician quoted in the aforesaid statement alludes to implicit factors that are not captured in commonly used written protocols whose urgency categories reduce clinical choices to 'red, orange and green'. These implicit dynamics were often couched in terms of 'tribal' differences between professions (Degeling *et al.*, 2003). The severity of these power dynamics is evident from the following extracts (extracts 14–17).

Extract 14

Nurse: Some [surgeons] get very impatient and make a lot of noise . . . and we have used the anaesthetic department sometimes to adjudicate.

Extract 15

Anaesthetist: If a surgeon came in and said, 'Look, my case is in column one, urgency two, subsection four, code red', I wouldn't care.

Extract 16

Anaesthetist: [Surgeons] think they are important . . . [If] you are an anaesthetist, you must have experienced these sorts of surgeons who feel their list is all important.

Extract 17

Surgeon: It's basically a situation where the nursing staff are really not making any decisions about patients; it's purely related to the medical team.

To a degree, these statements point to a shared perception of hierarchical differences between professions (Riley and Manias, 2005; Szirom *et al.*, 2004; Buchanan and Wilson, 1996) and within professions. As extracts 18 and 19 bear out, our respondents intimated that surgeons are perceived to be of higher status than anaesthetists by health care professionals, including doctors themselves (Mackenzie *et al.*, 1994, Gaba *et al.*, 1994).

Extract 18

Surgeon: I regard [theatre scheduling] as political. I regard the anaesthetists as a service industry... They are there to serve the needs of the surgeons and the patient... But, in general terms, the anaesthetist says, 'Look, I'm giving anaesthetic and that's the way it's going to be done.'

Extract 19

Anaesthetist: You're dealing with surgeons and they've got egos that are this big, so you're never going to do achieve anything, you know, when surgeons are involved, it's basically their egos are very big and they will always think that their case is the most important... You still have to fight on a regular basis to get the case booked.

These perceptions of professional hierarchy are backed up with accounts such as the following (extract 20):

Extract 20

Nurse: Surgeons tell fibs about what might be an emergency to suit themselves. That makes decisions difficult because they don't care if they categorize something a little bit differently, because they might have something to do elsewhere. They actually come out and admit that, but then they stick to their guns, that, 'Yes this is an emergency.'

Claims about professional importance and privilege are frequently anchored to proficiency with advanced technology, particularly when general familiarity with such advanced technology is lacking. As the following comment suggests, however, such claims are not always taken at face value, therefore representing another source of contestation (extract 21).

Extract 21

Surgeon: I have stood in here, 45 to 50 minutes when [an anaesthetist] is buggerising trying to do an interscalene block, or trying to do a psoas block or something, because this is the fad in anaesthesia... there are people in anaesthesia who are faddists in that regard and they like to do blocks, but generally that can be a very time-consuming thing.

In summary, and in tension with shared conceptions about clinical hierarchy and with the statistically proven perception that there are distinguishable levels of urgency, the further the interview discussion moves from cases that are generally agreed on as deserving surgical primacy, the more interprofessional contestation becomes evident in respondents' comments.

The anaesthetist as intermediary

Besides foregrounding interprofessional sources of disagreement, the interviews also threw up ways in which clinicians attempted to circumvent these challenges. One which we will discuss here is the proposed intermediary role of anaesthetists (extract 22).

Extract 22

Anaesthetist: It just doesn't seem cost-effective to me, and I always think that you need to try to use the theatres as economically as possible... I think the nurses generally and the anaesthetists on the floor have a very good idea about getting things moving, and how to organize things.

Given the problem of interprofessional disagreements about the basis of arranging unplanned surgery, recent Australian research (Fitzgerald *et al.*, 2005) has suggested that within a multidisciplinary team, the anaesthetist may adopt an intermediary role, situated between nurses and surgeons, as articulated in extract 22 above. This proposal was derived from the fact that, especially for conditions of intermediate urgency, anaesthetist interviewees tended to express clinical opinions that were intermediate between those of nurses and surgeons (Gabel *et al.*, 1999). The viability of this role was confirmed in the present study as is evident from the comments cited below (extracts 23–25).

Extract 23

Nurse: The surgeons, when they booked the case, they say whether they need to do it within ten hours. But looking at it realistically, if the patient is category one and the patient is not bleeding to death, then the anaesthetist might have a word; you might have a word to them and say, 'Oh, come on!'

Extract 24

Surgeon: [Anaesthetists are] in a unique position, that they are the only ones who's heard about all the cases, so they are the only person who can prioritize. Whether they are good at it or not, it's impossible for me as a surgeon to prioritize... also I'm influencing and biased because I got my own case and I have reason wanting that done, but the anaesthetist hasn't got that bias and the anaesthetist's had the advantage of having listened to all of these other cases and made a decision that's impartial.

Extract 25

Nurse: We have used the anaesthetic department sometimes to adjudicate.

Despite the inter- and intraprofessional contestations and the expressions of professional power seen in the previous subsection of this chapter, anaesthetists may be uniquely placed to occupy an intermediary role between surgeons and nurses, and between competing surgeons. In effect, their frequent involvement in managing the queue of unplanned surgery positions them as a hybrid clinician-manager (D'Armour *et al.*, 2005).

Acknowledging and formalizing this intermediary position of the anaesthetist have significant implications, not least of which is the change to the traditional management structure in the operating theatre that is based on the assumption that, to date, surgeons are in charge.

On the other hand, it needs to be acknowledged too that not all of our anaesthetist respondents warmly embraced the clinician-manager role.

Extract 26

Anaesthetist: So what one surgeon may consider to be a true emergency, others may not. But we as anaesthetists defer that decision to the surgeons, which is a fairly politically-sound thing to do [as surgeons are on top of the pecking order]. The only concern is that the system itself is open to abuse [of power], in that surgical teams may alter the priority put on the patient in an effort to expedite that patient's operation... If the anaesthetist is actively involved in patient selection for the emergency list, clearly that opens up political issues with the surgeons involved, and that can create quite difficult circumstances. For instance, a surgeon may believe that his or her case is more important than what we believe it to be, therefore creating some enmity.

As is evident from extract 27, anaesthetists may regard their clinician-manager role as harbouring a guardian function with respect to the operating theatre resources:

Extract 27

Anaesthetist: So I try to protect the operating theatre for things – Caesareans and car crashes and triple A's (Acute Abdominal

Aneurysms) and stuff. I don't know if that's the philosophy other people will take.

It seems then that, as medical peers, anaesthetists are positioned to contest the professional jurisdiction of surgeons in a way that nurses are not. It is uncertain, however, to what extent anaesthetists generally would be willing to manage the lists of unplanned surgery cases for multiple surgical teams, since such a role puts the anaesthetist squarely at the centre of the negotiation and prioritization dilemmas of surgical queues. Our future research will seek to address this question.

Conclusion

The research presented in this chapter confirms that dialogue around negotiating unplanned surgery involves both clinical and non-clinical factors, with disagreement about these factors becoming exacerbated the more the discussion moves away from extreme urgency cases. The less clinical urgency is the determining factor, the more accessibility of space, the availability of theatre time and the availability of staff are seen to play a key role in the negotiation over unplanned surgery queues.

As respondents' comments reproduced above further revealed, decision-making processes are greatly influenced by the expressed power and authority of particular staff members. Doctors, in particular surgeons, claim special rights in clinical decision-making when scheduling unplanned surgical cases. This leads to complex interprofessional, intraprofessional and interpersonal dynamics affecting the scheduling of unplanned surgery. There appear to be unwritten rules that govern decision-making and prioritization, whereby dynamics between *and* within professions can hinder prioritization of cases. These contestations and unwritten rules, it appears, raise serious problems for a decision-making instrument that is positioned as *on its own* being able to facilitate the scheduling of unplanned surgery.

Our research suggests that such an instrument will only work if the combative nature of professional positionings, relationships and communications is addressed and resolved. Despite the differences in professional perspectives, respondents' comments expressed consensus on the need for a conceptual framework to resolve professional tensions. The dilemma here is the expectation that a formal framework might aid decision-making, whereas the main sources of disagreement, as seen above, are claims about hierarchical privilege, power, specialty expertise and surgical priority. In light of this, any triage tool would appear to be contingent upon clinician-professionals acknowledging that such a tool may fail to contain the elasticity needed to accommodate the complex relationships between clinical considerations and time, logistical considerations, as well as interprofessional and interpersonal dynamics.

Overall, this research also shows that a systematized decision tool may make points of tension explicit, and isolate those areas of unplanned surgery that are most contested. Perhaps, together with greater prominence for the anaesthetist as intermediary, a triage tool might limit occasions of contestation and struggle to instances where disagreement could not be avoided given the personalities, emotions and perceived urgencies involved, and where mediation would be unavoidable given clinicians' deeply personal and strongly professional investments in their work.

Appendix

Prototype tool

Case progresses along the timeline right to left; urgency 1 is imminent when maximum wait time has elapsed.

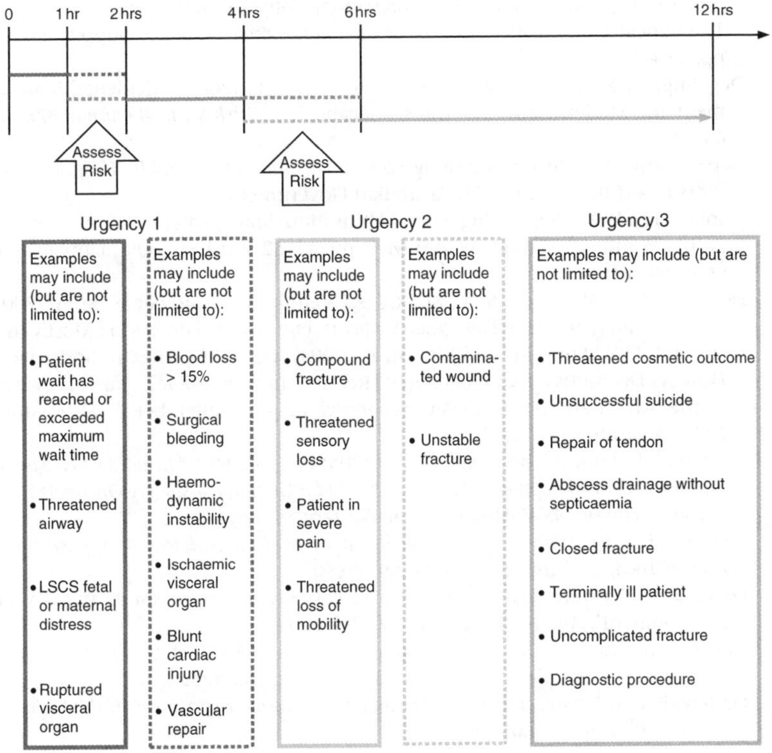

References

AIHW (Australian Institute of Health and Welfare) (2005) *Australian Hospital Statistics 2003–04*, Health Services Series No. 23 (Canberra, ACT: Australian Institute of Health and Welfare).

American Hospital Association (1992) *Special Member Briefing: Emergency Medical Treatment and Active Labor Act Requirements and Investigation* (Chicago: American Hospital Association).

Ashmos, D., Dennis, D. and McDaniel, R. (2000) 'Physicians and Decisions: a Simple Rule for Increasing Connections in Hospitals', *Health Care Management Review*, 25, pp. 109–16.

Audit Commission (2003) *Health Acute Hospital Portfolio: Operating Theatres: Review of National Findings* (London: Audit Commission).

Bogner, M. S. (1997) 'Naturalistic Decision Making in Health Care', in C. E. Zsambok and G. A. Klein (eds) *Naturalistic Decision Making*, pp. 61–9 (Mahwah, NJ: Lawrence Erlbaum Associates).

Buchanan, D. and Wilson, B. (1996) 'Re-engineering Operating Theatres: the Perspective Assessed', Occasional Paper 34 (Leicester: Leicester Business School).

Churchill, K. (1994) *Good Practice in Operating Theatre Management* (Leeds: NHS Executive).

D'Armour, D., Ferrada-Vodela, M., Rodriguez, L. S. M. and Beailieu, M. (2005) 'The Conceptual Basis for Interprofessional Collaboration: Core Concepts and Theoretical Frameworks', *Journal of Interprofessional Care*, 19 (Supplement 1), pp. 116–31.

Degeling, P., Maxwell, S., Kennedy, J. and Coyle, B. (2003) 'Medicine, Management and Modernisation: a "Danse Macabre"?', *British Medical Journal*, 326, pp. 649–52.

Department of Health and Ageing (2005) *The State of our Public Hospitals: June 2005 Report* (Canberra, ACT: Australian Government).

Doolan, L. (1997) 'Operating Room Utilisation Management', in P. Donnelly and L. Wadhwa (eds) *Access to Surgery*, pp. 43–52 (Brisbane, Qld: University of Queensland).

Ferrera, P. C., Colucciello, S. A., Marx, J. A., Verdile, V. P. and Gibbs, M. A. (2001) *Trauma Management: an Emergency Medicine Approach* (St Louis, Mo.: Mosby Inc).

Fitzgerald, J. A., Lum, M. and Kippist, L. (2004) 'Operating Theatre Bottlenecks: How are Decisions about Emergency Theatre Schedules Made?', paper presented at the 5th International CINet conference (25–27 September 2004) (Sydney, NSW: Australia).

Fitzgerald, J., Lum, M. and Dadich, A. (2005) *Professionals' Attitudes when Making Decisions: the Development of a Triage Model for Unplanned Surgery Queues* (Monograph) (Sydney, NSW: University of Western Sydney).

Freidson, E. (1988) *Profession of Medicine: a Study of the Sociology of Applied Knowledge* (Chicago: University of Chicago Press).

Gaba, D. M., Howard, S. K. and Jump, B. (1994) 'Production Pressures in the Work Environment', *Anesthesiology*, 81, pp. 388–400.

Gabel, R. A., Kulli, J. C., Lee, B. S., Spratt, D. G. and Ward, D. S. (1999) *Operating Room Management* (Woburn, Mass.: Butterworth-Heinemann).

Hadley, R. and Forster, D. (1993) *Doctors as Managers: Experiences in the Front-line of the NHS* (Harlow: Longman).

Hall, O. (1954) 'Some Problems in the Provision of Medical Services', *Canadian Journal of Economics and Political Science,* XX, pp. 456–66.

Kahneman, D. and Tversky, A. (1979) 'Prospect Theory: an Analysis of Decision under Risk', *Econometrica,* 47, pp. 262–91.

King, D., Kerridge, R. and Cansdell, D. (2004) *Ryde/Royal North Shore Hospital Review* (Sydney, NSW: MA International).

Kjekshus, L. E. and Hagen, T. (2005) 'Ring Fencing of Elective Surgery: Does it Affect Hospital Efficiency?', *Health Services Management Research,* 18, pp. 186–97.

Lennox, D. R. (1997) 'Management of Elective Surgery', in P. Donnelly and L. Wadhwa (eds) *Access to Surgery* (Brisbane, Qld: University of Queensland).

Lian, O. S. and Kristiansen, I. S. (1998) 'Ventetidsgarantien mellom medisin og byråkrati', *Tidsskrift for den Norske Lægeforening,* 118, pp. 3921–6.

Lindgaard Laursen, M., Gertsen, F. and Johansen, J. (2003) *Applying Lean Thinking in Hospitals: Exploring Implementation Difficulties* (Aalborg, Denmark: Centre for Industrial Production, Aalborg University).

Mackenzie, C. F., Craig, G. R., Parr, M. J., Horst, R. L. and Level One Trauma Anesthesia Simulation Group (1994) 'Video Analysis of Two Emergency Tracheal Intubations Identifies Flawed Decision-making', *Anesthesiology,* 81(3), pp. 763–71.

Martin, D. and Singer, P. (2003) 'Canada', in C. Ham and G. Robert (eds) *Reasonable Rationing: International Experience of Priority Setting in Health Care,* pp. 42–63 (Berkshire, England: Open University Press).

Matchar, D. B. and Samsa, G. P. (2000) 'Linking Modeling with Health Policy Formation and Implementation', in G. B. Chapman and F. Sonnenberg (eds) *Decision Making in Health Care: Theory, Psychology, and Applications,* pp. 145–57 (Melbourne, Vic.: Cambridge University Press).

Mayer, T. A. (2001) 'Trauma Team Response: Management and Leadership', in P. C. Ferrera, S. A. Colucciello, J. A. Marx, V. P. Verdile and M. A. Gibbs (eds) *Trauma Management: an Emergency Medicine Approach,* pp. 684–93 (St Louis, Mo.: Mosby Inc).

Midttun, L. and Martinussen, P. (2005) 'Hospital Waiting Time in Norway: What is the Role of Organizational Change?', *Scandinavian Journal of Public Health,* 33, pp. 439–46.

National Confidential Enquiry into Patient Outcome and Death (2004) *The NCEPOD Classification of Interventions* (London, UK: National Confidential Enquiry into Patient Outcome and Death (NCEPOD)).

NSW Health (2002) *NSW Health Operating Theatre Management Project Report* (Sydney, NSW: NSW Health).

Redelmeier, D. A., Rozin, P. and Kahneman, D. (1993) 'Understanding Patients' Decisions: Cognitive and Emotional Perspectives', *Journal of the American Medical Association,* 270, pp. 72–6.

Riley, R. and Manias, E. (2005) 'Governing the Operating Room List', 3rd International Conference on Communication, Medicine and Ethics and the 8th Annual Seminar of the Centre for Values, Ethics and Law in Medicine (30 June–2 July 2005) (Sydney: Australia).

Szirom, T., King, D. and Desmond, K. (2004) *Barriers to Service Provision for Young People with Presenting Substance Misuse and Mental Health Problems* (Canberra, ACT: National Youth Affairs Research Scheme (NYARS)).

Wadhwa, L., Mitra, S., Rockett, J. and Donnelly, P. (1997) 'Systems Analysis of Patient Flow and Theatre Utilisation', in P. Donnelly and L. Wadhwa (eds) *Access to Surgery*, pp. 63–81 (Brisbane, Qld: University of Queensland).
Western Canada Waiting List Project (2001) *From Chaos to Order: Making Sense of Waiting Lists in Canada: Final Report* (Edmonton: WCWL Project, University of Alberta).

6

Personality Disorder in UK Mental Health Care: Language, Legitimation and the Psychodynamics of Organized Surveillance

B. J. Brown and Paul Crawford

Introduction: formulating distress, deviance and disorder

Approaching health care situations through the lens of critical linguistics provides us with many informative ways of looking at how language is used to characterize vulnerable clients. In this chapter we will draw upon critical language study, including the work of Fairclough and the Nottingham Health Language Research Group, to examine how the clients and indeed the health professionals involved in the treatment of borderline personality are being subtly reformulated in line with broader changes in the policy framework and wider society. In order to make sense of the implications this has for the way we think about social processes and how notions of mind, self and society fit together, we will be drawing on Michel Foucault (for example, 1977) and Nikolas Rose (for example, 1990) who have done much to integrate questions relating to what we think of as the mind to larger-scale structures, events and policies. This, we believe, has important implications for clinicians and scholars of health care and hospital language and communication.

The story of personality disorder over the last one and a half centuries tells us much about how the mind has been conceptualized and embraced within discourses of policy, practice and responsibility, as well as personhood, philosophy and the post-Enlightenment sociopolitical milieu. In particular, scholars of the contemporary social scene in the UK have pointed to processes of individuation and detraditionalization (Beck, 1992; Beck and Beck-Gernsheim, 2002; Giddens, 1990, 1998).

The concept of the self that these thinkers see as important under contemporary conditions is a reflexive one. Society is becoming less traditional – indeed the present-day social condition, which is variously characterized as 'late modernity' or 'advanced liberalism', is one where we are systematically detached from what might once have been our cultural and community moorings. The reflexive self has arguably become more important in the context of these emerging 'post-traditional' settings. Reflexive self-awareness provides the individual with the opportunity to construct self-identities without the shackles of tradition and culture, which previously created relatively rigid boundaries to the options for one's self-understanding. Moreover, reflexive selves are constantly revising and reforming themselves in the light of new information or circumstances (Giddens, 1990, p. 38). This preamble into contemporary sociological theory is presented by way of a benchmark, so the reader can see the sort of self-aware, self-governing, skill-acquiring selves that are supposed to flourish under present-day social conditions.

While this is going on in the realm of high theory, health care is itself taking a rather different turn. Borderline personality disorder, after all, represents a failure of this reflexive self project. In contemporary mental health practice, the protocols, guidelines and assessment strategies that health professionals are encouraged to use to characterize the living conditions and problems of people with so-called personality disorder are at once constraining but at the same time productive. Health professionals are encouraged to look for signs of dirt, smells and cigarette burns in a client's home. They are encouraged to construct the client's subjectivity in terms of problems which require 'managing', and are drawn into a linguistic repackaging of distress in terms of such phrases as 'expressing suicidal intent'. This reformulation of human situations in terms of needs, 'risk' and 'issues' which need to be 'addressed' helps to create a particular kind of consciousness on the part of both the client and the health professional which is intimately bound up with notions of control and governmentality. In a sense, the attention of health care professionals is being directed towards something that has apparently failed in the reflexive self. They are exhorted to try to reconstruct it via the assiduous application of protocols, rating scales, contracts and 'dialectical behaviour therapy' regimes. We will also attempt to show, via a reflexive engagement with discourses surrounding this particular facet of health care, that by developing awareness of the operations of power we can pave the way to a more client-centred, emancipatory mental health practice.

This chapter is informed by three major strands of evidence which we have been assembling towards a larger study of the mental health service user movement in the UK. To this end, we will, in best Foucauldian, fashion, be drawing upon:

1 Historical evidence, for a cornerstone of this approach is the premise that to understand a concept one needs to grasp how it was created historically or genealogically;
2 Contemporary documents from policy makers and the professional literature, for we aim to show how the issue is constructed in contemporary terms as an object of inquiry or policy manipulation by relatively powerful groups such as government, health professionals and researchers;
3 Interview materials based on studies of practitioners and service users who, as part of a larger ongoing study of service users in the UK, were questioned about the care and therapeutic activity in which they were involved. The question of personality disorder was frequently a matter of concern to them and appeared to have been a predominant means of making sense of distress in the UK's health service over the previous few years.

Armed with these sources of information then, we can begin to build up a picture of how the question of disordered personalities, or insanity in the moral and medical sense, was built up, structured and restructured and linked to the operations of powerful or symbolically influential groups in the society. Whereas Foucauldian theory is notoriously short of specific advice about how analysis may be undertaken (Carabine, 2001), this can usefully be supplemented by discourse analysis which is broadly concerned with studying the performative use of language in the production of meaning (Edwards and Potter, 1992; Parker, 1994; Traynor, 1996). In this sense discourse analysis views language as a social process of constituting phenomena – a 'construction yard' (Potter, 1996) – rather than words simply acting as descriptions of things (Burr, 1995). Yet discourse analysis itself is a rather imprecise term that covers a number of disparate theories and methodologies (Hammersley, 2002; Wetherell *et al.*, 2001). In this chapter therefore we have adopted a variant of the method which is informed also by critical discourse analysis with its emphasis upon exposing the way in which linguistic practices reproduce and support oppressive ideologies (Fairclough, 1995a, b, 2001; Van Dijk, 1998). Critical discourse analysis pays special attention to extraneous factors such as the social context and intentions which provide a framework in which language occurs (Van Dijk, 2000), and asks how particular organizations of discourse might support powerful social interests. It is this synthesis then that informs our approach to the raw material of discourse about 'personality disorder'.

Our analysis will attempt to synthesize this selection of surviving written accounts, contemporary policy and scientific documents and first-hand experience to make sense of how the social and linguistic organization of health care for this client group becomes possible. This style of analysis enables us to link the legacies of history with the formulations of problems and people which abound in the present. It also encourages us to think about how forms of social organization shape, and are themselves afforded by, the accounts which their members deploy. These accounts may offer formulations of the nature of the persons, the qualities of their problems, and the courses of action which appear to them to be appropriate. Once we have identified this symbolic framework, it becomes possible to imagine other discourses, forms of arrangement and patterns of consciousness which might offer the possibility of beneficial change in both language and the organizations in which it is used.

Histories of the past, histories of the present

First, then, we are faced with the task of making sense of the history of a construct. Some of the roots are near the present, yet we also find that the genealogical history of these ideas can be traced back nearly two centuries. The sense of novelty and scientific discovery builds on commonsensical notions of what it means to be a person which have a much older pedigree. Like Antonio Gramsci (1971) famously wrote of common sense, it: '. . . is strangely composite; it contains elements from the Stone Age and principles of a more advanced science, prejudices from all past phases of history at the local level and intuitions of a modern philosophy . . . ' (Gramsci, 1971, p. 324). The ground, then, has been carefully prepared by these earlier, primordial discourses.

A feature of the modern era, which Rose characterizes as 'advanced liberalism' (Rose, 1990), borderline personality disorder (BPD) made its entry into the American Psychiatric Association's *Diagnostic and Statistical Manual* in 1980 (American Psychiatric Association, 1980). Currently 15–25 per cent of hospital and outpatient cases receive the diagnosis in the US. About three-quarters of those diagnosed with BPD are women. In this chapter we are not seeking to confirm or deny the 'reality' of BPD, neither do we wish to deny that those diagnosed with it experience distress. Rather, we wish to follow Wirth-Cauchon's (2001) ambition to 'deconstruct the meaning claims in order to look for the modes of power they carry and to force open a space for the emergence of counter-meanings' (p. 27).

Within the literature on BPD then, we may read about it in terms of its characteristics, incidence and prevalence. For example, the point of the prevalence in North America of people meeting diagnostic criteria for BPD is believed to be between 1 and 2 per cent, with Swartz *et al.*'s (1990) figure of 1.8 per cent of 19–55-year-olds often being used as a benchmark. According to the American Psychiatric Association (1994), 75 per cent of those diagnosed as having BPD are female. Moreover there are suggestions that the prevalence and severity are increasing in Western cultures (Millon, 1991; Paris, 1992, 1996). This alleged increase is supported by those who argue that it is linked to the increase in suicide, especially youth suicide, and aligned with the growing proportion of people meeting criteria for diagnoses of antisocial personality disorder and substance use disorder (Krawitz and Watson, 1999). This much is part and parcel of any introduction to the subject. But notice how these kinds of statements about personality disorder – or in our case BPD – tell us a whole lot more. They are more than simple renditions of how many people might meet the criteria. They also unfold an epistemological story about the condition as an entity – what Hosking might call an 'entitative myth'. That is, individual behaviour and attributes are theorized independently of context, and the extent to which context shapes behaviour and behaviour shapes context is curiously absent from this formulation (Hosking and Morley, 1991).

Having established the reality of BPD as a clinical entity in its own right, it then becomes possible to delineate for the reader its contours and textures. In the UK, the *Lancet* in 2004 carried an article by Lieb *et al.* (2004) in which they counselled gravely:

> Borderline personality disorder is a serious mental disorder with a characteristic pervasive pattern of instability in affect regulation, impulse control, interpersonal relationships, and self-image. (Lieb *et al.*, 2004, p. 453)

> Patients with borderline personality disorder have a range of intense dysphoric affects, sometimes experienced as aversive tension, including rage, sorrow, shame, panic, terror, and chronic feelings of emptiness and loneliness. These individuals can be distinguished from other groups by the overall degree of their multifaceted emotional pain. (Lieb *et al.*, 2004, p. 453)

Looking at the terms used in Lieb *et al.*'s account above we can see that this is overwhelmingly a vocabulary of interiority, reflecting what Smail (2005) has called a 'luxuriant interior jungle', replete with rage, sorrow and anger among other emotions. The question of personality disorders and their precursors such as moral insanity have for nearly two centuries presented psychiatry and jurisprudence with the problem that something seems to be awry in the arrangement of the sufferer's mental furniture, yet the implications for how these people were to be dealt with when they came into conflict with the law were often contested. In a sense the phenomenon struck at the very heart of the Enlightenment, post-industrial-revolution notion of the person as a participant in the social contract, and the medical notion of what it meant to have an illness.

In the early to middle nineteenth century, psychiatry was widening its ambit and increasingly large tracts of the human condition were being defined as mental disorders (Darjee and Crichton, 2003). Among these was 'moral insanity', first described by Prichard (1835), which included individuals who would probably today be diagnosed as suffering from 'personality disorder'. At that time Prichard (1842) in England and Ray (1838) in the USA were concerned with how such individuals might best be managed, and wrote of the relationship between moral insanity and criminal responsibility. According to Tadros (2001), the emerging concept of moral insanity influenced the courts in the nineteenth century and the acceptability of the insanity defence itself. Prichard's concept was seen as threatening to undermine the criminal law by defining as insane individuals who displayed repetitive antisocial behaviour.

Henry Maudsley (1873) distinguished between what he called 'instinctive insanity' which was an 'aberration and exaggeration of instincts and passions'; moral insanity which was a defect of the moral qualities along a dimension of 'viciousness to those extreme manifestations which pass far beyond what anyone would call wickedness'; and moral imbecility, identified by 'the total defect of moral faculties from birth and always associated with violent mischievous and criminal acts' (p. 289). Maudsley believed that the moral faculties were most recently evolved, and as a result they were the most vulnerable to disease. They were 'the finest flowers of evolution, the finest function of mind to be affected at the beginning of mental derangement of the individual' (Maudsley, 1873, p. 244).

Despite this fragility, the likelihood of acute distress and propensities to egregious or criminal activity, the individual with personality disorder has often not been deemed a suitable candidate for psychiatric treatment. A number of influential thinkers have argued that they are not and should not be the psychiatrist's main concern. At the end of the nineteenth century Koch (1891), who coined the term 'psychopathic', was convinced that these 'inferiorities' were not illnesses: 'Even in the bad cases the irregularities do not amount to mental disorder.'

The capacity of such patients to display periods of apparent normalcy, and their tendency to fall both into psychiatric and forensic categories, was a source of puzzlement. Here is Dr Sturrock, describing the situation in Scotland:

> At present there are several inmates in the Department whose insanity is only determined in association with the tendency of recent years to recognize as within the border line of insanity those peculiar forms of excessive irritability, impulsive conduct, destructiveness and other meaningless reactions to discipline which may be classified under some such term as Emotional Insanity, but which are extremely difficult to differentiate from exhibitions of ungovernable and some anti-social conducts. (Sturrock, 1909; quoted in Darjee and Crichton, 2003, p. 397)

The question then was where the boundary should be drawn between the territory of insanity on the one hand and the matter of 'ungovernable' and 'anti-social conducts' on the other. The 'steadily-increasing class of explosive prisoner' was regrettably apt to 'commit cunning and vicious thefts, and exhibit no sign of what is commonly called defective self-control till they come into the hands of the police or under the discipline of the prison warder' (Sturrock, 1911; quoted in Darjee and Crichton, 2003, p. 397). The apparent insanity, then, was accompanied by a tendency towards explosiveness and the likelihood that they would commit 'cunning and vicious thefts' – the moral insanity of the patient is reflected in the moral loading of the lexicon used to describe them. The lexical choices apparent here show that this problem is being framed as something that is under the will or conscious control of the patient and does not, for example, reflect mere confusion, but an inferred suite of reprehensible motives. It is this ambiguity over the intelligibility or otherwise of the person's actions that has been at the heart of the ambivalence mental health theorists and practitioners have felt towards them.

Later in the twentieth century, the influential Kurt Schneider (1950) argued that the intelligibility of the motives often attributed to people with personality disorders meant that they were merely 'abnormal varieties of sane psychic life'. Contemporary British psychiatry is often in agreement with this view, and as Kendell (2002) notes, the diagnosis of personality disorder is often used as a justification not to accept an individual for treatment. Moreover, as Lewis and Appleby (1988) describe, when patients were identified as having a 'personality disorder' they are often disliked by professionals. Their behaviour, especially suicide attempts, was seen as 'manipulative' and under voluntary control and the patients were seen as irritating, attention seeking and unlikely to comply with treatment recommendations.

The eruption of personality disorders onto the stage of public debate and policy in recent years is strange, as throughout much of the twentieth century they were, as we have seen, often not considered within the ambit of psychiatry. Instead, they were most fulsomely theorized within the field of psychoanalysis. Significantly, from our point of view, personality disorder was considered to be a deeply personal and profoundly individual issue, intimately linked to psychoanalytic accounts of identity. For example, we can see the implicit normative understandings of personality and identity at stake in the work of Erik Erikson (1963, 1968), who popularized the term in his discussion of 'identity crises' in adolescence. According to Erikson, identity includes role commitments and a sense of personal continuity or sameness over time and between situations. Also important is a presumed sense of inner agency, acknowledgment of one's role commitments, and a sense of how one is viewed by the community as a whole. Thus, the notion of the responsible, committed citizen is inscribed and conflated with notions of 'health', whereas its opposite is seen as a kind of disorder. 'Healthy' identities include the ability to choose an appropriate line of work, achieve intimacy with another, and find a place in the larger society. Conversely, the opposite pole of this involves 'identity confusion' or 'diffusion' manifested as: (1) a subjective sense of incoherence; (2) difficulty committing to roles and occupational choices; and (3) a tendency to conflate one's own feelings, and desires with those of other people and hence to fear a loss of personal identity when an intimate relationship dissolves. In line with the prevailing Western notion of the responsible individual, Westen (1985, 1992) identified the major components of identity as being a sense of continuity over time; emotional commitment to a set of self-defining representations of self, role relationships, and core values and ideal self-standards; development or acceptance of a world view that gives life meaning; and some recognition of one's place in the world by significant others. Wilkinson-Ryan and Westen (2000) write:

> . . . terms such as fragmentation, boundary confusion, and lack of cohesion . . . describe the experience of self in borderline personality

> disorder . . . the most severe identity problems are found in people with identity diffusion, who may have had multiple identity crises, chosen a succession of careers or religions, or may not even be aware of their lack of a cohesive identity. (Wilkinson-Ryan and Weston, 2000, p. 528)

Fonagy *et al.* (1991) examined borderline patients and maltreated children, identifying the failure of patients with BPD to 'develop the capacity to step inside the mind of another' (p. 214) and to imagine the way the other experiences the patient. For their part, Adler and Buje see the personality disordered individual as suffering from a sense of incoherence and disjointed thinking, feelings of loss of integration, concerns about 'falling apart', and a subjective sense of losing functional control over the self and other forms of 'self-fragmentation'. From a self-psychological perspective, these patients are said to lack an ability to internalize many aspects of their primary caregivers that would allow them to develop a cohesive sense of self (Adler and Buie, 1979; Buie and Adler, 1982).

All these formulations of the core problem of the personality disordered individual then posit a disorder at the level of what it is that makes a good citizen under advanced liberalism, or in the form of something awry with the purported sense of self that is valued in post-Enlightenment Western societies. Thus, being compromised in terms of what is valued by contemporary societies, being a 'problem person', and thus invalidated, may enhance the very difficulties in 'taking responsibility' for the things they can personally change (Warner and Wilkins, 2004). Warner and Wilkins also note that clients often report multiple experiences of having their thoughts and feelings invalidated, and feel that they are usually seen as being 'the problem'. Psychiatric labelling can further contribute to clients' negative sense of self because the focus is on disorder rather than adaptation. As Gergen (1991) argues, the tendency to pathologize can lead to 'a spiral of infirmity', which also exaggerates clients' passivity (Drewery and McKenzie, 1999). This then is particularly likely when clients are viewed as being essentially damaged by virtue of their biology, their pasts or their faulty psychodynamic machinery, their 'low self esteem' or their 'responsibility issues'.

The present: stigma, uncertainty and exclusion

Thus, while questions remain about the validity of the diagnosis of personality disorder and its various subdivisions, this particular client group find themselves marginalized, oppressed and frequently rejected from the UK's mental health services (Fraser and Gallop, 1993; Lewis and Appleby, 1988; Nehls, 2000). In such cases, the stand-alone term 'borderline' is commonly used in mental health settings and has assumed pejorative connotations that reflect these commonly held beliefs about such clients (Cleary *et al.*, 2002). They are seen as 'frequently self-harming, high users of costly services' (Blackshaw *et al.*, 1999, p. 9) and the 'costs in human and financial terms' of engagement with them are significant (Langley and Klopper, 2005). A widely held conviction is that people with BPD are both difficult and disruptive (Horsfall, 1999). Hence, once a decision has been taken to involve a person with so-called personality disorder in treatment, they are seen as presenting mental health practitioners with unique challenges.

In similar vein to this judgemental lexicon used to describe the burdens of caring for the client with so-called personality disorder there are some suggestions in the literature that this process of negative typification is a pervasive feature of health care work. Mohr's (1999) deconstruction of psychiatric nursing reports argues that these are written more from presupposition and ritual than proffering an account of the patient's experience. Only 1 per cent of over 4000 entries gave positive renditions of patients, while 20 per cent were categorized as 'pejorative, punitive, inane and nonsense' (p. 1055), containing entries such as 'is controlling and engages in power plays with staff' or 'mostly superficial and manipulative'. Mohr implies that nurses are largely to blame for this eventuality, suggesting that nurses should simply amend their practice in localized ways, rather than contesting the wider impress of power.

Parker (1992) argues that people might 'make discourse, but not in discursive conditions of their own choosing' (p. 32). Nursing has often been argued to be a subaltern profession (Porter, 1998) which is embedded within the managerialist aspirations of late capitalist economic rationalism (Crowe, 2000; Delacour, 2000; Traynor, 1999). Waitzkin (1991) suggests that it is these distal oppressive structures that are reproduced in the relations between health professionals and patients. Thus, perhaps rather than simply exhorting nurses to write more kindly about their charges, we need to reflect upon the broader social forces which place people in these positions and which predispose the typification of clients in these terms to begin with.

To understand this, we must pursue the suggestion that the language of record keeping in health care settings is arguably influenced by management concerns. Heartfield (1996) argues that managerialism informs medico-nursing documentation, which in his view is not so much about describing nursing care as assisting the more powerful medical and managerialist hegemony. Likewise, Foucault (1988) suggests that the 'technologies of government' may rule the individual or fashion conduct into the forms desired by powerful interests. The 'technologies' may be broadly defined as 'any set of social practices that is aimed at manipulating the social or physical world according to identifiable routines' (O'Malley, 1996, p. 205). Thus, the managerialist definition of health care, which privileges matters of cost efficiency, risk management and resource constraints, aims to direct health care practice according to routinely and systematically evaluated, managerially approved guidelines, manuals and codes of practice. More importantly from the point of view of our inquiry, these managerial standards represent a 'governmental technology' of health care (Wong, 2004) which seeks to control the work, and indeed the consciousness, of caregivers by securing their active consent and subjugation. The discourse of 'managing' a condition such as BPD, like 'managed care', 'best practice', 'evidence-based care' or even 'empowerment', creates new responsibilities which, in turn, unfold new kinds of subjectivity on the part of practitioners and clients. As well as formally desirable typifications of clients it also affords a much more pejorative informal vocabulary of terms such as 'bed blockers', 'timewasters', 'fakers' or otherwise undesirable patients. This type of managerialist subjectivity produces certain forms of health care practice that gives form and content to the engagement between clients, nurses and other caregivers, hence informally affording the management of beds and the hopefully 'docile bodies' of clients and staff.

One facet of these processes is that the notes made by practitioners under the UK's Care Programme Approach are often written so as to mesh with the requirements inherent in the process of diagnosing and treating 'mental disorders'. For example, they contain information such as 'response to medication', and are uncritically relayed in conversations in the ward, handovers and rounds. This may be enhanced by the increasing shift towards nurses adopting classificatory linguistic systems which privilege the needs of managers above those of patients or nurses. Crowe (2000) argues that mental health nursing's adherence to this kind of psychiatric discourse delimits the profession's therapeutic potential, and that reifying distress as 'disorder' along the lines of the *Diagnostic and Statistical Manual* (American Psychiatric Association, 1994) reduces nurses to assisting in the 'treatment' of 'disorders', rather than, for example 'reconnecting people to the social web of life' through an understanding of illness narratives.

Thus, documentary versions of clients with a diagnosis of BPD, as well as being overly judgemental, may also operate in more subtle yet equally delimiting ways. Within a framework of artfully constructed objectivity, accounts can neuter any political or personal significance that the client's experience has. For example, given that most people with a diagnosis of BPD are both female and reported to be the victims of parental neglect or childhood abuse (Krawitz and Watson, 2003; Silk *et al.*, 1995; Wonderlich *et al.*, 2001), this might say something significant about our social organization. Therefore, from a critical perspective (Fairclough, 2001), we might say that constructing BPD in terms of personal pathology can detract from a politicized understanding of the position of women within dominant social forms. Diamond and Quinby (1988) adopt a feminist perspective to explore how masculine and patriarchal power subjugates women both linguistically and through their bodies. An understanding of how language territorializes subjectivity enables a rereading of BPD, away from the notion of an internal disorder towards understanding it as a response to material trauma and perceived powerlessness (Wilkins and Warner, 2001). Thus, while Rosewater (1995) argues that personality disorder could be seen as an adaptive response to an aberrant event, professionals are encouraged to see their clients in terms of what has gone awry in relation to the dominant script of personhood, or indeed femininity. As one mental health support worker said in an interview:

> I know we're supposed to see whether the house is clean and stuff, and the cigarette burns and everything but you go in and that, I mean that's not the major problem. There was this client the other day and she'd just had her foot amputated so she wasn't getting around and she'd wet herself but that was understandable really, that was the least of her problems.

Here, the discourse of using domestic arrangements to 'read off' the dispositional complaisance of the client is subverted by the practitioner, who points instead to the circumstantial problems which eclipse questions of personal hygiene and who therefore appears to be resisting the dominant inscription. However, in other cases it is possible to see how the relationship between nurse and client has been more thoroughly infused with this agenda. Here is a Midlands-based community mental health nurse who has more fully imbibed this view of clients:

> I saw one woman last week and I know, I can tell what she's been up to by the state of the house, I went in and there was clothes

all over the floor and you know, overflowing ashtrays and the baby was crawling around on a filthy carpet, and I said straight away 'you haven't been taking your medication have you?'

This was followed by an account of the client's subsequent confession and her disclosure of a 'stash' of unused tablets. The state of the domestic sphere then was taken to be a window into the soul. The story was complete with a denouement or coda consolidating this apparent wisdom, and confirming the complaisance of the client in the face of the astute clinical gaze – she confessed.

The workshop within: reconfiguring clients and professionals

The therapeutic scrutiny of people with BPD has been governmentally encouraged in recent years. In the UK the policy and legislative framework has increasingly directed the attention of mental health practitioners towards clients with BPD after the period of relative neglect which we have documented.

This scrutiny has, it is true, often focused on offending behaviour, but from our point of view the interesting thing is how the internal characteristics and personal qualities of the client and to some extent the professional are formulated through the network of concepts and terms that go to make them up. Around the middle of the twentieth century the by then 100-year-old concern with a lack of moral sense had begun to be populated with new characteristics. Hervey Cleckley (1941), a mid-twentieth-century proponent of the term 'psychopath' and originator of the phrase 'the mask of sanity', was particularly interested in these apparently sane yet profoundly disruptive individuals, especially the more socially deviant variants of what eventually came to be known as personality disorder, and he described in some detail the characteristics. For example, such people were:

> ... grandiose, arrogant, callous, superficial, and manipulative... short tempered, unable to form strong emotional bonds with others, and lacking in empathy, guilt, or remorse... irresponsible, impulsive, and prone to violate social and legal norms and expectations... (Hart and Hare, 1997, pp. 22–3)

This putative quality of manipulativeness meant that when such a person was in contact with therapeutic services, all manner of chaos could ensue, as if by contagion. In his classic paper, 'The Ailment', Tom

Main (1957) described how in his view and that of the colleagues with whom he discussed difficult patients, these patients were responsible for 'splitting' or creating rifts between staff. Main's theoretical impetus in understanding this process derived from the object relations school of psychoanalytic psychotherapy, and conceived of the patient as dividing and conditioning the staff team. According to Main, upon the admission of a personality disordered patient to a ward or unit, such patients become 'special' to one or two members of the staff, via sentimental appeal, the arousal of 'omnipotence' and 'paranoid' sensitivity, aspects of the self which were supposed to exist in early childhood, which these patients somehow evoke in the staff. The sharing of confidential secrets between the patient and the 'special' members of staff also contributes to the rifts which begin to appear between the staff. Eventually a split between the staff would occur, often involving pre-existing lines of disagreement between nurses who viewed the patient as a special case requiring extra care and attention, and other staff who viewed the patient as troublesome or a time waster. Main believed the source of this 'splitting' process to be the dysfunctional relational style of the patients themselves, originating from early childhood experiences. He suggests that they have suffered severely in the past, and are now 'tormented by childlike needs and rages', needs for affection and love, and rages at the apparent inability of others to provide that love. The more love the nurses provide, the more it is mistrusted, tested and spoiled by the patient, prompting nurses into ever greater shows of commitment, fidelity and affection. Such constant demands for love, and the methods used to extort it from others via self-depreciation, shows of suffering and guilt induction, are said, by Main, to be the result of primitive sadistic impulses. He calls this the 'aggressive use of suffering'. Meanwhile, staff who resist these demands look on in horror at the overinvolvement and lack of 'boundaries' or 'objectivity' of those who they see to have been seduced into this emotional process. Conflict occurs between the two staff factions over their actions towards the patient.

Indeed, the durability and persistence of the pattern displayed by the so-called 'personality disordered patient' are carefully established in the literature. For example, its independence of the clinical or institutional context is established by Bowers (2003):

> For even outside contact with psychiatry, the daily behaviour of some PD individuals is characterized by an interpersonal style dominated by manipulation, in which others are ruthlessly exploited, conned and bullied into fulfilling their needs. (Bowers, 2003, p. 331)

It is an elementary matter to point to the pejorative language here. However, slightly more subtle is the implied voluntarism of terms like 'ruthlessly exploited'. The staff, it seems, are relatively vulnerable and this is reflected in the extensive 'supervision' they are theorized as needing in many therapeutic regimes addressed to clients putatively suffering with BPD (Linehan, 1993; Verheul *et al.*, 2003) which is described as being unusually taxing.

Yet despite the accounts of 'borderlines' as problematic, the health professional of today is repeatedly enjoined to attend to them as objects for the penetrative clinical gaze, with perhaps revealing clues about the nature of the conjectured personality dynamics involved. Here is a pamphlet published by the UK's Royal College of Psychiatrists:

> The personality can be likened to an onion, with each outer layer an attempt to cover up the strains of an inner layer. People with dangerous personality disorders are often deeply anxious and depressed though this may not show. It may be easier to sort out problems when the cover-up is stripped off and the issues are faced more directly. Anorexia nervosa is often an obvious form of rigid self-control and avoidance but in someone who underneath is terrified of their inner impulses. Alcoholism allows a man to become dependent on his mates in a 'masculine' fashion and can unlock habitual violence. (Hill, 2005, p. 2)

Here are the underlying forces after the veneer is 'stripped off' – anxiety, depression, terror of one's impulses, dependency – the entire psychodynamic bestiary from the late nineteenth century is presented in a near-perfect state of preservation in Hill's account. What is needed then, following this logic, is a systematic and disciplined way of laying open this disordered structure, indexing, rearranging and re-educating the individual, infusing them with 'skills', 'confidence', an understanding of 'boundaries' and 'responsible', 'appropriate' behaviour.

The road to enlightenment: the discourse and politics of 'responsibility'

There have been various attempts at addressing these therapeutic objectives in recent years. Perhaps the most noteworthy, because of its national impact in the UK, is the development and implementation of the Care Programme Approach or CPA, a policy introduced in 1991 and reformed in 1999. It is intended to enhance the care of people with mental health problems, and the desirability of the involvement of 'service users' in compiling care plans is made explicit (Department of Health, 1990, 1999). This care management process for mental health service users requires people needing an enhanced level of care to have the following: (i) an assessment of their needs; (ii) a comprehensive multidisciplinary care programme; (iii) a written care plan; (iv) a care coordinator; and (v) regular reviews. The self-identified principle was to offer a good, coordinated, integrated service to users and their carers, both in the community and as inpatients. The National Institute for Mental Health (2003a) recommends that people with diagnoses of personality disorder are subject to the CPA. Concern has been expressed that these reforms emphasized the bureaucratic aspects of care coordination rather than the therapeutic role and relationship of the coordinator (Simpson *et al.*, 2003). Others suggest the CPA is little more than a post-liberal response to control the dangerous mentally ill (Morrall, 2000), despite tentative evidence of its benefits, such that clients may feel more involved in care delivery and receive a more consistent service response (Fallon, 2003).

The uneven and variable implementation of the CPA (Social Services Inspectorate, 1999) indicates that such favourable results may not be found everywhere. Haigh (2003) found that people with a diagnosis of personality disorder experienced the CPA as poorly applied or unhelpful. McDermott (1998) and Lawson *et al.* (1999) argue that the CPA, while it drew upon the language of user-centredness, in practice was rather difficult to adjust to users' expressed preferences and needs. The UK's Commission for Health Improvement (2003) confirmed the inconsistent application of the CPA, and identified a need for greater patient involvement in care planning.

In any event, the kinds of frameworks into which clients are installed as part of this process are not necessarily ones which vouchsafe their autonomy. As one woman of 28 with a turbulent history of involvement with mental health services told us:

> Well they said you've got a personality disorder and you can have dialectical behaviour therapy. Now I'd not heard of myself being described as a personality disorder before, it had always been depression or something like that, but it was a personality disorder now and that's what I have to have.

The reinscription of the person into the diagnostic category and therapeutic frame means that they have to learn a new identity and a new discourse about themselves. This new label and role imposed from outside are at odds with the sense of continuity and coherence which is supposed to characterize the healthy reflexive self that Beck (1992) and Giddens (1990) believe is needed to flourish in late modernity.

Such is the zeal of some contemporary reformers that they seek to remedy not only the condition but the way it is seen by others. In the landmark publication *No Longer a Diagnosis of Exclusion* (NIMHE, 2003a), the argument is enhanced and authenticated by the inclusion of focus group material from service users themselves:

> No mental disorder carries a greater stigma than the diagnosis 'Personality Disorder', and those diagnosed can feel labeled by professionals as well as by society. There was a strong feeling that many professionals did not understand the diagnosis, and often equated it with untreatability. (NIMHE, 2003a, p. 20)

As a facet of this process of dealing with BPDs, staff themselves are encouraged to adopt the relentlessly upbeat approach as described in the UK's *Capabilities Framework* (NIMHE, 2003b) with staff themselves being reconfigured to acquire skills and ascend the 'escalator' of growing expertise:

> The escalator approach aims to open up opportunities for groups of staff whose developmental needs have been overlooked hitherto and is therefore a rational workforce-planning tool in relation to the development of personality disorder services. (NIMHE, 2003b, p. 18)

Rationality, planning and development will supervene over the division and strife described by Main (1957). This will be explicitly headed off by the myriad capabilities identified in the capabilities framework. For example, the 'technologies of the self' to which staff are enjoined are not just skills in the traditional manual or cognitive sense, but include aspects that are related to the workplace culture itself: 'Capable of developing a positive networking culture and strategies for sharing good practice in developing services to people with PD (personality disorder)' (NIMHE, 2003b, p. 31).

The multiple 'capabilities' to which the professionals are exhorted are, as we have intimated, paralleled by a variety of personal characteristics which are cajoled out of the clients. There is, for example, a relentless focus on responsibility. A few examples should suffice to illustrate its ubiquitous appeal to clinicians and authors on the subject. Flewett *et al.* (2003) advocate the development of a planned approach, where the therapeutic regime for each client is 'encapsulated in a management plan – a behavioural intervention to minimize reinforcement of hazardous behaviours and promote self-responsibility' (Flewett *et al.*, 2003, p. 79).

Similarly, the approach to clients may be designed to 'encourage them to take more responsibility for their own actions' (Horsfall, 1999, p. 428). In this respect it is as if therapy tries to reconstruct in miniature the processes that Beck (1992) and Giddens (1990) see as taking place in wider society as people are increasingly divested of traditional community supports and are thrown back on their own personal resources. This idea of 'responsibility' on the part of clients has repeatedly emerged as a point of contention in our field research and deserves further elaboration, for it is here that the ambivalences and disjunctures surrounding the idea what it is to be a service user with a personality disorder are particularly prominent.

The theme of trying to get patients to be 'responsible' continues through much contemporary literature. For example:

> ... patients are expected to assume a greater responsibility for and an active role in the management of their health and lifestyle. Their expectations, experience and expertise must be acknowledged, respected and form the basis of care. (Langley and Klopper, 2005, p. 24)

The taking of responsibility is reported to be valued by clients too, even when it comes to the rather fraught question of what to do about people who might be at risk of making suicide attempts. As a client is described as saying in Krawitz *et al.* (2004):

> Hospital became a place which was too safe, where I took no responsibility for myself and had no need to take control of my life. This fed my belief that I was inadequate and unable to cope with life. The more my needs were met in hospital, the less I believed I could manage my own life. This led to an increased frequency and duration of admissions, leading me to believe I was getting 'sicker', thereby needing more help, etc., etc. – a never ending cycle of helplessness and hopelessness. (Krawitz *et al.*, 2004, p. 13)

As one might expect, devices to enhance responsibility-taking by clients were popular with clinicians:

> Clinician participants all advocated using a contract to reinforce the mutuality of the partnership and the client's responsibility, and to help empower the client, emphasize limits and boundaries and state who could be informed of the client's condition at specific times and instances when the client could contact the therapist: '... it's all about responsibility; based on the contract and the fact that there's honesty. The responsibility is theirs.' (Langley and Klopper, 2005, p. 28)

Yet the nature of 'responsibility' itself assumes a notional level playing field where the actors are roughly equal in the powers that they may exercise over themselves and their circumstances. Yet, as Greener (2002, p. 697) points out, to 'pretend that we have empowered actors allowed to behave in a reflexive way may serve to conceal the deep-seated structural power relationships that exist'. In other words, insisting that clients should 'take responsibility' is to gloss over questions of whether they have the material powers to practically do so. Sometimes the practice of taking responsibility is incompatible with the political, legal or health care regime in which the client finds him or herself. As one service user said to us in interview:

> I try to take responsibility like they're always telling me but there's only a certain extent they'll let you take it. Like with the tablets I was like 'they make me sleepy, I don't want to take them' and they were like 'well you've got to' so where's the responsibility in that?

The neatly manicured internal architecture of a fully responsible Enlightenment soul is therefore sometimes difficult to achieve. From the clients' point of view it may appear to be at odds with the more mundane constraints of the therapeutic regime. At the same time this petulant questioning of staff decisions and attention to contradictions may serve to confirm the symptoms of the presumed 'disorder'.

Furthermore, urging clients to take responsibility makes more subtle assumptions about how the mind should work. As Newnes and Radcliffe (2005) note, in telling clients to 'take responsibility', social workers, family therapists and mental health staff are taking a position that emotions do not or should not affect the will, and thus, one's ability to act 'responsibly'. The client then is enjoined to act responsibly however he or she feels. Sometimes, even when clients are detained compulsorily under mental health legislation – which is a way of saying in legal terms that they are not responsible – they are still urged to take 'responsibility' even though legally this power has been taken away from them (Newnes and Radcliffe, 2005). Furthermore, children and adolescents in the UK are in a remarkably complex legal and policy framework governing the decisions they are allowed to make and the extent to which they may be held responsible for their actions. Yet as Newnes and Radcliffe (2005) note, here too practitioners can be found urging them to be more responsible.

At the same time, some practitioners can be found voicing concerns about the extent to which the idea of responsibility was being promoted. As another of our interviewees, a senior occupational therapist, observed: 'if we deem the mentally ill responsible, it absolves us of our responsibility to help them'. Or as Clarke (2005, p. 453) puts it, '*responsibility* appears as a smokescreen behind which the state is systematically divesting its responsibilities' (original emphasis).

In our research so far there are a great many such disjunctures between the vision presented in the official documentations or the academic literature and the experience on the ground which has been described to us. A further example will help to reinforce the point. Here are Swenson *et al.* (2001, p. 320) describing their proposed regime for treatment: the '. . . atmosphere helps to reduce shame and to empower the patient with validation, respect, and practical tools'.

Yet here is an experienced 35-year-old community mental health nurse describing an incident in her therapeutic liaison with a young man who was a 'dual' – that is, he had a substance use problem as well as a personality disorder:

> I suppose the first mistake I made was I gave him my phone number because, well, he seemed that much more vulnerable than a lot of the others, you know and I was genuinely worried about him, but then it was one thing leading to another and in the end he was just calling me all the time, like I couldn't get a minute with my kids without the bloody mobile going off and it was him and he was like 'I want to go and score, I'm trying not to, but I want to go and score.' I don't know what I was supposed to do about it. Or there were these texts that he used to send me. I had to get the mobile number changed and in the end I had him transferred to the forensic team.

Now of course this event did not occur within the team Swenson *et al.* (2001) were describing and in most teams, if such a thing had accidentally happened, then no one else would get to hear about it. Nevertheless it illustrates how the actual process of relating to clients is far more stressful and chaotic than is described in the vignettes presented in the official literature. Yet perhaps the disjunctures here are not just accidents but reflect more socially and politically significant fault lines in the very fabric of what the interventions are trying to achieve. As Hinshelwood (1999, p. 188) observes, the term 'difficult patient does not connote a configuration of clinical signs and symptoms . . . but is a way of describing the state of the professional'.

The organization of care for people with BPDs then is geared towards the reconfiguration of their psychic architecture – it is an aspect of what Miller and Rose (1994) called the 'orthopaedics of the soul'. This is aligned with the project of governments in many developed nations to make their citizenry more responsible for their own welfare (Clarke, 2005) and continually remodel themselves in line with the needs of business culture. Thus on the one hand we have increasingly refined and detailed attempts via the CPA and through dialectical behaviour therapy to reconstruct this alleged interior architecture of the disordered individual. Yet on the other we notice, in the guise of getting clients to 'take responsibility', that in some areas there seems to be a retraction in service provision; as if practitioners and policy makers were stepping back from some kinds of intervention. Taking a calculated risk in the case of suicidal intent, allowing clients to come into conflict with the law, or reducing the access they gain to services are promoted in the interests of getting clients to develop the kind of personality which is desired. The focus on the internal psychodynamic organization of personality disorders derived from early medico-legal and psychoanalytical work has tended to direct the professional gaze inwards, rather than outwards to any material constraints on clients' conduct or on their ability or opportunity to be responsible. The lessons from critical perspectives espoused by Fairclough, or Foucauldian work on governmentality, are that more therapy, personal development, responsibility and empowerment do not necessarily lead to liberation. Rather they represent new modes of subjection associated with the transition from expansive, welfare-oriented politics to advanced liberalism (Clarke, 2005).

Instead, perhaps it would be possible to redress the asymmetry and understand not only clients' psychic structure but also the hitherto underexplored social and political field within which 'BPD' occurs. The reflexive capacities celebrated by Giddens and Beck could be used to explore with clients why and how it is that they are prevented from 'taking responsibility', and how they might address the institutional, corporate and statutory powers ranged against them. By co-creating an account of the clients' and practitioners' social context, the hitherto bewildering swings of emotion, the sense that one is depersonalized or losing control, the neediness and anger, may be less terrifying and begin to make sense.

Conclusion: towards a reconfiguration of mental health care surveillance

In this chapter we have tried to examine how the notion of personality and its disorder has evolved over the last two centuries from the surviving written accounts of the syndrome and a selection of contemporary evidence. An ongoing theme is the apparent contradiction between the apparent sanity and rationality of a person who can at times appear alert, oriented and even affable, and at others seem mean, 'manipulative' and actively destructive of self or others. Far from there being any consistent disorder of mood or disengagement from consensual experiences or rationalities, the personality disordered individual has been a perpetual enigma. At once regarded as deeply disturbed yet at the same time often excluded from mental heath care, the client thus diagnosed has in the UK recently been subject to a variety of state-sponsored therapeutic interventions. The overall thrust of many of these has been to try to micro-manage the consciousness and psychic machinery of the client into a form that resembles the boundaried, responsible, self-determining individualized self of the kind that is believed to flourish in late modernity and which harmonizes with the corporate enterprise milieu. As the constraints and supports of occupational security and family roles are progressively dismantled and increasingly survival is framed as a matter that the individual should take into his or her own hands, then 'borderline personality disorder' is an apposite term for those who cannot live up to these demands. Their desperate attempts to inveigle themselves into a social network, to get others to do their bidding, and to elicit increasingly elusive desiderata such as 'love', 'respect' or 'fulfilment', yield instead frustration and 'emptiness' (Smail, 2005). When people in this position find their way into what, following Foucault (1975) we might call 'the clinic', they may well be confronted by an orthopaedic process of reconstruction (Rose, 1990) where they are encouraged to have 'responsibility' through techniques which will just as likely prevent it, or have their 'self-esteem' raised via techniques which remind them at every turn of their inferiority. It is surely no coincidence that personality disorder has been viewed as 'untreatable'.

The way in which a problem is formulated is important in terms of how it influences the vocabularies which are usable, the kinds of identity which can be experienced for both client and practitioner, and the implications for the treatment regimes that can be offered. As we have seen, the field of BPD plays out in miniature the kinds of drama which can be identified in the wider body politic. It involves the dilemmas of sovereign autonomy of the self, self-disclosure, responsibility and self-government that are part of the Enlightenment project and which have been re-emphasized in Western political regimes of the twenty-first century.

The idea of the 'reflexive self' (Beck, 1992) includes the notion that being a person is a 'continuous process of identity construction' (p. 180).

Thus undergoing 'detraditionalization' can be understood in such a way as to be an extension of the person's reflexivity and individualization. As Beck (1992) argues: 'Individualization of life situations and processes thus means that biographies become *self-reflexive*; socially prescribed biography is transformed into biography that is self-produced and continues to be produced' (Beck, 1992, p. 135; original emphasis).

If we were to take Giddens and Beck in a strong form we might see the non-personality disordered individual harvesting cultural resources in a knowing, self-aware way to enhance their skills, confidence and employability under advanced liberalism. By contrast, the borderline personality disordered individual is somehow unable to fulfil these kinds of demands. The rational–economic core to the individual, which is presupposed by much political and therapeutic discourse, where individuals are assumed to be willing and able to grow, gain skills, resolve conflicts and go onwards and upwards, seems to be awry in the personality disorders – at least it does if all we do is look inwards to the presumed intrapsychic space. On the other hand, armed with the insight from Foucault, Rose and critical linguistics we might do well to turn the question around. Perhaps one way through this maze is to see the personality-disordered person not as somehow alien but as having similar policies and desires as the rest of us. Clues as to the importance of language in this quest were provided by Krawitz and Watson (1999):

> Words are important carriers of information and significantly shape the future. Some commonly used terminology such as 'PD, worried well and just behavioural' invalidates clients, is offensive and almost certainly, leads to poorer outcome. We need to explore terminology, which is more helpful. 'Attention seeking' might be better replaced with *in need of attention*, 'manipulation' with *manoeuvre* and 'greedy' with *in need.* (Krawitz and Watson, 1999, p. 40; original emphasis)

Here, the recommended language is emphasizing familiarity, sameness and intelligibility and rather than dysfunction, otherness and deficiency. This humanization of the language surrounding BPD is welcome but still leaves us with the question of how we are to tackle the distress and difficulty itself. Perhaps in this case it is important to look at the organizational languages of the professions and identify how these may be contributing to the distress. Using the insights of critical theory and critical linguistics clients and practitioners may begin to unpack the multiple ways in which organized human activity systematically places the means of 'taking responsibility' or developing as a self-governing individual beyond the client.

In this view, rather than being a matter of incompetence, 'personality disorder' or ill will, clients may not be able to change because the material powers to change themselves and their world are quite literally beyond them. Amidst a mass of discourse about 'empowerment', clients seldom succeed in gaining the power to achieve such change. Therefore, perhaps one way of making progress would be for concerned practitioners to explore with clients how the social formations and institutions with which they are engaged often assist in disempowering them. The conceptual tools we have made use of in this chapter can be used to assist in important therapeutic work as we unpick not the client, but the client's context – the clinics, hospitals and prisons, the families, peer groups and communities – that make up their social world. Giving form to their frustration and alienation and giving them strategies to make sense of their context is perhaps a small step towards getting them to the stage where they no longer have to be subject to regimes of scrutiny or urged to 'take responsibility'. Perhaps, in this uniquely social, linguistic and political condition it is attention to language that will unravel the enigma and enable clients and practitioners to find new ways to transcend 'responsibility', by ensuring that the means to enjoy responsibility in their life world cannot be taken away from them in the first place.

References

Adler, G. and Buie, D. (1979) 'Aloneness and Borderline Psychopathology: the Possible Relevance of Child Development Issues', *International Journal of Psychoanalysis*, 60, pp. 83–96.

American Psychiatric Association (1980) *Diagnostic and Statistical Manual of Mental Disorders* (3rd edn) (Washington, DC: American Psychiatric Association).

American Psychiatric Association (1994) *Diagnostic and Statistical Manual of Mental Disorders* (4th edn) (Washington, DC: American Psychiatric Association).

Beck, U. (1992) *Risk Society: Towards a New Modernity* (London: Sage).

Beck, U. and Beck-Gernsheim, E. (2002) *Individualization: Institutionalized Individualism and its Social and Political Consequences* (London: Sage).

Blackshaw, L., Levy, A. and Perciano, J. (1999) *Listening to High Utilisers of Mental Health Services: Recognising, Responding to and Recovering from Trauma* (Salem, Ore.: Office of Mental Health Services).

Bowers, L. (2003) 'Manipulation: Searching for an Understanding', *Journal of Psychiatric and Mental Health Nursing*, 10, pp. 329–34.

Buie, D. and Adler, G. (1982) 'Definitive Treatment of the Borderline Personality', *International Journal of Psychoanalytic Psychotherapy*, 9, pp. 51–87.

Burr, V. (1995) *An Introduction to Social Constructionism* (London: Routledge).

Carabine, J. (2001) 'Unmarried Motherhood 1830–1990: a Genealogical Analysis', in M. Wetherell, S. Taylor and S. J. Yates (eds) *Discourse as Data: a Guide for Analysis*, pp. 267–310 (Buckingham: Open University Press/Sage).

Clarke, J. (2005) 'New Labour's Citizens: Activated, Empowered, Responsibilized, Abandoned?', *Critical Social Policy*, 25(4), pp. 447–63.

Cleary, M., Siegfried, N. and Walter, G. (2002) 'Experience, Knowledge and Attitudes of Mental Health Staff regarding Clients with a Borderline Personality Disorder', *International Journal of Mental Health Nursing*, 11, pp. 186–91.

Cleckley, H. (1941) *The Mask of Sanity: an Attempt to Clarify Some Issues about the So-called Psychopathic Personality* (St Louis, Mo.: C. V. Mosby Co.).

Commission for Health Improvement (2003) *Mental Health Clinical Governance Reviews* (London: Commission for Health Improvement).

Crowe, M. (2000) 'The Nurse–Patient Relationship: a Consideration of its Discursive Context', *Journal of Advanced Nursing*, 31(4), pp. 962–7.

Darjee, R. and Crichton J. (2003) 'Personality Disorder in the Law in Scotland: a Historical Perspective', *The Journal of Forensic Psychiatry Psychology*, 14(2), 394–425.

Delacour, S. (2000) 'The Construction of Nursing: Ideology, Discourse and Representation', in G. Gray and R. Pratt (eds) *Towards a Discipline of Nursing*, pp. 335–54 (Edinburgh: Churchill Livingstone).

Department of Health (1990)*The Care Programme Approach for People with Mental Illness Referred to Specialist Psychiatric Services*, HC(90)23/LASSL (90)11, Joint Health and Social Services Circular (London: Department of Health).

Department of Health (1999) *Effective Care Co-ordination in Mental Health Services: Modernizing the Care Programme Approach. A Policy Booklet* (London: Her Majesty's Stationery Office).

Diamond, I. and Quinby, L. (eds) (1988) *Feminism and Foucault: Reflections on Resistance*, pp. xi–xiv (Boston: Northeastern University Press).

Drewery, W. and McKenzie, W. (1999) 'Therapy and Faith', in I. Parker (ed.) *Deconstructing Psychotherapy*, pp. 132–49 (London: Sage).

Edwards, D. and Potter, J. (1992) *Discursive Psychology* (London: Sage).

Erikson, E. (1963) *Childhood and Society* (2nd edn) (New York: W. W. Norton).

Erikson, E. (1968) *Identity: Youth and Crisis* (New York: W. W. Norton).

Fairclough, N. (1995a) *Critical Discourse Analysis: the Critical Study of Language* (London: Longman).

Fairclough, N. (1995b) *Media Discourse* (London: Edward Arnold).

Fairclough, N. (2001) 'The Discourse of New Labour: Critical Discourse Analysis', in M. Wetherell, S. Taylor and S. J. Yates (eds) *Discourse as Data: a Guide for Analysis*, pp. 220–66 (Buckingham: Open University Press/Sage).

Fallon, P. (2003) 'Traveling through the System: the Lived Experience of People with Borderline Personality Disorder in Contact with Psychiatric Services', *Journal of Psychiatric and Mental Health Nursing*, 10(4), pp. 393–400.

Flewett, T., Bradley, P. and Redvers, A. (2003) 'Management of Borderline Personality Disorder', *British Journal of Psychiatry*, 183, pp. 78–9.

Fonagy, P., Moran, G. S., Steele, M., Steele, H. and Higgitt, A. C. (1991) 'The Capacity for Understanding Mental States: the Reflective Self in Parent and Child and its Significance for Security of Attachment', *Infant Mental Health Journal*, 13, pp. 200–16.

Foucault, M. (1975) *The Birth of the Clinic: an Archeology of Medical Perception* (A. M. Sheridan Smith, trans.) (New York: Vintage Books).

Foucault, M. (1977) *Discipline and Punish: the Birth of the Prison* (Harmondsworth, Middlesex: Penguin Books).

Foucault, M. (1988) 'The Political Technology of Individuals', in L. H. Martin, H. Gutman and P. H. Hutton (eds) *Technologies of the Self: a Seminar with Michel Foucault*, pp. 145–62 (London: Tavistock)

Fraser, K. and Gallop, R. (1993) 'Nurse's Confirming/Disconfirming Responses to Patients Diagnosed with Borderline Personality Disorder', *Archives of Psychiatric Nursing*, 7, pp. 336–41.

Gergen, K. L. (1991) *The Saturated Self* (New York: Basic Books).

Giddens, A. (1990) *The Consequences of Modernity* (Cambridge: Polity Press).

Giddens, A. (1998) *The Third Way: the Renewal of Social Democracy* (Cambridge: Polity Press).

Gramsci, A. (1971) *Selections from the Prison Notebooks* (London: Lawrence and Wishart).

Greener, I. (2002) 'Agency, Social Theory and Social Policy', *Critical Social Policy*, 22(4), pp. 688–705.

Haigh, R. (2003) *Services for People with Personality Disorder: the Thoughts of Service Users* (London: Department of Health).

Hammersley, M. (2002) *Discourse Analysis: a Bibliographical Guide*. http://www.cf.ac.uk/socsi/capacity/Activities/Themes/In-depth/guide.pdf/(accessed 29 December 2003).

Hart, S. D. and Hare, R. D. (1997) 'Psychopathy: Assessment and Association with Criminal Conduct', in D. M. Stoff, J. Breiling and J. D. Maser (eds) *Handbook of Antisocial Behaviour*, pp. 22–35 (Chichester: Wiley).

Heartfield, M. (1996) 'Nursing Documentation and Nursing Practice: a Discourse Analysis', *Journal of Advanced Nursing*, 24, pp. 98–103.

Hill, O. (2005) *Personality Disorder and its Treatment* (London: Royal College of Psychiatrists).

Hinshelwood, R. D. (1999) 'The Difficult Patient: the Role of "Scientific Psychiatry" in Understanding Patients with Chronic Schizophrenia or Severe Personality Disorder', *British Journal of Psychiatry*, 174, pp. 187–90.

Horsfall, J. (1999) 'Towards Understanding Some Complex Borderline Behaviours', *Journal of Psychiatric and Mental Health Nursing*, 6(6), pp. 425–32.

Hosking, D. M. and Morley, I. E. (1991) *A Social Psychology of Organising* (Brighton: Harvester Wheatsheaf).

Kendell, R. E. (2002) 'The Distinction between Personality Disorder and Mental Illness', *British Journal of Psychiatry*, 180, pp. 110–15.

Koch, J. L. A. (1891) *Die Psychopathischen Minderwertigkeiten* (Dorn: Ravensburg).

Krawitz, R. and Watson, C. (1999) *Borderline Personality Disorder: Pathways to Effective Service Delivery and Clinical Treatment Options* (Wellington, New Zealand: New Zealand Mental Health Commission).

Krawitz, R. and Watson C. (2003) *Borderline Personality Disorder: a Guide to Treatment* (Oxford: Oxford University Press).

Krawitz, R., Jackson, W., Allen, R., Connell, A., Argyle, N., Bensemann C. and Mileshkin, C. (2004) 'Professionally Indicated Short-term Risk-taking in the Treatment of Borderline Personality Disorder', *Australasian Psychiatry*, 12(1), pp. 11–17.

Langley, G. C. and Klopper, H. (2005) 'Trust as a Foundation for the Therapeutic Intervention for Patients with Borderline Personality Disorder', *Journal of Psychiatric and Mental Health Nursing*, 12, pp. 23–32.

Lawson, M., Strickland, C. and Wolfson, P. (1999) 'User Involvement in Care Planning: the Care Programme Approach from the Users' Perspective', *Psychiatric Bulletin*, 23(9), pp. 539–41.
Lewis, G. and Appleby, L. (1988) 'Personality Disorder: the Patients Psychiatrists Dislike', *British Journal of Psychiatry*, 153, pp. 44–9.
Lieb, K., Zanarini, M. C., Schmahl, C., Linehan, M. M. and Bohus, M. (2004) 'Borderline Personality Disorder', *The Lancet*, 364, pp. 453–61.
Linehan, M. M. (1993) *Cognitive Behavioral Treatment of Borderline Personality Disorder* (New York: Guilford Press).
McDermott, G. (1998) 'The Care Programme Approach: a Patient Perspective', *Nursing Times Research*, 3, pp. 47–63.
Main, T. F. (1957) 'The Ailment', *British Journal of Medical Psychology*, 30, pp. 129–45.
Maudsley, H. (1873) *Body and Mind: an Inquiry into their Connection and Mutual Influence, Specially in Reference to Mental Disorders* (New York: Macmillan).
Miller, P. and Rose, N. (1994) 'On Therapeutic Authority: Psychoanalytical Expertise under Advanced Liberalism', *History of the Human Sciences*, 7(3), pp. 29–64.
Millon, T. (1991) 'The Borderline Construct: Introductory Notes on its History, Theory and Empirical Grounding', in J. F. Clarkin, E. Marziali and H. Munroe-Blum (eds) *Borderline Personality Disorder: Clinical and Empirical Perspectives*, pp. 3–26 (New York: Guilford Press).
Mohr, W. K. (1999) 'Deconstructing the Language of Psychiatric Hospitalization', *Journal of Advanced Nursing*, 29(5), pp. 1052–9.
Morrall, P. (2000) *Madness and Murder: Implications for Psychiatric Disciplines* (London: Whurr Publishers).
National Institute for Mental Health in England (NIMHE) (2003a) *No Longer a Diagnosis of Exclusion* (Leeds: National Institute for Mental Health in England).
National Institute for Mental Health in England (NIHME) (2003b) *Breaking the Cycle of Rejection: the Personality Disorder Capabilities Framework* (Leeds: National Institute for Mental Health in England).
Nehls, N. (2000) 'Recovering: a Process of Empowerment', *Advances in Nursing Science*, 22(4), pp. 62–70.
Newnes, C. and Radcliffe, N. (2005) *Making and Breaking Children's Lives* (Ross on Wye: PCCS Books).
O'Malley, P. (1996) 'Risk and Responsibility', in N. Rose (ed.) *Foucault and Political Reason: Liberalism, Neo-Liberalism and Rationalities of Government*, pp. 189–208 (Chicago: University of Chicago Press).
Paris, J. (1992) 'Social Risk Factors for Borderline Personality Disorder: a Review and Hypothesis', *Canadian Journal of Psychiatry*, 37, pp. 510–15.
Paris, J. (1996) 'Cultural Factors in the Emergence of Borderline Pathology', *Psychiatry*, 59, pp. 185–92.
Parker, I. (1992) *Discourse Dynamics: Critical Analysis for Social and Individual Psychology* (Routledge: London).
Parker, I. (1994) 'Discourse Analysis', in P. Banister, E. Burman, I. Parker, M. Taylor and C. Tindall (eds) *Qualitative Methods in Psychology: a Research Guide*, pp. 76–93 (Buckingham: Open University Press).
Porter, S. (1998) *Social Theory and Nursing Practice* (Basingstoke: Macmillan).
Potter, J. (1996) *Representing Reality: Discourse, Rhetoric and Social Construction* (London: Sage).

Prichard, J. C. (1835) *Treatise on Insanity and Other Disorders Affecting the Mind* (London: Sherwood).

Prichard, J. C. (1842) *On the Different Forms of Insanity in Relation to Jurisprudence* (London: Bailliere).

Ray, I. (1838) *A Treatise on the Medical Jurisprudence of Insanity* (Boston, Mass.: Little).

Rose, N. (1990) *Governing the Soul: the Shaping of the Private Self* (London: Routledge).

Rosewater, L. B. (1995) 'Reminiscences, Recollections and Reflections: the Making of a Feminist Foremother', *Women and Therapy*, 17(3–4), pp. 407–17.

Schneider, K. (1950) *Die Psychopatischen Persőnlichkeiten* (9th edn) (Vienna: Deuticke).

Silk, K. R., Lee, S., Hill, E. and Lohr, N. E. (1995) 'Borderline Personality Disorder Symptoms and Severity of Sexual Abuse', *American Journal of Psychiatry*, 152, pp. 1059–64.

Simpson, A., Miller, C. and Bowers, L. (2003) 'Case Management Models and the Care Programme Approach: How to Make the CPA Effective and Credible', *Journal of Psychiatric and Mental Health Nursing*, 10(4), pp. 472–83.

Smail, D. (2005) *Power, Interest and Psychology: Elements of a Social Materialist Understanding of Distress* (Ross on Wye: PCCS Books).

Social Services Inspectorate (1999) *Still Building Bridges: the Report of a National Inspection of Arrangements for the Integration of the Care Programme Approach with Care Management* (London: Department of Health).

Swartz, M., Blazer, D., George, L. and Winfield, I. (1990) 'Estimating the Prevalence of Borderline Personality Disorder in the Community', *Journal of Personality Disorders*, 4, pp. 257–72.

Swenson, C. R., Sanderson, C., Dulit, R. A. and Linehan, M. M. (2001) 'The Application of Dialectical Behaviour Therapy for Patients with Borderline Personality Disorder on Inpatient Units', *Psychiatric Quarterly*, 72(4), pp. 307–24.

Tadros, V. (2001) 'Insanity and the Capacity for Criminal Responsibility', *Edinburgh Law Review*, 5, pp. 325–54.

Traynor, M. (1996) 'Looking at Discourse in a Literature Review of Nursing Texts', *Journal of Advanced Nursing*, 23(6), pp. 1155–61.

Traynor, M. (1999) *Managerialism and Nursing: Beyond Profession and Oppression* (Routledge: London).

Van Dijk, T. A. (1998) *Ideology: a Multidisciplinary Approach* (London: Sage).

Van Dijk, T. A. (2000) *Ideology and Discourse: a Multidisciplinary Approach.* http://www.discourse-in-society.org/teun.html/ (accessed 1 January 2004).

Verheul, R., Van Den Bosch, L. M., Koeter, M. W., De Ridder, M. A., Stijnen, T. and Van Den Brink, W. (2003) 'Dialectical Behaviour Therapy for Women with Borderline Personality Disorder: 12-Month, Randomised Clinical Trial in The Netherlands', *British Journal of Psychiatry*, 182, pp. 135–40.

Waitzkin, H. (1991) *The Politics of Medical Encounters: How Patients and Doctors Deal with Social Problems* (New Haven: Yale University Press).

Warner, S. and Wilkins, T. (2004) 'Between Subjugation and Survival: Women, Borderline Personality Disorder and High Security Mental Hospitals', *Journal of Contemporary Psychotherapy*, 34(3), pp. 265–78.

Westen, D. (1985) *Self and Society: Narcissism, Collectivism, and the Development of Morals* (New York: Cambridge University Press).

Westen, D. (1992) 'The Cognitive Self and the Psychoanalytic Self: Can We Put Our Selves Together?', *Psychological Inquiry*, 3, pp. 1–13.

Wetherell, M., Taylor, S. and Yates S. (2001) *Discourse Theory and Practice: a Reader* (London: Sage).

Wilkins, T. M. and Warner, S. (2001) 'Women in Special Hospitals: Understanding the Presenting Behaviour of Women Diagnosed with Borderline Personality Disorder', *Journal of Psychiatric and Mental Health Nursing*, 9, pp. 289–97.

Wilkinson-Ryan, T. and Westen, D. (2000) 'Identity Disturbance in Borderline Personality Disorder: an Empirical Investigation', *American Journal of Psychiatry*, 157, pp. 528–41.

Wirth-Cauchon, J. (2001) *Women and Borderline Personality Disorder* (Piscataway, NJ: Rutgers University Press).

Wonderlich, S. A., Crosby, R. D., Mitchell, J. E., Thompson, K. M., Smyth, J., Redlin, J. and Jones-Paxton, M. (2001) 'Sexual Trauma and Personality: Developmental Vulnerability and Additive Effects', *Journal of Personality Disorders*, 15(6), pp. 496–504.

Wong, W. H. (2004) 'Caring Holistically within New Managerialism', *Nursing Inquiry*, 11(1), pp. 2–13.

7 Renegotiating Disjunctions in Interorganizationally Provided Care

Hannele Kerosuo

Introduction

The increasing complexity of work and organization raises new challenges for service production in traditional organizations. New organizational forms and practices created to meet the demands of organizational effectiveness challenge conventional and familiar practices of working and organizing work. However, many institutions, particularly those in health care, are still trapped inside organizational models and practices that derive from conventional management thinking, according to which 'work and organizations can be thoroughly planned, broken down into units, and optimized' (Plsek and Greenhalg, 2001, p. 625; see also Morgan, 1997). Plsek and Wilson (2001) suggest that following the principles of whole system thinking in terms of complex adaptive systems would be more productive. Complex adaptive systems emphasize the dynamic interactions among parts of the system. On the level of clinical work, this implicates a holistic approach in patient care (Wilson and Holt, 2001). Complex adaptive system thinking in health care does not, however, tell us what the transition from hierarchical and functional organizations means in interorganizational practice. Neither does it investigate how the interaction between providers representing different organizations can be arranged in work practices.

In this chapter, I will suggest that besides the complexity inherent in diseases and illnesses and the complexity emerging in clinical practice, organizing health care service is complex in that it requires new organizational forms linking multiple providers. The integration of multiple services is often contingent on their respective histories and prospective futures. New types of links across organizations create challenges for employees who are expected to expand their customary ways of talking and doing work (Iedema and Scheeres, 2003). Employees need new communicative tools in order to learn practices involving the negotiation and the discursive construction of these new kinds of work (Engeström *et al.*, 2003).

In this chapter I investigate the learning of new work practices using an intervention that aimed at improving interorganizationally provided care in Finland. An interorganizational form of working represents a new way of organizing care on the multiple levels of primary and specialized hospital care in the health care system. I explore the complexities related to the care of patients with multiple illnesses. These patients require a kind of interorganizational care provision that is commonly lacking, but that our research sought to realize as intervention. Both members of primary and specialized care and patients participated in this intervention. The intervention created a hybrid space for interaction, that is, a social interface (Long, 2001), which led me to uncovered tensions embedded in interorganizational encounters, but that also promoted learning and the development of the care practice under study. Consequently, the intervention created an 'artificial' process of interorganizational communication in which 'members of an organization do not necessarily perceive their interdependence *a priori* the intervention and have not yet developed shared conceptions of their respective roles' (Rodríguez *et al.*, 2003, p. 149). The disjunctions that arose were investigated using the following research questions:

1 What kinds of disjunctions emerged as a result of new socio-organizational interfaces?
2 How could these disjunctions be addressed?
3 What kinds of new organizational arrangements might minimize these disjunctions?

The methodology of the study combines organizational discourse analysis (Iedema and Wodak, 1999) and activity theory (Engeström, 1999a; Engeström and Middleton, 1996). The data of the study are six videotaped gatherings in which the details of ten patients' care provision were discussed as part of an intervention. The ethnographic data collected during the intervention are also included in the study to provide background and contextual information about the research context. The ethnographic data (observations and interviews) are complemented with organizational reports and documents, journal articles, national and local histories.

In what follows I first describe the background of health reform in Finland. I then offer a description of the research setting, following which I will present the methodology and the key concepts of the study. I will then present the methods and the procedures of the study, leading to specifying the selection and description of the data. The subsequent section elaborates the findings. The chapter's conclusion brings these themes together, before advocating the importance of integrating new approaches into health care organization.

Background: health care organizational interfaces as historical traces

The division of primary and secondary care can be traced back to the history of health care organization in Finland. The Health Care Act of 1939 (Act 197/1939) secured public medical service provision throughout the country, with municipal physicians and registered nurses as the main providers of public health (Pesonen, 1980, pp. 414–18). Strengthening this, the implementation of the Primary Health Care Act of 1972 (Act 66/1972) created a system of primary health care in Finland that covered the whole population. The practical implication of the Public Health Act was a nationwide project to build health centres. Health centre clinics were able to integrate diverse practices such as shared consultation spaces for physicians, maternity and child welfare clinics, and dental as well as laboratory and X-ray services (Pesonen, 1980, p. 693). The health centre physicians who worked at the health centre clinics did patient visits, provided maternity and child-welfare clinics as well as services at health centre hospitals, and took responsibility for emergency services. By and large, however, services in primary care focused on single, isolated health visits. In the 1980s, criticism of this practice led to the creation of a personal physician system in which the object of health care expanded from a single visit to a care relationship in primary care units.

Secondary and tertiary hospitals gradually developed alongside primary care organized by the municipality (Pesonen, 1980). The development of diagnostics and medication in these sites exacerbated the divisions between specialized hospital care and primary care provided by health centre physicians. Moreover, the internal differentiation of specialties had already begun in the 1930s when the profession of medicine was conceded the right to control its specialties and many professional colleges were established (Pesonen, 1980, pp. 669–70). In 1932, there were 11 specialties; the number of specialties increased to 79 by

1998, at which time the number was reduced to 49 due to EU regulations (Pylkkänen, 2002). More recently still, specialties have again become more internally diversified (Pylkkänen, 2002).

This increasing specialization simultaneously advances and complicates the delivery of care. The progress of medical knowledge and skill enables the cure of serious and complex diseases while at the same time the specialties and subspecialties complicate the organization of the overall delivery of care by increasing the total number of providers. Therefore, recent developments in the reorganization of secondary and tertiary hospital and outpatient care ideally involve a transition towards integrated care processes or critical pathways of care. In the Finnish context, critical care pathways are care plans that detail the essential steps and responsibilities in care provision with a view to describing the expected progress of the patient (Renholm *et al.*, 2002, p. 196).

In the capital area of Helsinki, and following the 1990s economic downturn, demand for effectiveness and cost containment motivated further reorganization of health care services. In particular, the overlaps in specialized services provided simultaneously by the university hospitals and secondary care hospitals owned by the city of Helsinki were reorganized. The intervention project under focus here was carried out during this reorganization. This reorganization brought about changes in the functioning of the local health care centres as well as in the division of labour between primary, secondary and tertiary care. The biggest change was, however, the merger of general hospitals and secondary care hospitals. One consequence of the structural change in health care practice was the establishment of consultation clinics representing the secondary care in health centre hospitals as an intermediate level between primary, secondary and tertiary care. By making these changes, political decision-makers and health care management sought to improve the cooperation between primary and secondary care. However, as our data below will show, cooperation between these levels of care remains problematic.

The research context: an intervention to improve the care for patients with multiple illnesses

The study reported on here is part of an intervention project in which new collaborative tools (a care calendar, care map and care agreement) and a new care practice (flexible teamwork or 'negotiated knotworking') were implemented and developed in the care of patients with multiple illnesses.[1] To date, a number of providers treat these patients simultaneously in both primary and secondary care. Despite the structural changes referred to in the previous section, the organization of care is often fragmented with no one seeing the overall picture or having the ultimate responsibility for the care of the patients (Engeström, 2001; Engeström *et al.*, 1999, 2001; Kerosuo, 2001; Saaren-Seppälä, 2004). The demand to enhance cross-service collaboration is urgent because the number of adult patients with multiple illnesses is presently increasing due to an ageing of the population, and patients' need for more and more complex services.

The intervention project applied what Yrjö Engeström has termed the 'change laboratory' method (Engeström *et al.*, 1996). This is a participatory method for developing work based on approaches derived from activity theory and developmental work research (Engeström, 1987), about which I will say more in the next section of this chapter. The implementation of the care agreement and the negotiated way of working in the present project were carried out in two phases. During the first phase in 2000, we gathered information about the care of 16 patients who had heart, pulmonary or renal disease, rheumatoid arthritis, or diabetes as a primary disease alongside other secondary diseases and symptoms.

The medical doctors recruited for the project discussed here chose the patients for the intervention from among their own patient population. The criteria for the selection were that the patients were volunteer participants, that they have multiple illnesses, that they live in the capital of Finland and that the professional had assessed their care as involving problems of collaboration in the care provision. We interviewed the patients and their providers, traced the patients' visits to doctors and collected their patient documents from different providers. Then we analysed the interview data and constructed the patient's care history (the care calendar) and present care locations (the care map), and invited the patient and his or her providers to a change laboratory session. We invited all care providers, because ordinarily the different parties do not meet each other personally, since the communication between primary and secondary care is secured through formal referrals and care feedback forms. Altogether nine sessions were arranged with ten different patients. In the change laboratory sessions, we presented our findings and started the discussion about the problems in the patient's care provision. The findings were presented most often as edited video clips, lists of case histories and organizational maps. During phase one, we gained an extensive view of the problems in the information exchange and in the overall care provided to these patients (Engeström *et al.*, 2001).

The second phase of the project began with the formation of a pilot group. The pilot group was made up of general practitioners and nurses from primary care units and internists and nurses from the health centre hospitals. Those recruited from secondary and tertiary care organizations included clinicians and nurses working in the areas of pulmonary disease, cardiology, nephrology, renal disease and endocrinology. Overall, the pilot group members were drawn from two health centres involving six primary care units, two health centre hospitals representing primary and secondary hospital care, and five clinics from two tertiary care hospitals (university hospitals).

The group members were then invited to choose a patient from among their patients and apply the new tools (the care calendar, care map and care agreement) and the new cross-service approach of providing care to the patient. Ordinarily, a piloting physician extended the routine focus of a patient visit by making extra questions concerning the patient's history of diseases and illnesses and other providers. Furthermore, physicians contacted the relevant other providers in order to secure the collaborative processes of the care provision. Finally, the piloting physician presented the results of the exploration at the change laboratory meeting. The discussion of various cases improved and clarified the new collaborative practice during the intervention.

The pilot group attended a total of nine change laboratory meetings. In the first meeting, the research group presented the findings of the first phase of the project. The presentation was followed by a general discussion about the new tools and the arrangements needed in the experiment. The following six meetings involved case presentations of ten patients and further elaboration of the tools and practice. Finally, the tools and the new way of sharing information were discussed in the eight and ninth meetings (for more details see Kerosuo and Engeström, 2003). The findings and the outcomes of the whole process were presented in a seminar that was arranged for members of both organizations. The processes ended with the heads of both organizations deciding on how to apply the tools and the practices in the health centres and in secondary and tertiary care hospitals in Helsinki.

Theoretical and methodological issues

The methodology of this study is based on cultural historical activity theory (Engeström, 1987, 1999a) and organizational discourse analysis (Iedema and Wodak, 1999; Wodak, 1996) as part of a developmental ethnography (Kerosuo, 2006). This methodological constellation enables the analysis of interaction in which new meaning and sense of activity is created in close connection to practical activity (Engeström, 1999a, p. 170; Engeström and Middleton, 1996).

Organizational discourse analysis investigates (1) the genesis of the discourses and practices in organizational life, (2) the contribution of these discourses and practices to organizational life, and (3) the effect of increasingly objectified and depersonalized meanings to specific discursive practices (Iedema and Wodak, 1999, p. 13). Interaction is approached as 'talking work' (Iedema and Scheeres, 2003) and as embedded in the context of interaction by focusing on 'how "objectivity" is construed, achieved and contested' in its historically derived connection (Iedema and Wodak, 1999, pp. 12–13).

For its part, cultural historical activity theory (CHAT) shares with organizational discourse analysis an interest in the historically derived objectivity constructed in everyday interactions and actions. Thus, the genesis of the organizational structures currently dominating Finnish health care is traced to reveal those structures' historical origins. However, CHAT differs from organizational discourse analysis by using specific concepts in the definition of context, objectivity and development as follows. In CHAT, social and historical context are conceptualized as *activity systems* (Engeström, 1987). These involve elements of activity such as subjects, for example medical doctors focusing on an object, such as the care of a patient. The actions that emerge are mediated by the concepts and instruments applied in medical work practices. The object as well as the mediating artefacts are embedded in a community that is governed by specific rules and divisions of labour. The dynamics inherent in and between activity systems provide methodological resources for the analysis of development, learning and change in the practical activity that is discussed below.

The concept of 'object' has a specific meaning in activity theory deriving from Russian and German philosophy. The 'object is simultaneously an independently existing, recalcitrant, material reality *and* a goal or purpose or idea that we have in mind' (Adler, 2005, p. 404). 'An object (*Gegenstand*) may, therefore be understood in the framework of activity theory as a collectively constructed entity, in material and/or ideal form through which the meeting of a particular human need is pursued' (Foot, 2002, p. 134). However, an object is rarely unequivocal since participants of an activity may have different perspectives of an object. For instance, different specialties focus on different objects: cardiologists focus on the treatment of cardiac diseases while renal specialists focus on renal diseases. The German concept of *Gegenstand* captures the object's embeddedness in activity as distinct from the notion of mere *Objekt* referring to its materiality (Engeström and Escalante, 1996, pp. 361–2). Hence, objects of activity are involved in social relationships and these relationships need to be functionally coordinated in order to be able to create coherence and stability of the object (Miettinen, 2005, p. 60). In this study, new objects (such as the care map) invite the members of the pilot group to invest new meaning and sense into new kinds of collaborative activity. Part of this is that they come to identify disjunctions that prevail between them in the lab sessions. Solutions to these disjunctions come to represent the emergent new object of the interorganizational practice.

For its part, the concept of interface (Long, 2001) allows us to conceptualize the discursive space that emerges as a result of such an organizational intervention. Social–organizational interfaces emerge typically at the intersections of different and conflicting life worlds, organizational fields, or institutional domains and arenas of social action (Long, 2001, p. 65). From the perspective of this study, interorganizationally provided care produces interfaces that emerge between providers in their everyday practices and interactions. These social interfaces emerge as 'sites of struggle' where diverse understandings, interests, values and power are negotiated and contested. Such interfaces arise across and within many different institutional domains and arenas of social action when 'struggles over social meanings and practices take place' (Long, 2004, p. 15). My focus on practical activity as harbouring activity systems enables the exploration of social interfaces as interorganizational points of tension. The interface that is explored in this study emerges between the activity systems of primary and specialized care and of the patient's life world.

In this study, disjunctions emerging in the interaction between providers and patients represent manifestations of developmental contradictions. Disjunctions are ruptures in the interorganizationally provided care. For example, a disjunction emerges when a patient or one of the providers observes that a relevant part of a patient's care provision is neglected. Such disjunction arises from contrasting perspectives on what needs to happen held by general practitioners, specialists and patients, and is fuelled by the asymmetry of power between professional and lay knowledge. Discovery of such disjunctions may lead to 'bridge building', for example, fixing a rupture and working out who needs to do what to enhance the health care that is provided. The investigation of situated interaction where we encounter people trying to repair ruptures is important from the perspective of learning and development, because it is at these interfaces that we may find not just possible but also creative solutions. This brings me to the data and methods of this study.

Data and methods

The data presented here include transcripts of the six change laboratory sessions in which the cases of the pilot patients were discussed. A research assistant transcribed the data from digital tapes. The transcribed data of the laboratory session were then divided into speech turns of each individual speaker in order to be able to locate the gaps in the interaction data.

Table 7.1 presents an overview of the change laboratory sessions held. The interactions of the first, eighth and ninth sessions are not analysed here because I want to focus on that part of data where the health care provision of concrete patients was discussed. The first session was a preparatory gathering in which the process was explained to participants and the findings of the first phase were presented. The eighth and the ninth sessions concluded the process and involved reflecting on the experiments with the new tools.

Altogether 39 persons participated in the sessions. This number includes 7 patients and one relative of a patient; 7 primary care physicians, 5 nurses and one manager; one secondary care nurse and 2 internists; 12 tertiary care staff (7 specialists, 2 head nurses and 3 nurses), and the research team. Twelve employees from various organizations participated only once in cases they were involved with. The descriptions of the seven patients who participated in the intervention in phase two are provided in Table 7.2. Pilot patients two, four and eight did not participate in the sessions. A close relative of patient two participated in the session to replace her.

The discussion at the change laboratory sessions followed the agenda set out by the pilot group member presenting the case and by the researchers. One of the researchers chaired the session. At the beginning, the purpose and the agenda of the session as well as the change laboratory method were usually presented and discussed. The pilot doctor or nurse presented the patient's illnesses and locations of care using the care calendar and map. The discussion topics that followed included the main ailment of the patient, the flow of information, the responsibility for care, and the care agreement. Researchers showed the video clips related to the experiment in most cases after the pilot doctor's presentation. Following these presentations, there was discussion of the patient's

Table 7.1 Description of the change laboratory data

Meeting	*Date of the session*	*Pilot patient*	*Number of turns*	*Other data presented in the session*
1. Not included in the analysis	4.1.2001	–	590	Findings of problems in the care of patients during the first phase of the project
2.	15.2.2001	Pp 1 and Pp 2	453	Meeting with the patient (the specialist, the nurse and the researcher), negotiation between the specialist and the GP (Pp1) Meeting with the patient (GP and Pp2)
3.	10.5.2001	Pp 3 and Pp 4	599	Planning meeting (the GP and the researcher), meeting with the patient (the internist, the GP and the researcher), interview with an endocrinologist (the endocrinologist and the researcher) (Pp3) Two interviews on the telephone (Pp4 and the researcher), planning meeting (the specialist and the researcher)
4.	20.6.2001	Pp 5	706	Planning meeting (the GP and the researcher), the researcher's interview with a specialist, meeting with the patient (Pp5, GP and the researcher)
5.	9.10.2001	Pp 6 and Pp 7	561	Meeting with the patient (Pp6, the internist and the researcher), care negotiation after the change laboratory session (Pp6) Meeting with the patient (Pp7, GP and the researcher)
6.	14.11.2001	Pp 8	416	The researcher's interview with Pp8, planning meeting between the pilot nurses and the researchers, meeting between the cardiologist, GP and the home care representative
7.	13.12.2001	Pp 9 and Pp 10	615	The patient's visit with a specialist (Pp9, the researcher also present) The researcher's interview with the patient (Pp10), the patient's visit with the specialist, the researcher's interview with an internist (Pp10)
8.	29.1.2002		831	Evaluation of the experiments with the tools, outline of the negotiated care practice
9.	25.2.2002		Not transcribed	Further discussion on the new tools and the practice, creation of the process model for the negotiated practice

Table 7.2 Description of the patients participating in the intervention

Pilot patient	*Primary disease or symptom*	*Other diseases and symptoms*
P1 Female 61	Rheumatoid arthritis	Asthma, fracture of vertebra, fainting
P2 Female 79	Heart disease	Hemiplegia, epilepsy, dementia, arthritis, fracture of the thigh bone
P3 Female 64	Heart disease	High blood pressure, high lipids, diabetes type II, stomach troubles, infections, pain in the leg
P4 Male 54	Diabetes type II	High blood pressure, history of heart infarctions, eye trouble, knee problem
P5 Male 71	Diabetes type II	High lipids, high blood pressure, polyneuropathy, retinopathy, foot infections
P6 Female 45	Nephropathy	Diabetes mellitus, infections
P7 Female 59	Stomach trouble	Diabetes type II, high blood pressure, high cholesterol, hiatus hernia, obstruction, joint trouble
P8 Female 66	Pulmonary symptoms	Coronary artery disease, diabetes type II, COPD, swellings
P9 Male 47	Nephropathy	Diabetes, retinopathy, neuropathy, allergy to penicillin
P10 Female 73	Asthma	Gastritis, brain infarct, osteoporosis, glaucoma

care provision. It was usually during the pilot doctor's or nurse's presentation that disjunctions in the care provision became evident, although they also at times became apparent as a result of the subsequent discussion. This, in turn, made it possible to begin addressing how to negotiate the disjunctions affecting the care provided.

I pinpointed the disjunctions affecting patients' care by reading through the transcripts several times. The pilot physicians and nurses tended to refer to disjunctions during their presentation, often to the surprise of the other providers. For instance, the other providers were unaware that the information was not being transferred properly, or that the responsibility for some part of the provision was not assigned to anyone. However, some of the disjunctions were taken as given; for instance, there was an assumption that patients do not and will not understand organizational procedures. It appeared particularly difficult for staff to acknowledge that patients may not know about procedures that are transparent and self-evident to their health care providers.

After identifying the disjunctions in my data, I marked these and the ways they were discussed in the transcripts. This enabled me to compare the cases and their disjunctions and retrieve people's suggestions for how to deal with them. The final stage of my analysis was to locate my findings on a single map and connect them as part of an activity system. This enabled me to address my third research question: how do these disjunctions relate to the new organizational forms proposed?

The discussion below addresses how the various disjunctions were discussed during the intervention. From that, I summarize solutions that were put forward for overcoming the disjunctions that were discussed, and I offer some thoughts on how they relate to the study's innovative organizational intervention method.

Disjunctions in interorganizational care

This section presents a discussion that answers the first research question: what kinds of disjunctions emerge in existing social–organizational interfaces that define contemporary Finnish health care? I begin by listing the disjunctions as they were presented and discussed during each patient case (see Table 7.2).

Pilot patient one received arthritis care from the rheumatology clinics at the tertiary care hospital and from the personal physician at the primary care health centre. It soon became clear that communication between the primary and the tertiary care providers was deficient. When the rheumatologist went to meet the personal physician before the laboratory session, he found out that this person was not informed about the care procedures at the tertiary care site. For instance, the changes in medications were not communicated, although the medication that the patient used was such as to require the health centre clinic to engage in follow-up surveillance. This was a surprise for the rheumatologist. The patient was also unaware of the disruption in the information exchange because she had signed a form giving permission to the rheumatology clinic to deliver her patient files to her personal physician, and she assumed that they had been delivered.

In the *second patient case*, the pilot doctor reported on her patient, an old lady with memory problems. The lady's care provision included treatments for a thigh bone fracture, pleura in her lungs, and convulsions, for which she received care at three hospitals separated by short intervals. The communication travelled well between the transferring and receiving care locations, whereas the personal doctor responsible for the coordination of the overall care was not informed. Because of the lack of information and the patient's forgetfulness, the appointment set for neurological examinations at the fourth hospital was missed. In excerpt 1, the personal physician gives an account of the incident.

Excerpt 1

Personal physician I went for a visit to the patient's home and the patient said that someone had called on the phone but she did not know who it was. The person on the phone had said that she [the patient] does not have to visit the outpatient clinic after all. Then I thought that **there must be a disruption in the flow of information**. Nobody at the home care or the folks at home had information about a visit to the outpatient clinic. The information was somehow lost. (15 February 2001)

The care of the *third pilot patient* involved a lack of treatment for the patient's leg. No one was treating the pain the patient felt in her leg after the care process at the health centre hospital was concluded. The personal physician was not aware of this particular ailment; it was overshadowed by various other diseases and illnesses that the patient presented with.

Patient case four sheds more light on the effects of communication disjunctions between providers when the patient is not particularly active, in contrast to the first and third pilot patients who were active themselves, and the second patient who had relatives acting on behalf of her/him (gender is left unspecified for confidentiality reasons). Patient four suffers from diabetes, heart failure and hurting knees. During his history of illness, this patient made several visits to the hospital because of heart trouble, and he was recently referred for further examinations of his heart condition when he participated in a health study at the cardiology clinic in the tertiary care. However, clinicians at the health centre clinic that treated the patient's diabetes assumed that the patient was treated at the secondary care hospital. They lacked the information about the referral to cardiology and did not know about the heart failure. The patient thought that the information had been sent to the health centre clinic from cardiology. He had also been wondering why it was taking so long for the cardiology clinic to give him an appointment because his symptoms were getting worse. He was afraid that he was going to have another heart infarction before receiving cardiology treatment. But he did not know that the health centre clinic could have expedited the referral. He also missed his hypertension follow-ups and tests for blood consistency at the health centre clinic, because the cardiology clinic did not ask him to have the examinations and the tests done. In fact, he did not know that it was important to have the tests. The head nurse of the health centre clinic and the specialist from cardiology thought that the patient had become non-compliant when in fact the patient's absences were due to him not knowing how the health care system worked.

Overall, these disjunctions between providers occurred more as a rule than an exception in the pilot cases. In *case five*, there was a gap in the flow of information that caused a discontinuity in diabetes follow-ups. This resulted from a disruption in the communication between endocrinology and angiopathic surgery. Endocrinology suggested a surgical stocking for the patient, while angiopathic surgery asked the patient not to use them. The patient was caught in-between two specialties and did not know whose advice to adopt.

The providers of *pilot patient six* did not have information about her renal condition in acute care, and the patient herself could not inform the providers about her medication because of her condition. However, she was worried about receiving medication that would harm her kidneys. *Pilot patient seven* was the only patient who did not have gaps in her care provision. Her personal physician constructed an overall image of the patient's care organization during the patient's visit (as is described in Engeström *et al.*, 2003). Therefore, any disjunctions that might have affected the care provision of patient seven were prevented. The care of *pilot patient eight* included miscommunications between the patient and providers and between providers that were similar to those that affected the care provision of patient four. Pilot patient eight had coronary artery disease, diabetes, COPD, swelling and pulmonary symptoms. The patient felt that the personal physician at the health centre clinic was busy and difficult to reach, that the home care nurses kept changing and that some of them were useless. The professionals at the tertiary care hospital emphasized that they could not help the patient because she did not follow orders. The patient did not take the medication prescribed for her to diminish the swelling. She did not care about stabilizing her blood sugar and she ate whatever she liked, including sweets. She gained weight instead of losing it, although it was important to lose weight for her condition to improve. The disjunctions affecting this case were in fact established before the laboratory session in a meeting with the tertiary hospital internist, the health centre physician and the home care nurse. An example used at the subsequent change laboratory session, excerpt 2 relates how the major disjunctions in the patient's provision became evident.

Excerpt 2

Health centre physician I have seen her every now and then since 1993. (Although she was not the patient's personal physician)

Internist Yes.

Health centre physician I talked with John[2] that even though **he thinks that the care** [of the patient] **is in principle provided at the tertiary care hospital.**

Internist Yes, and, as the last bit **in the transcript of the hospital recording shows, it says that the follow-ups are at the health centre** and they should specially focus on the care of diabetes and lipids.

Health centre physician Yes.

Internist But we have not agreed on any follow-ups at this stage.

(Meeting at the health centre, 8 November 2001)

The care of *pilot patient nine* involves a disjunction in the follow-up of the medication related to blood consistency. The nephrology clinic suggested that the health centre physician could take care of the follow-up as was agreed in the division of care responsibility between primary and tertiary care. But the health centre physician was not aware of the follow-ups. In this case, the patient did not realize that he ought to reserve the time for the tests at the health centre clinic. This patient was also affected by a more general kind of disjunction. The patient had a kidney transplant, neuropathy, retinopathy and an allergy to penicillin. The main providers were the nephrology clinic and the angiopathic surgery clinic at the tertiary hospital as well as the personal physician at the health centre clinic. However, despite the importance for all involved of knowing about the penicillin allergy, the kidney transplant and the macro angiopathy, none of the providers gained access to all the necessary patient documentation.

Finally, the *tenth patient* is an aged lady with a long history of many illnesses, and the pilot doctor, a lung specialist, had plans to transfer her asthma follow-ups from the tertiary care hospital to the primary care health centre. However, a discussion with the patient at reception caused her to be uncertain about the details of the transfer. The relationship between the patient and her personal doctor was apparently not functioning, and the network of care providers appeared to be acting without knowledge of what the other parties were doing. For instance, when the patient received a prescription for medicine in specialized care, the health centre physician advised her not to take the medicine. The patient felt that her care was 'in crisis'. She was uncertain about what to do and which advice she should follow.

In summary, there are two types of disjunctions in interorganizationally provided care that appear as ruptures in the patients' health care provision. First, there are disjunctions at the level of information exchange: providers follow the routine of sending referrals and providing feedback about the care between primary and secondary care, but this type of practice breaks down in cases that involve extended and more complex care procedures. Second, there are disjunctions in the overall responsibility of care, where providers may fulfil their share of the care provision, but the locus of overall responsibility for the care provided is often left undefined. This particularly affects patients who have multiple and parallel care episodes due to complicated diseases or symptoms.

The change laboratory sessions: addressing the disjunctions

This section discusses answers to the second research question: how can the disjunctions that have become evident be addressed? The change laboratory sessions enabled participants to reflect on the reasons why disjunctions emerged in the provision of care, what needed to be done, and why it was at times impossible to overcome these disjunctions. Group discussions raised a number of possible solutions. For example, one participant suggested a microchip in the national health insurance card; another elaborated on the idea of a chip card, and a third suggested a computer program that would stretch across organizational boundaries. Discussions also revealed that carrying out particular suggestions might be easy for one provider but difficult for another. For instance, primary and secondary care participants suggested that tertiary care providers ought to mail their patient documents following every single patient visit, not realizing that mailing such documents with such frequency would be an impossible task.

That said, two kinds of solutions emerged that were feasible: the first focused on appropriately communicating information, and the second dealt with breakdowns in care responsibility. I will present these in turn, using the elements of the activity system discussed above to link my discussion to more general organizational issues.

First, then, solutions were proposed regarding the communication of information. In effect, and to use the terms of activity theory introduced above, these solutions challenge the ways in which actors typically handle objects and construe purposes as part of their everyday activity. To some extent, of course, clinical information exchange is contingent on the patients' capability to act as conduits of their own information across the boundaries of multi-organizational care (Rodríquez *et al.*, 2003). But as we saw above, there were patients who emphasized that they are not capable of doing this (Pp6 and Pp9). Two pilot patients (Pp2 and Pp10) had problems with memory, while other patients (Pp1, Pp4, Pp5 and Pp8) harboured the expectation that the information would be delivered by health care providers.

At the laboratory session, people's comments about the need to fix information discontinuities were often accompanied by demands to formulate new rules or guidelines to govern the care process. But not everyone agreed with this suggestion. Whereas the primary and secondary care participants emphasized the need for new guidelines, tertiary care representatives stressed the need to condense the information and warned against information overload.

Aside from some suggestions that were not unanimously accepted, the pilot group participants proceeded to propose some practical ideas related to the use of a care agreement to streamline the information exchange. Here, the discussion addressed four kinds of potential problems affecting care agreements. Firstly, consideration was given to the problem of finding a contact person in tertiary care with whom to arrange the care agreement. The relationship between providers and patients was quite constant in nephrology, rheumatology, endocrinology and pulmonary diseases, while most of the contacts with cardiac patients were short with changing providers due to rapid rotation of junior medical staff. The difficulty of finding a contact in primary care resulted from the tertiary care practitioners not knowing the primary care system well enough. Secondly, it was proposed that the care agreement information needed to be sorted out according to its relevance, which could pose a problem (Pp1, Pp9). Thirdly, it was noted that a care agreement contains information that is of importance for multiple professionals, but it is impossible to have an information format that suits professionals and patients simultaneously (Pp1, Pp3, Pp9). Finally, participants noted that care agreements confront the difficulty of care providers not realizing that specific kinds of information need to be exchanged between them (Pp4, Pp5, Pp8, Pp9).

Finding a solution for these kinds of problems was, therefore, not easy. For instance, in case four presented above, the discussion with the patient about his care became urgent since the patient was not aware of the importance of some components of his care (follow-ups of hypertension and tests for blood inconsistency) and since there were also disjunctions affecting the information exchanges between his care providers. As excerpt 3 shows, a head nurse from secondary care suggested that the public health nurse might take time and explain to the patient the elements of his care. For the public health nurse this was impossible because she currently already had too many patients that 'drowned' in the health care system.[3]

Excerpt 3

Head nurse Could it be that the public health nurse [could meet the patient] regularly, that she could arrange a visit with him once a month? And discuss these things so that he understands this pattern of care.

Public health nurse Yes, it is for certain that it [the care relationship] has ended when the patient has been provided with tertiary care. Well, the information did not arrive this time but it can be [that a visit with him can be arranged]. But it is a question of these patients who have drowned [in the system], who are not really active themselves, there are many of them. So who has the time to catch them.

Head nurse But for this patient since we have noticed this [lack of communication], I am just thinking that a care agreement document between us could show, or what one could see from it, that it is easier this way that we ask the patient [for a visit] than that we ask the patient to contact us. He has contact with the health centre clinic when he comes for the laboratory tests. He is physically present then.

Public health nurse Yes, he is, but the laboratory belongs to tertiary care and is functioning separately from us. We do not know about their appointments. We are not even allowed into their computer system to see when the patient is coming [for tests]. It is only if we bump into each other in the corridor accidentally that we find out when he is coming.

(Meeting took place on 5 May 2001)

This extract shows that the physicians did not welcome the suggestion to ask patients to visit them. In fact, some were annoyed about the lack of initiative on the part of the patient. However, in session seven (Pp9), they supported the active role of some nurses in communicating with patients. When a patient's medication and care procedures are as complicated as in nephrology, the specialized nurses were expected to take a more active role with patients between their visits at the outpatient clinic. Another solution came from a pilot patient (Pp9) who brought up the problem of the multidirectionality in the flow of information. He had settled the problem by collecting a patient file himself and by personally delivering the documents to his three main providers.

The discussion that addressed disjunctions in the communication of information became intertwined with comments about how to clarify the locus of responsibility for specific patients. Securing continuous care for the patients with multiple illnesses is an aim that is shared between primary, secondary and tertiary care. Normally, coordinating the overall care is the task of the health centre physician. However, some health centre physicians consider patients with multiple diseases to be too complicated for the health centre clinic (for instance, the physician of Pp7; cf. Engeström *et al.*, 2003). One of the solutions suggested at the pilot group meetings in this regard was that geriatrics should take the overall responsibility of the care of these patients (Pp2). However, this suggestion came up against the problem of a general lack of geriatric physicians. Another member suggested that internists at the consultation clinics ought to have the overall responsibility for the patient's care provision (Pp10), an approach that was in fact adopted in some cases (for instance, Pp6).

This brings me to the third research question that informs this study. I asked: What kinds of new organizational arrangements might minimize these kinds of disjunctions? The groups' reflections on informational needs and the needs of overall care led to suggestions about new tools, rules and divisions of labour between providers to overcome the kinds of problems identified during the laboratory sessions. Seen from the perspective of expansive learning (Engeström, 1987), new tools should enable people to devise new organizational arrangements and practices. That is not to say, however, that these new tools, arrangements and practices might not create further contradictions. Generally speaking, changes result in unintended consequences due to the altered relationship between tools, object/motives and activities (Engeström, 1987), and not all of these consequences need be positive. Nevertheless, in this study group members were able to discover and articulate disjunctions due to the opportunity to experiment with new solutions during the laboratory intervention, and this was also the learning task of the intervention project.

This task, however, was far from a linear process of development and learning, and resembled rather a cyclic process involving returns to earlier contradictions and double binds as is characteristic of the developmental process. Engeström (1999b, p. 385) calls these developments miniature cycles and regards these as potentially expansive if they are successfully integrated into the learning processes on the level of organizational development. In the intervention focused on in this chapter, the results of the experiment were presented at a seminar after the experimentation phase. The managing directors of the primary and secondary care signed a statement to implement the care agreement tools and related practices in both organizations. Unfortunately, however, despite the evidence provided by the miniature cycle of learning, the new tool and the new practice were not adopted for general use.

Concluding discussion

This chapter has presented a study of social interfaces in interorganizational care provision. The study demonstrated that it was possible to alert clinical providers to disjunctions in information and care responsibility. The study also showed that discussions with primary and specialized care providers could produce various solutions, and that participants were able to reflect on and explore the potential problems inherent in those solutions. While directors of the different services agreed to initiate a care agreement that would ensure better continuity of care, it is thus far unclear what the final form of this care agreement will be (see Kerosuo, 2006).

On a theoretical front, this study was initiated in recognition that the organization of contemporary health care is becoming increasingly complex, requiring increasingly interdependent clinical treatment practices (Plsek and Greenhalg, 2001; Plsek and Wilson, 2001; Wilson and Holt, 2001). The organization of contemporary care is complex because it presumes that clinical practitioners dealing with chronic and complex disease are able to coordinate, organize and manage what they do while at the same time enacting their specific expertise. In Finland, as in many other post-industrial nation states, chronic and complex disease provision requires the creation of organizational structures and alternative organizational arrangements that supersede specialty and service boundaries. But rarely are organizational development and learning recognized as central to the enhancement of clinical care. This study shows, however, that the informal learning that emerges from clinicians together exploring organizational double binds may produce important elements central to the conceptualization of new organizational forms. As seen, the members of the pilot groups provided many suggestions for overcoming the discontinuities of care, but their suggestions remained captive to the local practice level because the link between developing health care practices and interorganizational intervention remained weak. Repairing the disjunctions in interorganizational health care is a complex challenge, requiring solutions that involve multiple providers and high levels of organizational and professional involvement and learning (Engeström *et al.*, 2003). No doubt these challenges necessitate new approaches to organizational development, new forms of research, and new approaches to educating twenty-first-century health care providers.

Notes

1 The research group from the Centre for Activity Theory and Developmental Work Research at the University of Helsinki was in charge of a project called *Developing a Negotiated Way of Working between Primary Care and Specialized Hospital Care in Helsinki* during the years 2000–2. The members of the research group were Yrjö Engeström, Ritva Engeström, Tarja Vähäaho (presently Saaren-Seppälä, a member of the research group until the end of the year 2000) and the author of this chapter.

2 John is the senior physician of the health clinic who normally sees the patient.

3 Note that patient 4 did not participate in the meeting.

References

Adler, P. S. (2005) 'The Evolving Object of Software Development', *Organization*, 12(3), pp. 401–35.

Engeström, Y. (1987) *Learning by Expanding: an Activity-Theoretical Approach to Developmental Research* (Helsinki: Orienta konsultit).

Engeström, Y. (1999a) 'Communication, Discourse and Activity', *The Communication Review*, 3(1–2), pp. 165–85.

Engeström, Y. (1999b) 'Innovative Learning in Work Teams', in Y. Engeström, R. Miettinen and R. L. Punamäki (eds) *Perspectives of Activity Theory*, pp. 377–404 (Cambridge: Cambridge University Press).

Engeström, Y. (2001) 'Expansive Learning at Work: Toward an Activity Theoretical Reconceptualization', *Journal of Education and Work*, 14(1), pp. 133–56.

Engeström, Y. and Escalante, V. (1996) 'Mundane Tool or Object of Affection? The Rise and Fall of the Postal Buddy', in Bonnie A. Nardi (ed.) *Context and Consciousness: Activity Theory and Human–Computer Interaction*, pp. 325–73 (Cambridge, Mass. and London, England: The MIT Press).

Engeström, Y. and Middleton, D. (1996) 'Introduction: Studying Work as a Mindful Practice', in Y. Engeström and D. Middleton (eds) *Cognition and Communication at Work*, pp. 1–14 (Cambridge: Cambridge University Press).

Engeström, Y., Virkkunen, J., Helle, M., Pihlaja, J. and Poikela, R. (1996) 'The Change Laboratory as a Tool for Transforming Work', *Life Long Learning in Europe*, 2, pp. 10–17.

Engeström, Y., Engeström, R. and Vähäaho, T. (1999) 'When the Center does not Hold: the Importance of Knotworking', in S. Chaiklin, M. Hedegaard and U. J. Jensen (eds) *Activity Theory and Social Practice: Cultural–Historical Approaches*, pp. 345–74 (Aarhus: Aarhus University Press).

Engeström, Y., Engeström, R. and Kerosuo, H. (2001) 'Neuvottelevan työtavan kehittäminen. Väliraportti. Helsingin kaupungin terveysvirasto' *Raportteja*, 2001(5) [Development of the Negotiated Way of Working, Report, City of Helsinki Institute for Health, *Reports 2001(5)*. In Finnish].

Engeström, Y., Engeström, R. and Kerosuo, H. (2003) 'The Discursive Construction of Collaborative Care', *Applied Linguistics*, 24(3), pp. 286–315.

Foot, K. A. (2002) 'Pursuing an Evolving Object: a Case Study in Object Formation and Identification', *Mind, Culture, and Activity*, 9(2), pp. 132–49.

Iedema, R. and Scheeres, H. (2003) 'From Doing Work to Talking Work: Renegotiating Knowing, Doing, and Identity', *Applied Linguistics*, 24(3), pp. 316–37.

Iedema, R. and Wodak, R. (1999) 'Introduction: Organizational Discourses and Practices', *Discourse and Society*, 10(1), pp. 5–19.

Kerosuo, H. (2001) 'Boundary Encounters as a Place for Learning and Development at Work', *Outlines: Critical Social Studies*, 3(1), pp. 53–65.

Kerosuo, H. (2006) *Boundaries in Action: an Activity-Theoretical Study of Boundary Dynamics of Development, Learning and Change in Health Care for Patients with Many Illnesses* (Helsinki: Helsinki University Press).

Kerosuo, H. and Engeström, Y. (2003) 'Boundary Crossing and Learning in Creation of New Work Practice', *Journal of Workplace Learning*, 15(7/8), pp. 345–51.

Long, N. (2001) *Development Sociology: Actor Perspectives* (London and New York: Routledge).

Long, N. (2004) 'Actors, Interfaces and Development Intervention: Meanings, Purpose and Powers', in T. Kontinen (eds) *Development Intervention: Actor and Activity Perspectives*, pp. 14–36 (Helsinki: Hakapaino).

Miettinen, R. (2005) 'Object of Activity and Individual Motivation', *Mind, Culture, and Activity*, 12(1), pp. 52–69.

Morgan, G. (1997) *Images of Organization* (2nd edn) (Thousand Oaks, Calif.: Sage).

Pesonen, N. (1980) *Terveyden puolesta – sairautta vastaan: Terveyden- ja sairaanhoito Suomessa 1800- ja 1900-luvulla* (Porvoo: WSOY) [For Health – Against the Illness: Health Care and Nursing in Finland during the 19th and 20th Century, Porvoo: WSOY. In Finnish].

Plsek, P. E. and Greenhalg, T. (2001) 'The Challenge of Complexity in Health Care', *British Medical Journal*, 323, pp. 625–8.

Plsek, P. E. and Wilson, T. (2001) 'Complexity, Leadership, and Management in Healthcare Organizations', *British Medical Journal*, 323, pp. 746–9.

Pylkkänen, K. (2002) 'Erikoisalaprofession sata järjestäytymisen vuotta', *Suomen Lääkärilehti*, 57(16), pp. 1819–23 ['Hundred Years of Organizing Specialties', *The Finnish Medical Journal*, 57(16), pp. 1819–23. In Finnish].

Renholm, M., Leino-Kilpi, H. and Suominen, T. (2002) 'Critical Pathways: a Systematic Review', *Journal of Nursing Administration*, 32(4), pp. 196–202.

Rodríquez, C., Langley, A., Béland, F. and Denis, J. L. (2003) 'Managing across Boundaries in Health Care: the Forces for Change and Inertia', in N. Paulsen and T. Hernes (eds) *Managing Boundaries in Organizations: Multiple Perspectives*, pp. 147–68 (Basingstoke: Palgrave Macmillan).

Saaren-Seppälä, T. (2004) *Inter-organizational Medical Care: a Study about New Practices and Relationships between GP, Hospital and Children's Parents*, Acta Universitas Tamperensis, 1052 (Tampere: University of Tampere) (In Finnish).

Wilson, T. and Holt, T. (2001) 'Complexity and Clinical Care', *British Medical Journal*, 323, pp. 685–8.

Wodak, R. (1996) *Disorders of Discourse* (London: Longman).

8
Anaesthetic Talk in Surgical Encounters

Catherine Pope, Maggie Mort, Dawn Goodwin and Andrew Smith

Introduction: anaesthetic talk and anaesthetic work

Anaesthetists form the largest single hospital speciality and are involved in the care of two-thirds of all hospital patients. Their work is technically complex and is often compared to aviation: indeed, it shares many features with this work – it is highly dynamic, characterized by uncertainty, time pressures, and complex human–machine interactions. Anaesthetic work is 'specialist-manual' labour, rather than emotional labour (James, 1989, 1992) and perhaps because of this little attention has been paid to anaesthetic talk and the interactions that take place between anaesthetists and patients. The Association of Anaesthetists of Great Britain and Ireland issues guidance on various aspects of anaesthetic practice, including obtaining consent, but is silent about anaesthetists' communication skills. Kopp and Shafer (2000) discuss the importance of communication skills and different communication formats in anaesthetic work, Lingard *et al.* (2002) and Hindmarsh and Pilnick (2002) look at talk among anaesthetic teams, but no study of the specific communication between practitioners and patients around emergence and induction, the focus of this chapter, has been published.

What does anaesthetic work in surgical settings entail? The main task is to prepare the patient for surgery. The anaesthetist, assisted by other members of the anaesthetic and theatre team, must render the patient unconscious, insensitive to pain, but at the same time alive: vital functions must be maintained and the patient must be kept in this state of suspended animation for the duration of surgery and brought back to consciousness afterwards. The doctor–patient encounter in anaesthesia differs considerably from other medical encounters. In general practice (where much of the work on doctor–patient interactions and communication has been conducted) the patient is conscious. In much surgery the surgeon deals with an unconscious patient in the operating theatre. Anaesthetic work in surgical settings straddles the boundary between consciousness and unconsciousness, and anaesthetic talk must manage both these states and the transitions in between them.

Of course, anaesthetists also work outside the operating department. Anaesthetists play an important role in preoperative assessment, engaging in face-to-face interactions with patients prior to surgery in outpatient clinics and on wards. They may also take responsibility for aspects of intensive care and they specialize in running pain management clinics. This chapter does not look at talk in these latter settings.

Expertise in anaesthesia: settings and methods

This chapter is based on data from an ethnographic study of expertise in anaesthesia. The study aims were: to observe, describe and define the nature of expertise, with a particular attention to tacit knowledge, and to trace the acquisition and transmission of knowledge and expertise. We used observation and interviews and the study took place in two English hospitals: one principal site where we spent most of our time and a second comparative site. There were 25 anaesthetists at the main site and 39 in the comparative site, including trainees. The study drew in other individuals associated with everyday anaesthetic work, principally nursing and theatre support staff.

We obtained ethical approval from all the relevant local Research Ethics Committees and we invited staff to take part, initially via departmental meetings, and then by contacting individuals. Verbal consent was obtained, with staff being given opportunities to decline part or all of the study. In the event, none declined to be observed, and two declined to be interviewed. Although the focus of the study was on staff and their work, that work involved patients, so all patients on operating lists we observed were informed about the study and written consent was obtained to observe their operations.

We conducted observation in anaesthetic preparation rooms, operating theatres, recovery rooms, wards, clinics, the Intensive Care Unit, seminars, audit meetings and teaching sessions. Settings were purposively sampled to cover a range of different types of surgery and anaesthetic practice and levels of anaesthetic expertise from trainee to highly experienced practitioner. Our observations were targeted to capture different kinds of action, sometimes trailing the anaesthetist from one operation to another, sometimes following a complete patient episode, sometimes staying in particular locations such as the operating theatre or recovery room. The observations were conducted principally by DG but also by CP and MM, with some paired observation (DG with MM or CP). Handwritten notes of what was said and what happened were taken during observation, and written up in full immediately afterwards. We conducted approximately three observation periods per month yielding a total of 133 hours.

Semi-structured interviews were conducted with a cross section of medical, nursing and support staff. These lasted 30–120 minutes, averaging one hour in length and were tape recorded. They were guided by a topic list which was based on questions and themes identified in our literature review and initial observations. Less formal conversations were recorded near verbatim during or immediately after the event, and two 'debriefing' interviews allowed two anaesthetists to read our notes about a session they were involved in and to talk though the events that took place.

Data excerpts and preliminary interpretations were reported back to the anaesthetic department teams during the course of the study and their comments and questions were discussed and incorporated into the analyses.

Transitions: induction and emergence

For the anaesthetist an operative event has three distinct phases: induction of anaesthesia, maintenance of anaesthesia during the operation, and withdrawal of anaesthesia (emergence). For this chapter, we are interested in talk around general anaesthesia where the patient is rendered unconscious for the duration of a surgical procedure, rather than local or regional anaesthesia where the patient remains 'awake' and only that part of the body undergoing surgery is anaesthetized.

Induction begins with the transfer of the patient from a ward to the operating area and the administration of pharmacological agents to induce anaesthesia. This typically takes place in an anteroom, adjacent to the operating theatre, some 15 minutes before the patient is taken into the theatre. The anaesthetic team, usually consisting of an anaesthetist and operating department practitioner/assistant (ODP/ODA), attach monitoring equipment to the body; they may insert tubes into the body of the patient (for example, a cannula in the back of the hand as a means of administering drugs during the operation) and a breathing tube to deliver gases. We refer to the talk which occurs during this phase as *induction talk*. This talk may be directed to the conscious or semi-conscious patient, or it can be 'about' the process or the patient and addressed to another member of the team.

Once general anaesthesia is established the operation takes place and the anaesthetist acts to maintain the patient's vital functions and ensure that unconsciousness is maintained and that surgery is pain-free. Talk here is to the other theatre staff, surgeons, nurses, ODP/ODAs, porters and other anaesthetists. It may be about the patient, but it also includes other forms of informal talk such as gossip, discussion of sports or news-worthy events and jokes.

When the operation is completed the anaesthetist must restore all vital functions to the patient, which involves bringing them back from 'sleep' and supervising their transfer out of the operating theatre to a recovery area, prior to their transfer to a ward. Talk here may be directed to the patient in order to establish the patient's return from unconsciousness, and to the patient and other members of the team to effect the transfer to recovery and the ward. This talk we call *emergence talk*.

It will be clear from the foregoing discussion that induction and emergence are transitions. In many cases induction and emergence are moments when the patient is physically transferred from one location to another. Metaphysically they are moments of transition between sleep/unconsciousness and waking/consciousness. Our argument is that the talk at these moments is special: it represents an important kind of practitioner–patient encounter, notwithstanding its routine and commonplace standing in the operative arena. The specific focus of this chapter is on induction and emergence talk.

Talk work

We observed 54 inductions of anaesthesia and saw 31 patients emerge from anaesthesia. We deliberately did not follow every patient's journey from induction to emergence as our observation was focused at various points on particular spaces such as the anaesthetic room where induction takes place, or on particular staff groups. There are different approaches that might be fruitfully employed to analyse these 'moments' of data about induction and emergence. Fox's (1992) discourse analysis of surgery is one possible approach. Hindmarsh and Pilnick (2002) used conversational analysis to explore how talk is structured and the moment-to-moment organization of the anaesthetic team interaction. Our approach was ethnographic. We see 'talk work' as one kind of work – others might be 'boundary work' or 'machine work' – that anaesthetists do. We are less interested in the structure of talk (so deliberately chose not to video-record interactions) than in the types of talk employed in this setting. In essence, we are following Goffman's taxonomic lead, but seek to move beyond his focus on 'the things people don't say' (Collins, 1980, p. 171) to explore 'what gets said'.

Our analysis began with close readings and rereadings of the observational and interview data. We individually annotated transcripts and began to identify themes and then collectively discussed, developed and refined these ideas, over a series of team meetings. We established the boundaries of the various analytic categories and searched for examples of divergent cases which were, in turn, used to revise our categories until all the data were accounted for. In this way we identified three categories of anaesthetic talk: descriptive, functional and evocative. Below we show how these occur in the induction and emergence phases of anaesthetic work.

Induction talk

As described, induction talk typically takes place in the anaesthetic room, adjacent to the operating theatre. The talk is often minimal yet it provides a mixture of information, instruction and comforting talk. We noted that induction talk had an incantatory quality, and was markedly different from the talk used during emergence.

Descriptive induction talk tells the patient what s/he might expect to feel, what is happening around and to them (I6 line 1), and the sensations which might be associated with injections (I6 line 5; I20 line 6), and the onset of anaesthesia, such as feeling sleepy (I20 line 8). (Transcription conventions are listed in this chapter's appendix.)

I6

1 ODP: This is the anaesthetic, not started yet though.
2 *The junior doctor programmes equipment called a syringe driver. Moves the drip stand and adjusts the trolley into the flat position.*
3 ODP [*to patient*]: Going to give you some oxygen to breathe
4 *Places a face mask over the patient's nose and mouth and turns a dial on the gases machine. The syringe driver is beeping.*
5 ODP: This might just feel cold up your arm

I20

1 Anaesthetist: Some oxygen to breathe, hold it [*mask*] with your right hand
2 *He turns the valve (positioned above the grey reservoir bag) and presses the oxygen flush, this makes a loud hiss.*
3 *ODP moves into his position between the anaesthetic machine and the patient.*
4 *Anaesthetist connects the 'giving set' from the pumps to the cannula.*
5 *He has a 2 ml syringe in his hand from which he injects into the tube.*
6 A: It will feel cold in the back of your hand.
7 *I can hear the pumps whirring, he picks up the other 2 ml syringe.*
8 A: Any second now you will be feeling sleepy and drowsy.

Some descriptions are also functional. The mention that the injected agent will 'feel cold' can serve to stop the patient responding inappropriately. The anaesthetist signals that this 'coldness' is expected and routine, and therefore the patient does not need to react to or report this sensation. Similarly describing the gas in the mask as 'oxygen' or saying that it 'might smell funny' signals that it can be safely inhaled. Sometimes these descriptions are half-truths or misrepresentations. The gas in the mask is initially oxygen, but will be mixed with other gases to effect anaesthesia (and these may have a characteristic smell). An alternative, but reasonable, interpretation of the feeling of the injected agent travelling up a vein might be 'pain', but 'cold' is preferred to explain this uncomfortable sensation. We will return to this point later and discuss how these phrases serve to maintain the integrity of the anaesthetic situation and ensure the smooth progress of induction.

Functional talk as suggested, may be descriptive, but also gives instruction, for instance, inviting patients to take deep breaths from the mask. Or it can serve to help the anaesthetist assess the depth of anaesthesia – by asking the patient to open their eyes (I33 lines 8 and 12) or saying their name (line 12) to see if there is a response. Here the anaesthetist also explains to a trainee (A2) that it is the absence of response to such requests that is important (line 13):

I33

1 Anaesthetist 1: My colleague is going to give you some oxygen to breathe.
2 Anaesthetist 2: *holds the mask over the patient's face.*

3 A1: a bit of pain killer
4 *A1 injects from 2 syringes, one with orange label and one with brown label. A1 says something about a 'non-steroidal' and asks A2 to cancel*
5 *the blood pressure monitor. This reduces the noise, and creates some additional*
6 *calm in the room. A2 leans over to do so, lifting the mask off.*
7 *A1 tells her to keep the mask on. A1 attaches the propofol syringe to the cannula.*
8 A1: Keep your eyes open as long as you can. Think about something pleasant.
9 *A1 injects about 10 ml propofol*
10 A1: Still with us?
11 *Patient's talking becomes muffled. A1 injects another 5 ml*
12 A1: Open your eyes Phillipa
13 A1 [*to A2*]: With propofol it's loss of voice awareness, you can still get eyelash response.

On one occasion (I39) functional talk was used not only to establish that the patient was unconscious, but it also enabled team members to determine that an injection had already been given, unnoticed by their colleague:

I39

1 *A crowded anaesthetic room. There are two registrars, a senior house officer and the consultant anaesthetist in the room.*
2 *The anaesthetist injects something into the cannula.*
3 *Someone appears at the door and anaesthetist joins him in the corridor to talk.*
4 *Meanwhile the registrar takes a green swab and wipes the patient's forearm, he inserts a brown cannula into the left forearm very quickly.*
5 *The patient is now lying with her head flopped back on the pillows, her mouth open, looking unresponsive.*
6 Registrar 2: MARGARET [*to the patient*]
7 *looks at the other registrar*
8 Registrar 2: He [*the consultant*] has given her something.
9 *The anaesthetist returns*
10 Registrar 1: You could have told us [*emphasis*] [*about the injection*] I was rather concerned then

Descriptive and functional induction talk are often intertwined. In I30 instructions are given, but the anesthetist also engages in 'small talk' with the patient (lines 3–4) as a way of establishing that the anesthetic is working – the patient's responses become slurred when he drifts off to sleep. Such talk is used as a distraction and is notable in I25 and I48 which are interactions with children:

I30

1 *Anaesthetist injects fentanyl.*
2 A: This will make you feel light-headed and drowsy, when we can see that working we'll get you off to sleep.
3 What would you normally have been doing today?
4 Patient: I'm a builder.
5 *The anaesthetist moves to the head and places the propofol syringe on the anaesthetic machine. He turns the oxygen on.*
6 *The patient's talk has become very slurred.*
7 A: Take big breaths of oxygen through this mask
8 *places the black mask over the patient's face and injects all 20 ml of the propofol.*
9 *The patient snores.*

I25

1 Anaesthetist 1: What's your favourite football team?
2 Child: Manchester United
3 A1: There's only one football team. Liverpool
4 *Anaesthetists talk to each other at the counter. A2 picks up the black mask.*
5 A1 [*to the child*]: You'll feel a bit sleepy.
6 A1: Who's your favourite player?
7 *Injects.*
8 Child: Don't have one.
9 A1: There aren't any decent players. Liverpool were robbed last season.

I48

1 *Child begins to cry*
2 Child: I don't want it
3 *ODP puts the BP cuff to one side. The anaesthetist hands the child the mask*

4 A: this is like what spacemen or pilots have
5 *shows the child the reservoir bag*
6 A: Can you blow it up?
7 *Child begins to breathe through the mask watching the bag move as he does so.*

As well as this functional and descriptive talk, induction contains examples of a third type of talk: *evocative talk*. This talk evokes pleasant or familiar images and appears designed to comfort and reassure the patient. Frequently, the effects of sedative or analgesic drugs given before induction are compared to those associated with alcohol (I46):

I46

1 Anaesthetist: A gin
2 Patient: No, I only drink Boddingtons Bitter
3 A: Okay. A Boddingtons, gone a bit flat, lost its head. Young man, do you know what is going to happen to you?
4 We'll take you into theatre and you'll wake up in recovery [*short pause*]
5 Boddies struck home yet? I'm going to put the back rest down.
6 *slowly lowers back rest*
7 A: and slide you up the bed. Okay young man
8 *injects propofol*
9 A: [*soft, hypnotic voice*] you're going to have fantastic dreams. Feel nice and warm.
10 You're on a golden sandy beach and wake up when it's all over.

In I13 the patient confirmed the accuracy of these evocations of the effects of alcohol (line 6):

I13

1 Patient: Is this it now? [*short pause*]
2 P: I'm not asleep yet
3 A: Yes, I know
4 *Anaesthetist picks up the propofol syringe and injects slowly, looks intently at the patient's face.*
5 A: How are you feeling now?
6 Patient: Drowsy. Pissed

For the patient, time 'stands still' during anaesthesia, but the anaesthetic staff use evocative talk to refer to the continuing progress of time and to signal beginning and end points in the process, saying things like 'You're going to go off to sleep now. We'll see you in an hour or so.' Evocative talk also contains other 'calming' referents, harking back to bedtime rhymes such as 'Night night. Sleep tight. Don't let the bed bugs bite.' I41 includes a reference (line 3) to the opening line from a children's BBC radio programme called 'Listen with Mother', which was used as a signal that a story was about to unfold:

I41

1 A2: Lie you flat
2 *puts the back rest down. A1 draws up an ampoule of fentanyl.*
3 A1: Are you sitting comfortably? Then we'll begin.
4 *injects the fentanyl, then midazolam*

Features of induction talk

Induction talk tends to be seen as unimportant in anaesthetic settings and has not been extensively studied. Yet, within these comparatively brief segments of conversation practitioner and patient construct an understanding of the situation. This understanding is constituted *in situ* by drawing on indexical features of language and by pulling in external references (which may be relatively obscure, such as line 3 in I41). The meaning of indexical expressions depends on some sort of explicit or implicit indication to and contribution by the surroundings of speaker and hearer (Goffman, 1974, p. 500). The expectation 'We'll see you in an hour or so' spoken by the anaesthetist depends on this occasion of use, it alludes to recovery from surgery and emergence from anaesthesia. But induction talk also contains references that have nothing to do with the surgical context such as functional 'small talk'. Likewise evocations may be designed to calm the patient, but on the face of it have little to do with the task at hand.

Induction talk is patterned depending on the individuals involved. Evocative talk about alcohol is particularly idiosyncratic. One practitioner employed the local vernacular for a beer (I46 line 5), others did not use images of alcohol. Several practitioners had a repertoire of 'stock' phrases they employed. Such talk was also contingent on the patient – talk to children in particular is tailored to them. Likewise, the reference in I41 has greatest resonance if the speaker and listener remember this particular radio programme.

On one level it would be easy to dismiss induction talk as peripheral. It creates a transient understanding of the situation and allows the work of anaesthesia to progress. However two interviews suggested that induction talk is central to induction. The first reported something we had not observed and is an instance of what we call 'broken' induction. The interviewee describes a case where the anaesthetist omitted to use descriptive, functional or evocative talk:

> There have been a couple of other cases where I've felt uneasy really. In one particular instance, the anaesthetist gave the anaesthetic without warning the patient and the patient panicked. I felt uneasy then. I felt very uneasy because the patient sat bolt upright and started grabbing hold of her throat and I felt bad because I hadn't warned the patient. I thought the anaesthetist was going to do it. The patient was scared stiff. If that was me I would have quite a phobia about coming into theatres now.

A second example, below, in our observation notes, shows how a potentially broken induction was 'repaired'. Here the ODA (Brian) described how, following the failure of the anaesthetist to engage in induction talk with the patient, he had to act to 'reassure' the patient:

> While we are waiting for the next patient, Brian talks to me in the corridor.
>
> He talks about what happened with the previous patient. He points out how the anaesthetist set the anaesthetic infusion going but didn't tell either him or the patient that she was going off to sleep.
>
> Brian noticed the infusion going, so he quickly moved to the side of the patient to hold her steady (as she was lying on her side) and reassure her.

This failure by the anaesthetist to deliver adequate talk was potentially harmful. It required intervention by the ODA to reassure the patient and to ensure that she did not roll off the trolley. The lack of induction talk meant that an important cue or signal for the ODA was missed and Brian suggests that it is only his alertness in 'noticing' the infusion that allowed him to respond.

Emergence talk

Like induction talk, emergence talk contains functional and descriptive elements, but it has a very different quality. Perhaps most significantly it loses its incantatory undertone and the relaxing and calming evocations disappear to be replaced with urgent summoning 'back to life'. A key feature of this talk is that it is loud. It often entails shouting and typically addresses the patient by name (as in E1 lines 1, 4, 6, 8 and E27 lines 2, 4 and 7). The aim of this talk – like functional induction talk – is to invoke a response. The difference is that during emergence the response must occur: some physical or verbal reaction is required to reassure the anaesthetist that the patient has regained vital physiological functions such as muscle strength, protective airway reflexes and breathing. There may be some attempt to reorientate or reassure the patient, but the enchantment is over:

E1

1 A [*to patient's ear*]: FIONA. HELLO.
2 *A and the ODA lie the patient down flat. A has a conversation with one of the surgeons about another case.*
3 *Scrub nurse removes sterile handles from operating lights. ODA brings in the bed and is asked to suction patient's mouth again.*
4 A [*to patient*]: FIONA.
5 A [*to team*] Let's get her into bed
6 A [*to patient*]: FIONA.
7 *A suctions patient's mouth.*
8 A [*to patient*]: WE ARE GOING TO TAKE THE TUBE OUT OF YOUR MOUTH.
9 OPEN YOUR MOUTH.
10 [*This loud talk is a bit like the caricature of talking to deaf people – extra loud and carefully enunciated. Meanwhile normal volume conversations*
11 *about the patient and other things take place very close to and sometimes across the patient.*
12 *These are partly audible from where I stand.*]

E27

1 *The patient moves, CO2 trace now going up and down.*
2 A: CARLY. DEEP BREATHS
3 *Nurse prepares the oxygen mask.*
4 A: CARLY
5 A [*to ODP*] Take the tube out when I'm happy that she is breathing regularly. [*short pause*] not quite yet.
6 *Patient is still again, the CO2 trace now flat.*

7 A: CARLY
8 *Patient gagging on tube, begins to chew it then stops, rubs her eye. CO2 trace goes up and down again.*

Emergence talk, then, shares features with induction talk. It is descriptive and functional. It entails telling the patient what is going on and what to do, and involves various tests designed to reassure the anaesthetic team that recovery has begun. E25 is a longer example covering approximately 15 minutes of interaction that displays each of these features:

E25

1 A3 [*deep voice to patient*]: Hello, operation's finished. Time to wake up
2 *A3 walks to anaesthetic machine. ODP1 goes into the anaesthetic room and then returns.*
3 A4: What's the reason we are not doing this lady in here? She is on her bed.
4 ODP1: Wee bit pear shaped
5 A3: Do you want to carry on in here?
6 ODP1: [*reply not heard*]
7 A4: just go with it.
8 *A3 squeezes the grey bag, repositions the pulse oximeter, ventilating, oxygen saturation flashing 74% then 86%.*
9 *12 people (including me) in theatre. Very noisy. Only A3, ODP1 and me looking at the patient.*
10 *Oxygen saturation measure on screen is 89%.*
11 A3: She de-saturates very quickly
12 *A3 is stood by the anaesthetic machine, ventilating.*
13 A3 What length is the tube in at?
14 ODP1: 24, 22 at the teeth.
15 A3: hmmm. Maybe just shifted.
16 *Saturation now 93%.*
17 A3 [*deep voice to patient*]: Mrs Mills, time to wake up, operation's finished, are you comfortable?
18 *Change in tone of beeps.*
19 A3: Desaturating again
20 *Saturation 91%. A3 walks back to anaesthetic machine, ventilates, oxygen saturation 89%.*
21 *ODP1 stood by the patient's head.*
22 A3: As soon as the sats drop she starts looking dark

23 *Saturation 89%. ODP1 and 2 others move the table away. A3 ventilates, saturation 88%.*

24 A3: Come on Mrs Mills

25 *Someone tries to take the suction away.*

26 ODP1: We are using that. Three people have tried to take it away.

27 A3: Mrs Mills, the operation's finished.

28 *Suctions. Patient coughing.*

29 A3: That's better

30 ODP1: Shall we swing the bed head to that end?

31 *(that is, towards the anaesthetic machine)*

32 A3[*to ODP1*]: Good thinking. [*to patient*] Mrs Mills, big deep breaths, operation's finished, open your eyes.

33 *A3 ventilates, saturation 89%.*

34 ODP2: What have you done to her?

35 A3: She's only had 6 of morphine

36 *Changes the position of the pulse oximeter, saturation 82%. Ventilates, patient coughs again,*

37 *saturation 79%. Turns the valve by the bellows.*

38 A3: Is there a stethoscope?

39 ODP1: Dozens of them

40 *Hands A3 a stethoscope that had been hanging on the anaesthetic machine.*

41 *A3 presses the stethoscope to the patient's chest, by her armpits and listens as he ventilates, the same on the other side. Patient coughing. A3 continues ventilating, saturation 87%.*

42 A3: Sounds all right. Have you got any suction catheters

43 ODP1: What size

44 A3: Nothing too brutal

45 *Ventilating. Frowning at the patient.*

46 A3 [*to patient*] Mrs Mills, wee tickle in the back of you throat

47 *feeds the catheter down the tube, ODP1 occludes the whole at the top and A3 pulls the catheter out.*

48 A3: Nothing to speak of

49 *Auxiliary nurse enters*: Will you be coming to join us in Theatre 4?

50 A3: Hopefully 5 minutes ago. Has A4 got the patient sedated? Two shakes. [*to patient*] Mrs Mills. Time to wake up

51 *Patient still coughing.*

52 A3: OK Mrs Mills, tickle in the back of your throat [*suctions*] big deep breath, another tickle

53 *A3 moves the tube fractionally, sats falling from 81%–76%, A3 ventilating, the cuff down.*

54 A3: sats a little bit higher before I extubate. [*to patient*] another wee tickle

55 *inflates the cuff again*

56 A3: I just don't understand why [*tails off*]

57 ODP1: Member of staff, always trouble. There's quite a lot of blood

58 [*blood tracking back up the IV line*] Just take the extension out?

59 A3: Let's work on the assumption it's the tube that's upsetting her, big cough on three, one, two, three [*extubates*] big deep breaths Mrs Mills

60 *A3 places the black mask over her face. Saturation climbs immediately to 96%.*

61 A3: Happier without the tube, anyway pain doesn't seem to be a problem, thankful for small mercies

62 *changes the black mask for a clear plastic oxygen mask*

63 A3: Look

64 *he points to saturation which is 99%.*

65 A3: Shall we go into Recovery, Mrs Mills, finished now

Much of the above interaction involves talk among the team about this patient who is not recovering as they would like. Their conversation relates to the activities and monitoring functions they undertake. This conversation is carried out at normal pitch. At line 17 the anaesthetist addresses the patient directly, there is a change of tone in his voice. The patient's physical signs do not suggest that she is emerging from anaesthesia and there is a flurry of clinical talk, with one of the team stood by the patient's head. At lines 24, 27 and 32 there are further attempts to engage a response from the patient which produce positive signs of coughing (line 28) but the patient's saturation level has still not reached a desired, stable figure. This engenders further clinical talk, despite the fact that the patient has shown signs of making the transition from unconsciousness to consciousness. Lines 36–48 involve talk and activity around listening to and then clearing the patient's lungs. At line 49 we see that the anaesthetist is meant to be elsewhere dealing with another patient and that this emergence is taking longer than planned.

The anaesthetist then engages in more talk directed to the patient while he makes a decision to remove the breathing tube, at which point the saturation level rises dramatically and they move to recovery (line 65) signalling the end of anaesthesia. All of this is accomplished without a response (other than coughing) from the patient and the patient was still unconscious at the point of transfer.

Functional emergence talk is particularly clear in the various instructions given to 'test' patient responsiveness in E25 and the next extract, E10. Instructions to 'open your eyes' are given (E10 lines 4, 7) but unlike in induction, they require a physical response:

E10

1 A: Vic, open your eyes, deep breaths now Vic.
2 *The patient beginning to cough now, his face is a purple-ish colour. A*
3 *picks up a syringe, empty – to deflate the cuff.*
4 A: Deep breaths now Vic, open your eyes.
5 *holds the tube in place. ODP on the left of the patient, nurse on the right. A asks*
6 *ODP for something. ODP goes into the anaesthetic room. ODP returns with an ampoule.*
7 A: Open your eyes, open your mouth
8 *extubates the patient and hands the tube to ODP who throws it away. A holds the black mask over the patient's face with 2 hands.*
9 *The grey bag inflates and deflates. Can hear the patient snoring.*
10 *ODP moves the bed out of the way and takes something out of the drawer of the anaesthetic machine – an ear probe.*
11 *The patient has his hands clenched and the finger probe is giving a poor trace.*
12 *The ear probe still gives a poor trace – reading 70%.*
13 *The patient looks a better colour now, still snoring, moving his head from side to side.*
14 A: Vic, stick your tongue out for me
15 *[I think A says this as he presses the mask over the patient's face and I think the patient says 'no']*
16 *ODP repositions the oxygen saturation probe – poor trace. The patient is snoring loudly.*

In only one case in our data set does emergence talk not seem to have occurred. The reasons for this are not clear, but unlike induction talk, its absence does not seem to have an adverse effect.

Purposes of talk

We have shown that anaesthetic talk in induction and emergence includes descriptive and functional talk, and that an additional category – evocative talk – occurs only during induction. Hindmarsh and Pilnick (2002) argue that talk directed to the patient is principally used as a resource by the anaesthetic team to organize their work. They suggest that the kinds of descriptive talk we have identified 'simultaneously makes features of an individual's work visible and available to their colleagues. Thus, talk to the patient can be used as a resource by colleagues to coordinate their own actions and activities' (2002, p. 148). They go on to say that the patient has the ability to disrupt work and that the team maintain cooperation by instruction and information giving – a point confirmed by our interview data about broken and repaired induction talk. The task of the anaesthetic team is to get job done quickly, but make the patient as relaxed as possible. Anaesthetic talk is thus used to present anaesthesia as a series of minor and unchallenging activities and to normalize a potentially threatening situation by distraction and presentation of routine. Our data, while not the same form as those used in conversational analysis, reinforce Hindmarsh and Pilnick's contention that talk provides mechanisms that ensure smooth progress of anaesthesia. We have been able to add to their analysis by outlining the different forms of talk used for induction and emergence. Induction has a gentle tone, like an incantation, it employs calming evocations, allusions to soporific states, refers to the passage of time, and engages in distraction. Emergence talk, by contrast, is loud and urgent, it is both descriptive and functional but crucially does not use evocation to bring the patient back to reality. Moreover we have shown that it is not only the patient who disrupts teamwork. The omissions and actions of members of the team, notably the anaesthetists, can affect the flow of activity. In addition, patients, as participants in this talk – engaging in small talk or responding to emergence 'tests' – rather than disrupting the work, facilitate its progress.

Anaesthetic etiquette

Anaesthetic talk is ritualized. It follows a conversational etiquette that ensures that impressions given by those involved are managed or controlled. What gets said is carefully structured to avoid placing strain on the situation. For example during induction no reference is made to the content of the upcoming operation or the competency or demeanour of the surgeon. Anaesthesia induces unconsciousness and the talk creates 'a little social system with its own boundary-maintaining tendencies' (Goffman, 1967, p. 113).

So what are the rules that govern these practitioner–patient encounters? We have shown that both induction and emergence use description and functional talk. Descriptive talk serves a dual purpose, informing the patient about the unknown and signalling tasks to the team. Functional talk, often itself descriptive, can be used in induction and emergence to issue instructions designed to elicit responses from the patient. Other forms of functional talk include conversation designed to distract attention away from the process of anaesthesia. We have described a third form of talk – evocation – but suggest that this only occurs in the induction phase. This form of talk provides a necessary soporific aspect in this phase of anaesthesia, helping to maintaining a calm atmosphere. While the preoperative phase may be one of anxiety or trepidation for patients, and of technically difficult procedures for the anaesthetic team, this is glossed over by the use of descriptive, functional and evocative talk. For the most part induction talk is effective, although we did note that it may be less so for children, who perhaps need to be analysed as 'special cases' (Dingwall and Murray, 1983). Here it is often the parent or carer to whom talk is addressed to elicit their help in the processes of anaesthesia.

Patient–practitioner encounters and 'uncivil inattention'

Not only does anaesthetic talk take on these different forms, it is also layered in the sense that there are often several conversations (and purposes) being attended to at once. Our data suggest that there are hierarchies of urgency within anaesthetic talk. Some anaesthetic talk is directed at team members and the anaesthetic process of which the patient is a recipient. Talk to ensure that technical processes are accomplished often takes priority over direct communication with the patient. Social niceties are forgotten at moments of crisis or urgency and the patient is typically 'talked over' rather than 'with'. This resembles Goffman's conceptualization of 'civil inattention' which he outlines using the example of ignoring a fellow passenger in a lift. Goffman argues that bystanders are often obliged to refrain from exploiting the communication position they find themselves in (1963, p. 156) and must act *as if* they cannot hear. Patients in the anaesthetic room are clearly required to engage in civil inattention. They are not expected to show interest in the talk around them unless it is directed to them. But patients are not only bystanders. They are indeed a captive audience, whose proximity to team communication means they may be obliged to attend to the talk around them, but as recipients of anaesthetic care, they have more than a passing interest in what is happening. Induction and emergence are transitional moments for the patient, they are simultaneously absent and present, at once ignored and attended to. The situation we have described may perhaps better be conceptualized as 'uncivil inattention' whereby practitioners act, at certain points, as if the patient cannot hear, and at other points, are forced to acknowledge or include the patient in their talk.

Conclusion

Why should we be interested in anaesthetic talk? These interactions between patients and practitioners are part of a wider patient experience in encounters with health services. Anaesthetic talk constructs and shapes that experience. The elements of anaesthetic talk are familiar but worthy of further examination. We argue that it is important to understand transitions and that transitional talk, of itself, is a category not previously examined. Hindmarsh and Pilnick have shown how the anaesthetic team and its work are constituted and structured by anaesthetic talk. We have suggested some approaches drawing on the work of Goffman to understand how talk manages anaesthetic transitions, but there seems scope for extending conversational analysis or other discourse analysis approaches as we have done.

The unremarkable character of anaesthetic talk is only visible when it breaks down, when a member of the team forgets to talk, and the flow of work is disrupted. How talk, and the processes of anaesthesia are managed in these situations requires work by members of the anaesthetic team and the patient. We have demonstrated that there is an underlying etiquette governing talk. Most noticeably if induction talk does not get done the work is likely to be disrupted. The participants in anaesthetic work must attend to talk and respond to silences yet there is little to guide them in this terrain. Communication between anaesthetic practitioners and patients is a core part of anaesthetic practice yet we are aware that much of the knowledge about communication during anaesthesia is tacit. Induction and emergence talk are seldom commented on and remain a largely invisible thread that holds the action of anaesthetic practice together. There is no formal teaching about this aspect of communication (in stark contrast to formal training programmes instituted for other medical practitioners). As a result talk retains idiosyncratic features and is 'learnt' or acquired through osmosis, copying teachers and through the telling of 'atrocity stories'. For us understanding anaesthetic talk is part of understanding the interplay of explicit and tacit knowledge of anaesthetic practice.

Appendix: Transcription key

Lower case	speech
CAPS	loud speech
Italics	researcher observations of action, summary of speech
[*italics*]	researcher comment, for example, direction of speech or meaning

Acknowledgements

The research on which this chapter is based could not have been undertaken without the participation of the anaesthetic teams who allowed us access to their world. Special thanks are due to Professor Graham Crow for his extremely helpful comments on an earlier draft of this chapter. The research was funded by NHS North West Research and Development.

References

Association of Anaesthetists of Great Britain and Ireland. http://www.aagbi.org/guidelines.html/ (accessed 11 May 2004).

Collins, R. (1980) 'Erving Goffman and the Development of Modern Social Theory', in J. Ditton (ed.) *The View from Goffman* (London: Macmillan).

Dingwall, R. and Murray, T. (1983) 'Categorisation in Accident Departments: "Good" Patients, "Bad" Patients and Children', *Sociology of Health and Illness*, 5, pp. 127–48.

Fox, N. (1992) *The Social Meaning of Surgery* (Milton Keynes: Open University Press).

Goffman, E. (1963) *Behaviour in Public Places: Notes on the Social Organisation of Gatherings* (New York: Free Press).

Goffman, E. (1967) *Interaction Ritual: Essays on Face to Face Behaviour* (New York: Doubleday).

Goffman, E. (1974) *Frame Analysis: an Essay on the Organisation of Experience* (Boston: Northeastern University Press).

Hindmarsh, J. and Pilnick, A. (2002) 'The Tacit Order of Teamwork: Collaboration and Embodied Conduct in Anesthesia', *Sociological Quarterly*, 43, pp. 139–64.

James, N. (1989) 'Emotional Labour: Skill and Work in the Social Regulation of Feelings', *Sociological Review*, 37, pp. 15–42.

James, N. (1992) 'Care = Organisation + Physical Labour + Emotional Labour', *Sociology of Health and Illness*, 14, pp. 488–509.

Kopp, V. and Shafer, A. (2000) 'Anesthesiologists and Perioperative Communication', *Anesthesiology*, 93, pp. 548–55.

Lingard, L., Reznick, R., Espin, S., Regehr, G. and DeVito, I. (2002) 'Team Communications in the Operating Room: Talk Patterns, Sites of Tension and Implications for Novices', *Academic Medicine*, 77(3), pp. 232–7.

9

Corridor Conversations: Clinical Communication in Casual Spaces

Debbi Long, Rick Iedema and Bonsan Bonne Lee

> Corridor conversations. God, the place runs on them. We call them Corridor Conferences – we have them just outside the ward, and in the corridor outside the kiosk, you're always meeting people there and getting things sorted out. And the things you get organized when you run into people at the coffee shop! You get more decisions made in Corridor Conferences than you do in meetings sometimes, I reckon.
>
> Infection Control Nurse Consultant

> [I]n authentic practice, people engage continually in informal activities and interactions and often . . . much work . . . happens despite . . . formal organization.
>
> (Breu and Hemingway, 2002, p. 147)

Introduction

Corridor consultations are 'part of the daily discourse of hospital medicine' (Heard *et al.*, 2003), however, in spite of being 'an integral part of physicians' medical culture . . . little is known' about this widespread and significant mode of clinical communication (Peleg *et al.*, 1999, p. 241), and corridor communications 'are often discussed as if they were of little formal value' (Downey *et al.*, 1997, p. 245). Communication modes in hospitals have been extensively studied: medical records, handovers, ward rounds, case management meetings, organizational meetings and doctor–patient communication (Iedema, 2005). Corridors, however, have so far been overlooked as a site of study for health communication. And yet mentions of corridor or hallway consultations or conversations are sprinkled throughout the medical literature, and it is evident from this that corridors act as important conduits of clinical information flow. It appears then that in some respects the interactions that take place in corridors are similar to interactions in other spaces. The focus of this chapter, however, is on how corridor conversations differ from other more frequently studied kinds of clinical information exchange, such as case conferences and ward rounds, and to investigate what is typical of interactions that take place in one specific hospital-based clinic's corridor space.

According to Johnson *et al.* (2000, p. 282), 'the setting in which discussions occur [is] as important as the more narrative elements of the story'. No doubt, this sensitivity informs comments from ethicists and clinicians about the inappropriateness of using corridors for negotiating end-of-life and palliative care decisions with families (Bliton, 1999; Johnson *et al.*, 2000). Similarly, Hanley (2003, p. 156) comments on the ethical and medico-legal implications of conversations being overheard in corridor space. Corridor consultations are further called into question because they are associated with lapses in administration and documentation (Heard *et al.*, 2003; Swan and Spigelman, 2003), and with gossip and prejudice (Chur-Hansen, 2004). Finally, corridors have also been judged to be inappropriate spaces for dealing with poorly performing or impaired practitioners (Reid, 2002) or for providing colleagues with health advice (Anderson, 1999; Davidson and Schattner, 2003; Shadbolt, 2002).

While doctor–patient corridor consultations are occasionally mentioned (Biderman and Antonovsky, 1988; Okamura *et al.*, 1998), references to colleague health consultations, or doctor–doctor corridor consultations are much more frequent. In a survey of over 100 practitioners, Peleg *et al.* (1999, p. 241) reported that 82 per cent of their respondents had experience of their colleagues requesting 'hallway medicine'. In another study, Shadbolt (2002, p. 19) writes that '"Corridor consultations" are common, with 22% of respondents admitting to requesting a prescription from a work colleague. Interestingly, more than 50% of respondents said they felt uncomfortable about being asked for a prescription by a colleague.' Authors from the NSW Doctors Health Advisory Service conclude that '[m]any doctors lack adequate medical care' themselves because they rely on ad hoc corridor advice, leading them to recommend that 'doctors . . . avoid "corridor consultations" . . . ' (Pullen *et al.*, 1995, p. 481). In a similar vein, Anderson (1999) recommends that doctor-to-doctor consultations should take place in 'optimal circumstances. This is not the corridor.' Shadbolt (2002, pp. 19–20) agrees, arguing that doctors are an at-risk group with poor health-seeking behaviour, and that doctor–doctor corridor consultations are a major contributor to this.

While clinicians using the opportunity of 'bumping into' a colleague to ask for medical advice for themselves is seen as problematic, there are other functions for corridor consultations which are seen to constitute good medical practice. Using the opportunity of a chance encounter to ask colleagues' advice about a patient is seen as an integral part of hospital life. Thus, Heard *et al.* (2003) ask:

> Should clinicians refuse to discuss patients outside the formal setting of a referral? The loss to patient care and to clinical practice could potentially be enormous. Perhaps it is necessary for the profession to consider the overall risk and loss to patient care were such exchanges lost, but at the same time, to assess the consequence of such exchanges taking place informally and as undocumented episodes of clinical care. (Heard *et al.*, 2003, pp. 46–7)

Lancashire *et al.* (2003) go further when they describe these interactions as important for clinicians socially, professionally and educationally. Speaking of education generally (not specifically medical), Hicks (1999, pp. 10–11) states that it 'could be argued that by far the greatest amount of instructional consultation takes the form of quite incidental and informal advice sought and received by colleagues in the faculty common room or the corridor'. Following this same philosophy, Pearce (2003) advocates for corridor teaching to be taken properly into account in medical education. Arguing that 'teaching during corridor consultations is an important and integral part of general practice training' (Pearce, 2003, p. 747), he reports that:

> While trainees have regular scheduled teaching sessions and release programs, an integral part of their learning is the casual, 'corridor' contacts during their consulting sessions.... This ad-hoc teaching usually occurs in response to a specific problem – a patient with a condition the registrar doesn't recognize or doesn't know how to treat. The response needs to be timely and appropriate... 'corridor teaching'... [is] an important area of learning that was underappreciated by policy setters.... An analysis of the literature revealed little on what is a core learning activity in vocational training.... We were not able to identify any studies looking at specific content... none of the literature seemed to address the specific needs of the corridor teaching experience [and] this significant area of teaching has

not to date been examined in any systematic way. (Pearce, 2003, pp. 745–6)

Discussing the role of nurse practitioners working in general practice, Watts *et al.* (2004, p. 47) found that 'GPs and nurses... agreed that communication mechanisms and systems (whether formalized in team meetings or non-formally through corridor conversations) were important to ensuring that nurses worked effectively in general practice'. As well as having implications for 'risk management... clinical governance and... [limiting] cross infection', Heard *et al.* (2003, p. 46) argue that studying corridor consultations is 'increasingly relevant in the context of multiprofessional ward rounds where advice may be given/heard by not only medical staff but also by other health care professionals'.

The value of these latter comments notwithstanding, there is at least one other aspect of corridor conversations that remains unexplored in the medical literature: the role of the corridor as 'liminal space' (cf. Turner, 1967: 93) in facilitating dynamic or *heterogeneous* communications in multidisciplinary teams. Specifically aimed at addressing the lack of empirical data available on this aspect of corridor conversations, this chapter focuses on providing in-depth examples of types of 'corridor talk' which were recorded in a multidisciplinary outpatients clinic. In doing so, the chapter highlights the centrality of corridor talk to the organization of the clinicians' work (Iedema *et al.*, 2005a).

The clinic

The clinic described in this chapter treats people with spinal cord injury who have developed pressure ulcers (Iedema *et al.*, 2006b). The clinical team is comprised of a doctor (staff specialist), nurse (clinical nurse consultant), occupational therapist, physiotherapist, dietitian, social worker and peer support worker. Other specialists are on call: an orthopaedic surgeon, plastic surgeon and/or infectious diseases staff specialists (or their registrars) attend when required. Apart from separate team meetings and case conferences, the team members come together in this particular space, an outpatients clinic in the hospital, every fortnight. They normally see three or four patients during any one clinic.

Due to the logistics of the type of care offered in the clinic (involving seeing multiple clinicians), and the patient population (special transport is frequently required, the timing of which can be unreliable), all patients are booked in on the same day and for the same time. Hence there is

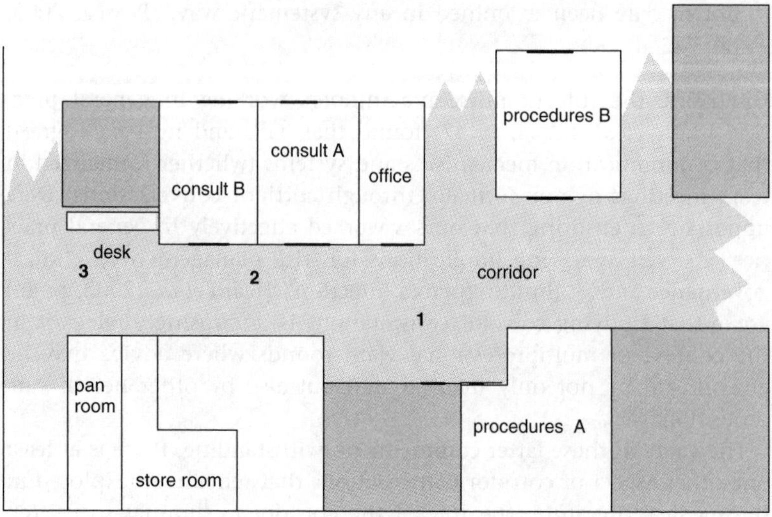

Figure 9.1 Layout of outpatients clinic

generally more than one patient being attended to in the clinic at any one time, and clinicians move between consulting rooms, conferring in the corridor as they move in and out of patient consultations. Figure 9.1 shows the layout of the clinic space. Conversations most frequently take place in the corridor space between the procedures room and the office (1 in the map produced as Figure 9.1), however they also take place in the corridor outside consulting rooms A and B (2 in Figure 9.1), or around the desk at the end of the corridor (3 in Figure 9.1).

Data collection, pseudonyms, abbreviations and affiliations

The data discussed in this chapter were collected as part of a video ethnography project exploring clinician identity in multidisciplinary health care teams (see Iedema *et al.*, 2006b for an overview). A researcher (Long) spent ten months observing and videoing a variety of interactions between team members, including a number of focused observations of the corridor space in the clinic. The excerpts presented are transcripts taken from video footage of two particular clinic sessions.

All names used are pseudonyms. The naming format among clinicians is consistent, that is, whether someone has used title and surname or first name has been reproduced in the pseudonyms. Speakers in the

Table 9.1 Abbreviations and pseudonyms used for clinicians

Abbreviation	*Profession/position*	*Gender*	*Pseudonym*
DR	Staff specialist	Male	Kim
CNC	Clinical nurse consultant	Female	
PT	Physiotherapist	Female	Nicky
OT	Occupational therapist	Female	Liz
SW	Social worker	Male	Don
DT	Dietitian	Female	
PS	Peer support worker	Female	Theresa
RN1	Registered nurse	Female	Marie
RN2	Registered nurse	Female	
RN3	Registered nurse	Female	Sasha
RN4	Registered nurse	Female	
OPCNC	Outpatients clinical nurse consultant	Female	
WM	Wardsman	Male	
	Relieving occupational therapist	Female	Collette
	Ward social worker	Female	Lisa
	Ward physiotherapist	Male	Steve

transcripts are identified according to their professional background, using the above abbreviations (Table 9.1).

Corridor communications

Discussions in the corridor included the expected exchanges of clinical information, as well as giving and receiving of instructions. In this clinic, however, corridor conversations also covered a wide variety of other topics, such as time management and work flow planning; discussions on equipment costs and purchasing (for both patients and the clinic); knowledge and skill exchange; affective talk including social or 'phatic' communication and conflict resolution talk, and reflections on attitudes and practices. Here we will review five prominent modes of corridor communication that we found to be central to effective multidisciplinary teamwork in a hospital: clinical, technological, organizational, affective and reflexive talk.

Excerpt 1 below shows the doctor briefing the peer support worker in the corridor outside consult room B prior to the peer support worker entering the consultation room and introducing herself to the patient. This is a typical ad hoc clinical information exchange taking place in the corridor.

Excerpt 1

DR He's healing conservatively, and we think he'll be right for seating assessment in about two months. Uh, he's also got respiratory issues so we sent him to a respiratory doctor, because he's got sleep apnea. We think the sleep apnea is compounded by his hyperscoliosis, so we've sent him to an orthopedic surgeon to look into his curvature of the spine.

These kinds of exchanges occurred frequently, providing the clinicians with ongoing updates about specific patients and their progress. Not much of this information was documented until at the end of the clinic or even later. Some of these exchanges were never recorded because they embodied what Downey and colleagues term 'nonascribable (off the record) but necessary information' (Downey *et al.*, 1997, p. 245) about emotional state, family problems or substance abuse.

In hospital-based health care in industrialized communities, clinical knowledge is inextricably intertwined with technology. Treatment and management plans inevitably involve technology in at least part of their planning and implementation. In the following excerpt, the occupational therapist tells the social worker about a discussion she had with a patient regarding a particular wheelchair that the doctor has recommended.

Excerpt 2

OT ... and then he said he understood why [doctor] wanted him to buy it [....] it means that you can get out of bed, and you can change the angle of how you sit and you can just be a little bit more interactive [.....]

Technology-oriented discussions in the corridor included clinical applications of technology, such as types of pressure-relieving mattresses and cushions that might be needed to suit particular patients' needs. They also included high-tech diagnostics, such as heat mapping photography equipment to track wound healing; evidence-based recommendations, such as the latest on types of bandaging for particular wounds; discussions about having tracks installed into particular treatment rooms to allow hoists to be used (to lift patients) and very pragmatic exchanges of skills, such as how to insert text boxes into word processing documents, or tips on navigating the newly introduced telephone note dictation service. Technology both facilitates (or hinders) communication in so far that the clinic's practices are heavily technology dependent, and for that reason technology also generates much additional (e.g. explanatory) communication, as shown in excerpt 2 above.

Elsewhere we argue that due to their apparently marginal status, corridors are open to facilitating conversations about all of these aspects of hospital work in a highly dynamic fashion (Iedema *et al.*, 2005a). In that sense, corridors are particularly important resources for clinicians working in multidisciplinary teams. As members of these teams, clinicians are to varying degrees required to take on oversight or 'post-bureaucratic' responsibilities in addition to their clinical ones (Iedema, 2003), requiring increased attention to the coordination, administration and organization of care processes. In this scenario, rather than clinicians undertaking clinical work and managers taking charge of organizational work, the advent of the post-bureaucratic clinician means that care organization has become a major component of many clinicians' daily work. As a closely knit clinical team, all clinicians in the clinic reported on here were required to be aware of the organizational implications of their treatment solutions, and management plans were negotiated among clinicians in ways which meant that all clinicians had to engage with the organizational aspects of patient care.

The corridor, it turns out, proved to be the site par excellence for enacting these new responsibilities and roles: it functioned as a 'meta-space' whose lack of interactive–communicative prescription and ritual definition enabled clinicians to adopt a bird's-eye view on their tasks and on patients' care trajectories, while relaxing their status and formal power habits in favour of attentiveness to the logic of the work. Consider the following excerpt that captures a mobile phone call received by the doctor in the clinic from the nurse manager of the ward. They discuss the timing of booking a patient into the ward so they can get ready for surgery. This decision requires both the doctor and the nurse manager to be aware of the status of all the patients on the ward (to know the likelihood of beds coming free in the near future), including the status of all patients awaiting admission, the relative financial, social, emotional and clinical outcome costs of delaying one patient's admission to facilitate another's, and the organizational and clinical needs of the surgical team.

Excerpt 3

DR ... Shall we get [patient E] in and lock the bed? *[pause]* yep *[pause]* yep *[pause]* yep *[pause]* yeah, I know *[pause]* I know, I know, I know. *[pause]* Yeah, well the bed's just going to get blocked if we're not going to take it. *[pause]* hmmm *[pause]* yep *[pause]* yeah *[pause]* Yep, no worries. Yes yes, I think . . . yes, you do have consensus. *[pause]* OK thanks. *[pause]* OK, bye.

As well as engendering this kind of complex organizational, communicative work, corridor conversations facilitated the negotiation of organizational minutiae as and when the need arose. As reported in workplace ethnographic studies such as those by Hutchins (1991) and Orr (1996), team members in the present study valued this informality for the flexibility it afforded them in how they communicate with colleagues.

At the same time, however, and without exception, the team members described the clinic as chaotic. This informality and perceived chaos appeared to impact particularly on the nursing staff who had an important coordinating role in the clinic. Interactions occurred around time management and planning for the flow of the clinic, most frequently between the clinical nurse consultant (CNC) in the multidisciplinary team, and the registered nurses (RNs) who worked in the outpatients clinic. Illustrating this is the following excerpt which displays communication between the nurse on the team (CNC) and one of the outpatient nurses (RN1).

Excerpt 4

RN1 Now [patient B] *[indicates vaguely up the hallway]*

CNC No, we've got another patient in *[indicates consult room C]*.

RN1 There? *[indicates procedures room]*

CNC No, there. *[indicates consult room C again]*

RN1 Well when he comes we'll use that bed *[indicating]*, and we'll either put him in there *[consult room A]* or there *[consult room C]*

CNC No, there's someone else in there *[consult room C]*

RN1 Oh really. Kim [the doctor] must have put him in there. Well when a wardsman turns up, that's what I'm going to do, I'm going to put him on this bed *[indicates bed in hallway behind hoist]*

CNC OK. So the dressing is done there? *[indicating procedures room]*

RN1 Eh?

CNC Is the dressing done there [procedures room]

RN1 Oh . . . it's happening. It's just that lady seeing him [peer support worker]

CNC Oh, OK. . . . can you also organize the follow up appointment for him? *[indicates procedures room]*

While this extract reproduces exchanges dealing with clinic-internal issues, quite a number of interchanges involved the organization of activities complementary to the clinic's main purpose. In one corridor conversation, the social worker explained to the occupational therapist how to access translation services. Accessing translator services generally occurs outside of the temporal–spatial framework of the clinic: that is, it requires a call from the occupational therapist's office (which is situated on a different floor and a long way from the outpatients clinic). The corridor becomes the place where the issue of a translator support service can be raised in dynamic response to specific patients' needs, further underscoring the *meta-clinical* orientation of much of the clinic's corridor talk.

Besides this meta-clinical communicative work that targets the coordination of clinical, technological and organizational details, the corridor also revealed considerable emotional or 'immaterial' labour (Iedema *et al.*, 2005b). The increasing complexity of hospital services leads not just to an intensification of clinicians' post-bureaucratic responsibilities, but also engenders more and more affective and reflexive work (Iedema *et al.*, 2006c). In this study, it is the perceived liminality of the clinic's corridor space, we suggest, that affords and facilitates these affective and reflexive kinds of communication (excerpt 5).

Excerpt 5

DR Did you have a good break?

SW Yes, I did. I went to [city]. Saw some friends there. Interesting chap. [. . .] He makes pianos. [name]

DR Oh, I've seen them, I've think I've seen a [name] piano.

SW They're beautiful. I couldn't believe it. He took me round his factory. It was, it was . . . I was humbled. The craftsmanship is just beautiful.

Social chats also occur when clinicians and/or other hospital staff run into someone they have not seen for a while, or don't usually see in the clinic. These chats particularly involved the occupational therapist and the physiotherapist, who had worked in the unit for many years, and the peer support worker, who was well known to many of the patients. A wardsman who had come to help move a patient from his chair to a bed, knew the peer support officer, but had not seen her for some time (excerpt 6).

Excerpt 6

PS	Hallo darling, how are you?
WM	Hallo, long time no see.
PS	Can I have a kiss?
WM	Yeah [bends over and kisses PS on cheek]. You're looking great.
PS	It's been a long time. I'm working here now.
	[. . .]
WM	How long's it been? How long have you been in the chair [wheel chair] now?
PS	Twenty-two years!
WM	Fair dinkum? Shit!
PS	Shit, yeah *[laughs] [introduces to researcher]* He was with me when I was an 18 year old. And they all got me introduced to the pub.
WM	You took to it really well!

Not all affective interactions were affectionate, however. Dissatisfaction was mostly expressed in muted ways among the multidisciplinary team and the outpatients nursing staff. There are no examples in the corridor data collected of multidisciplinary team staff directly and assertively questioning each others' performance in any way. We have some examples of team members expressing frustration about a lack of equipment funding, the broader hospital system, blockages to surgery or postoperative care, and occasionally about problems caused by other departments in the hospital. These dissatisfactions were rarely verbalized with overt anger, and mostly took the form of irony or sarcasm, often accompanied by a sad smile. For their part, outpatients nursing staff did on occasion express negative opinions if they felt someone was not pulling their weight. Yet they were also very open about supporting each other to achieve a fair task allocation (excerpt 7).

Excerpt 7

OPCNC	Are you using that trolley, Marie?
RN1	Just used it then, but you can have it if you want.
RN4	OK, thanks. [OP CNC moves out of earshot]
RN1	Is Sasha coming to help you?
RN4	[very slight head shake]
RN1	*[mutters]* She's supposed to. *[taps top of trolley]* Sorry I haven't washed that down yet.
RN4	That's all right.

Negative emotions were also recorded. Excerpt 8 captures how two clinicians initiated spontaneous conflict resolution. The occupational therapist had been on leave, and when she returned there was a misunderstanding about how the social worker had intervened in a complex and ongoing case during her absence.

Excerpt 8

SW Well, you didn't know, I think it was, well you'd just got back, and you didn't know what was happening, what we'd been doing

OT No, and I was just told . . .

SW No wonder you got a bit defensive, but that's OK.

OT I'm REALLY sorry.

SW That's OK, we fixed it.

OT I just got back, and everyone said 'he's going home next week, can you sort him out?' there was a big note on the chair, saying 'I'm not buying this chair' and I went 'WHAT?'

SW And you thought 'what's going on here?'

OT And then I was told he was buying it, and I was like, I don't know where I'm at! I was just trying to clarify things, to get my head around it.

SW Yeah, that's cool.

OT So I just wanted to find out.

SW Yeah, of course. I hope we're OK about it *[touches her arm]*.

OT Yeah, of course, yeah.

SW Oh good, thank you.

OT Oh yeah.

SW That's cool, no worries. *[pause]* It can be quite stressful coming back from holidays, especially long holidays.

OT Just trying to sort out where I'm at. . . . I just wanted to get round and talk to some people and sort out where things were at. Lisa had told me that you'd put in a hell of a lot of work to get him to agree to purchase it.

Finally, the perceived liminality of the corridor space also facilitated clinician reflexivity. In the following excerpt (9), the doctor consults with the CNC about a plan of action for a patient who is not healing as expected. This is not uncommon in this clinic: the patients present with extremely complex issues, and much exploration often takes place between the multidisciplinary clinicians to develop management plans that take into account as many factors as possible. Below, the doctor and CNC explore possible explanations, deciding that depression may need to be considered as a factor. They have just come from the procedures room, consulting with the patient with a number of the team members. The doctor mentioned depression to the patient, and discusses the patient's reaction with the CNC, reflecting that it may have been more appropriate not to raise depression in front of so many people.

Excerpt 9

DR Once Liz gets out we need to pow-wow about [patient F], I'm not convinced we have a full [picture]. [. . .] And he's had a year of [treatment], and it's still in this situation . . . so I think we need to look at . . . if there's another way we can break that . . . there's something going on here that's not allowing him to move forward. It may be cognitive as well.

CNC I know, it may be related to the depression.

DR Yeah, well, did you see what he did, what his behaviour was when I mentioned that? *[CNC grimaces and covers eyes with hand]* I was thinking 'I shouldn't have said this.'

CNC No. Maybe it would have been different if it was just you there . . . [the procedures room had a large number of clinicians with the patient at the time]

DR Let's have a talk about it, and then we can decide whether I go back in and talk to him again. If we can feel strongly that it's worth pushing for an antidepressant, then I'll sit down in there with him for as long as it takes and see if I can convince him, because there's something that's stopping this man moving forward and I just don't know what it is.

Some interactions involve all five of the characteristics we have argued are defining of this multidisciplinary team's communication: clinical, organizational, technological, affective and reflexive. The following excerpt (10) captures an interaction around infection control procedures, and illustrates how the various meta-clinical dimensions of corridor talk tend to become intricately intertwined. As a response to increased infection rates in their client population, changes to infection control protocols had recently been introduced into the clinic. Clinicians had agreed to try and remind each other to use gloves and gowns, and the CNC, whose awareness of infection control practice was an area of strength, was often relied upon to communicate best practice.

Excerpt 10

[Outside procedures room: doctor commences gowning, social worker enters procedures room without gown or gloves.]

DR Do you want a gown, Don?
[Social worker comes back, doctor hands social worker gown]

SW Oh thanks.
[Doctor gets gown for himself. Doctor and social worker gown up. Doctor walks up corridor tying apron around the front. Sticks head in consult room A [. . .]
Doctor walks back towards procedures room, CNC exits consult room A and follows]

CNC Um, Kim *[DR turns, CNC indicates apron]* Don't tie it round the front.

DR Uh, OK, sorry. *[Doctor reties apron at the back, hand gels outside procedures room. CNC joins him, gets gown and starts gowning.]*

Similarly, corridor conversations often shift from focusing on one patient to other patients. Particularly significant here is that not all patients discussed in the corridor need be in the clinic at the time: clinicians often update each other on developments of patients who are in between visits, or discuss patients who have been admitted as inpatients to wards elsewhere in the hospital.

Interactive heterogeneity

This conversational dynamicity manifests itself also in clinicians coming to join or leaving the corridor conversation. The following multi-message interchange (excerpt 11) begins with the doctor, dietitian and peer support worker, with the dietitian passing on information about a patient. The doctor updates them on another patient. The occupational therapist joins the discussion. The doctor informs all three about what is happening with the second patient, and formulates strategies to manage pressure areas in this patient with the occupational therapist. The occupational therapist and the doctor discuss another task they need to undertake, and then negotiate the time management around two joint tasks.

Excerpt 11

DT I've asked [the registrar] to do a vitamin D on [patient F] – he hasn't been out in the sun for five years!

DR By the way, [patient E] got sick again on the weekend

PS Oh no! *[. . . OT joins]*

DR [patient E] is back in intensive care.
[. . .]
He's still on ionotropes and still in intensive care, but the only other thing I could think of, is it might be worth swinging by there and just checking what mattress he's on.
OT In intensive care?
DR Yeah. *[makes comment about how important it is to provide good pressure relief in intensive care, to avoid pressure sores]*
OT I heard he was coming back up to the ward today?
DR No way.
OT That's not true?
DR *[shaking head – makes comment that patient can't come to ward while still needing ionotropes: he needs to stay in the intensive care unit for that]*
OT What's ionotropes?
DR It's something to keep your heart going.
OT . . . OK, so we need to swap the mattress again, if he's not on . . .
DR I think we should get him on to one of ours, if we can, Liz.
OT That's fine.
DR I know that's an easy thing to say but a hard thing to do . . .
OT . . . that's fine
DR I need to sit down with you and do that letter.
OT Yeah, when do you want to do that?
DR Do you have time now?
OT Do you want me to go to ICU now or do you want me to do the letter now?
DR Well, do you want to do the letter now, and then we can run to ICU after that?
OT Yeah.

On top of the corridor talk rapidly shifting in ideational focus, it is therefore also highly heterogeneous, interactively speaking. This heterogeneity, we suggest, provides another reason for the corridor talk being central to the quality of care achieved by and delivered in this clinic (cf. Iedema *et al.*, 2006b). Because clinicians can pick up on issues as needed with a variety of individuals in dynamic ways and without being unduly constrained by professional hierarchies, strict rituals or formalized routines, they are able to conceptualize their and their colleagues' care practices from the perspective of both their dynamically evolving details and their meta-clinical logic and cohesion.

Discussion

As can be seen from these examples, significant amounts of communication, much of it critical to the effective functioning of the clinic, takes place in the corridor. The extracts above demonstrate that the corridor provides a space where flexible, dynamic imparting of information, giving of instructions and making of decisions take place. Further, clinically important actions are decided: in excerpt 11 the doctor and the occupational therapist decide on a number of actions, including writing a letter and visiting a patient on the inpatients ward. They jointly decide to write the letter immediately after clinic, and then go together to the ward. The talk embodies dynamic shifts in what is important, highlighting the flexibility, as well as the associated potential for disruption and disorder, in the flow of corridor communication.

As some of the literature reviewed earlier suggests, there are multiple interdisciplinary teaching and learning opportunities in the corridor as a space where clinicians share from their area of expertise. In the excerpts shown above, reflexivity is expressed in a number of different ways. The doctor, social worker and occupational therapist, on advice from the CNC, adapt their practices with infection control precautions (excerpt 10); the doctor chastises himself for raising the sensitive issue of depression with a patient in a room crowded with other clinicians (excerpt 9). In the conflict resolution between the social worker and the occupational therapist, both reflect on why the situation developed the way it did, express understanding of each other's position, and come to a resolution (excerpt 8). This type of opportunistic learning and reflection is an acknowledged requirement of clinical work, and as Pearce (2003) notes most typically takes place in informal conversational spaces in hospitals such as corridors.

Organizational scholars of health care services are developing discourses with which to articulate non-linear approaches to complex clinical care (Iedema *et al.*, 2006a). Enriching these discourses, the examples of corridor communication that we have presented above represent much that is ironic, contradictory and complex about hospital-based clinician communication. These corridor conversations are dynamic, non-linear and heterogeneous. They take place in narrow, linear spaces (in that they go, mostly in a straight line, from somewhere to somewhere else) which also tend to be perceived as liminal spaces, we suggest, in that they are betwixt and between, defying spatial categorization as a sort of room-like spaces which are not rooms. Clinicians move through the corridors and (in our study) their physical movements appear to be associated with highly dynamic, quite economic and carefully targeted communications (Iedema *et al.*, 2005a). We believe that this link we have sketched between corridor space and dynamic and heterogeneous communication is as yet insufficiently appreciated: 'we still have little understanding of collaboration in action' (Reeves and Lewin, 2004, p. 318). Reeves and Lewin suggest that in hospitals collaborative action 'depends largely upon informal negotiated agreements between professionals' (2004, p. 318). In their ethnographic study of two hospital wards, they found that 'interprofessional collaboration consisted largely of short, unstructured and often opportunistic interactions' (2004, p. 221). The examples given above of the clinic corridor provide depth and scope of such 'opportunistic interactions' in the team we studied.

Conclusion

Learning and reflexive practice as well as complex clinical decision-making are often strongly facilitated by the types of everyday, opportunistic, heterogeneous communications which take place in informal hospital spaces such as tea rooms, corridors, car parks and coffee shops. We argue that corridor communication needs to be taken more seriously in hospital communication studies. Corridor talk pulses through the very heart of most clinical communication, and yet has been neglected in the study of hospital communication. For clinicians to work safely and effectively, they require facilitative, dynamic and heterogeneous modes of communication by means of which they monitor, adjust and refine their medical and patient management plans. Where formalized modes of clinical communication have been well studied, the more liminal phenomena presented in this chapter have received little to no attention. This is an important area of future research, we suggest, to clarify how (effectively) clinicians make decisions, implement them, reflect on their day-to-day practice, and are responsive to their dynamic clinical environments and patients' variable kinds of progress.

References

Anderson, W. (1999) 'Doctoring Doctors', *British Medical Journal*, 319 (July 31). http://bmj.bmjjournals.com/ (accessed 27 April 2006).

Biderman, A. and Antonovsky, A. (1988) 'The Submerged Part of the Iceberg and the Family Physician', *Family Practice*, 5(3), pp. 174–6.

Bliton, M. J. (1999) 'Ethics Talk, Talking Ethics: an Example of Clinical Ethics Consultation', *Human Studies*, 22, pp. 7–24.

Breu, K. and Hemingway, C. (2002) 'Collaborative Processes and Knowledge Creation in Communities of Practice', *Creativity and Innovation Management*, 11(3), pp. 147–53.

Chur-Hansen, A. (2004) 'Experience of being Gay, Lesbian or Bisexual at an Australian Medical School: a Qualitative Study', *International Journal of Inclusive Education*, 8(3), pp. 281–91.

Davidson, S. K. and Schattner, P. L. (2003) 'Doctors' Health-seeking Behaviour: a Questionnaire Survey', *Medical Journal of Australia*, 179(6), pp. 302–5.

Downey, G. L., Dumit, J. and Traweek, S. (1997) 'Corridor Talk', in G. L. Downey and J. Dumit (eds) *Cyborgs and Citadels: Anthropological Interventions in Emerging Sciences and Technologies*, pp. 245–63 (Sante Fe: School of American Research Press).

Hanley, J. (2003) 'Ignorance of the Law Excuses No Man', *Directions in Psychiatry*, 23 (lesson 12), pp. 151–8.

Heard, S. R., Roberts, C., Furrows, S. J., Kelsey, M. and Southgate, L. (2003) 'Corridor Consultations and the Medical Microbiological Record: Is Patient Safety at Risk?', *Journal of Clinical Pathology*, 56, pp. 43–7.

Hicks, O. (1999) 'A Conceptual Framework for Instructional Consultation', *New Directions for Teaching and Learning*, 79, pp. 9–18.

Hutchins, E. (1991) 'Organizing Work by Adaptation', *Organization Science*, 2(1), pp. 14–39.

Iedema, R. (2003) *Discourses of Post-Bureaucratic Organization* (Amsterdam/Philadelphia: John Benjamins).

Iedema, R. (2005) 'Medical Discourse: the Organization of Doctoring', *Encyclopedia of Language and Linguistics*, pp. 745–51 (Oxford: Elsevier).

Iedema, R., Long, D., Carroll, K., Stenglin, M. and Braithwaite, J. (2005a) 'Corridor Work: How "Liminal" Space can be a Focal Resource for Handling Complexities of Multi-disciplinary Health Care', in M. Muetzelfeld (ed.), *Proceedings of the Asia Pacific Researchers in Organization Studies Conference* (Melbourne: Victoria University).

Iedema, R., Rhodes, C. and Scheeres, H. (2005b) 'Presencing Identity: Organizational Change and Immaterial Labor', *Journal of Organizational Change Management*, 18(4), pp. 327–37.

Iedema, R., Jorm, C. M., Braithwaite, J. Travaglia, J. and Lum, M. (2006a) 'A Root Cause Analysis of Clinical Errors: Confronting the Disjunction between Formal Rules and Situated Practice', *Social Science & Medicine*, 63(5), pp. 1201–12.

Iedema, R., Long, D., Forsyth, R. and Lee, B. B. (2006b) 'Visibilising Clinical Work: Video Ethnography in the Contemporary Hospital', *Health Sociology Review*, 15(2), pp. 156–68.

Iedema, R., Rhodes, C. and Scheeres, H. (2006c) 'Surveillance, Resistance, Observance: the Ethics and Aesthetics of Identity (at) Work', *Organization Studies*, 27(8), pp. 1111–30.

Johnson, N., Cook, D., Giacomini, M. and Williams, D. (2000) 'Towards a "Good" Death: End-of-life Narratives Constructed in an Intensive Care Unit', *Culture, Medicine and Psychiatry*, 24, pp. 275–95.

Lancashire, W., Hore, C. and Law, J. A. (2003) 'The Hospitalist: a US Model Ripe for Importing?', *Medical Journal of Australia*, 179(1), p. 62.

Okamura, H., Uchitomi, Y., Sasoko, M., Eguchi, K. and Kakizoe, T. (1998) 'Guidelines for Telling the Truth to Cancer Patients', *Japanese Journal of Clinical Oncology*, 28(1), pp. 1–4.

Orr, J. (1996) *Talking about Machines: an Ethnography of a Modern Job* (Ithaca: Cornell University Press).

Pearce, C. (2003) 'Corridor Teaching: "Have You Got a Minute . . . ?" ', *Australian Family Physician*, 32(9), pp. 745–7.

Peleg, A., Peleg, R., Porath, A. and Horowitz, Y. (1999) 'Hallway Medicine: Prevalence, Characteristics and Attitudes of Hospital Physicians', *Israeli Medical Association Journal*, 1(4), pp. 241–4.

Pullen, D., Lonie, C. E., Lyle, D. M., Cam, D. E. and Doughty, M. V. (1995) 'Medical Care of Doctors', *Medical Journal of Australia*, 162(9), p. 481.

Reeves, S. and Lewin, S. (2004) 'Interprofessional Collaboration in the Hospital: Strategies and Meanings', *Journal of Health Services Research and Policy*, 9(4), pp. 218–25.

Reid, A. M. (2002) 'Overview: the Experience of the New South Wales Medical Board', *Medical Journal of Australia*, 177, pp. 25–6.

Shadbolt, N. E. (2002) 'Attitudes to Healthcare and Self-care among Junior Medical Officers: a Preliminary Report', *Medical Journal of Australia*, 177, pp. 19–20.

Swan, J. and Spigelman, A. D. (2003) 'Audit of Surgeon Awareness of Readmissions with Venous Thrombo-Embolism', *Internal Medicine Journal*, 33(12), p. 578.

Turner, V. (1967) *The Forest of Symbols. Aspects of Ndembu Ritual* (Ithaca: Cornell University Press).

Watts, I., Foley, E., Hutchinson, R., Pascoe, T., Whitecross, L. and Snowden, T. (2004) *General Practice Nursing in Australia* (Sydney, Australia: Royal Australian College of General Practitioners and Royal College of Nursing).

10
The Role of Signs and Representations in the Organization of Medical Work: X-rays in Medical Problem Solving

Per Måseide

Introduction

Modern medicine represents what Karin Knorr Cetina (1999) has termed an 'epistemic culture'. Medical institutions and practitioners produce and warrant medical expert knowledge and insights; hospitals function as expert organizations and much of the medical work is conducted through expert processes. Significant parts of medical work require collaboration between doctors and other professionals with different kinds of expertise. To borrow a formulation from Knorr Cetina (1999), many of the collaborative activities may be described in terms of different social and discursive 'machines' that are at work within medical expert systems. This chapter will deal with the collaborative production of clinical knowledge and ventures within a hospital context. A bottom-up perspective will focus on the local and situational organization of problem-solving activities. In the following pages the hospital will be seen as an 'expert organization', consisting of different kinds of expert systems, working at different organizational levels.

An integrated part of medical problem solving is the production and reproduction of a medical order conforming to the professionalized and institutionalized order of biomedical problems (Atkinson, 1997). The medical expert organization has a bureaucratic structure that is supposed to recreate such order and adjust to other forms of order. Bureaucratization and other principles of management are supposed to rationalize medical work economically and in terms of medical output (Gray and Harrison, 2004). As shown by Berg (1995) and Timmermans and Berg (2003), various kinds of expert systems are developed for these purposes.

They include technological equipment, networks of professional experts, various decision-support systems, and various tools for standardizing, rationalizing and regulating medical care.

In the bottom-up perspective of this chapter, medical problem solving comes out as an emergent and complex process that is essentially associated with situational, differentiated and practical conceptions of medical problems. Collaborative medical problem solving uses and generates expert systems; it is practised and organized as 'a social system of distributed cognition' (Engeström *et al.*, 2003; Hutchins, 1995; Resnick, 1994); and it may be studied 'through the window of social discourse' (Cicourel, 1990) in the form of 'situated activities' (Suchman, 1987). In these perspectives collaborative medical work is not only regulated by organizational, institutional and professional principles; it is also regulated by situational requirements and restraints and by principles regulating social interaction. Among the latter are the normative order that Goffman (1983) termed the 'interaction order'. The situated activities of problem solving form collaborative systems similar to what Goffman (1961) called 'situated activity systems' and the micro systems of distributed cognition called 'activity systems' by Goodwin (1994). Such activity systems represent situationally restricted medical expert systems.

Within activity systems professional actors collaborate with other professionals, but also with equipment, technology, representations, discursive forms and other signs. But a comprehensive part of medical problem work is not conducted in direct relation to patients and their bodies. Most of the medical problem work is conducted in relation to signs, marks or representations. Representations are also signs and they function as 'cognitive artifacts' (Hutchins, 1995). X-ray pictures are important representations in medical problem solving. They make parts of the patient's body visible in a medically relevant manner and regulate the problem solving activities. X-rays serve as evidence in concrete medical problem solving, but in a different sense from the one that this term has in 'evidence-based medicine'. Here, evidence is a local, interactive phenomenon that provides actors with resources necessary for conducting and continuing their interactions (Garfinkel, 1967). The first and major part of this chapter focuses on how X-rays become part of medical activity systems and how they are used within such activity systems. Following from these analyses, the chapter will finally point to aspects of the local, interactive and emergent organization of medical work as it relates to medical sign systems.

The background for the chapter is fieldwork data from the thoracic ward of a university hospital in Norway. My data consist of audio recordings and field notes from diverse ward conferences, and in particular from a regular conference called 'the thoracic meeting' where different medical specialists meet in order to make medical decisions. The first section of the chapter introduces theoretical concepts and perspectives and the second gives a general description of the cultural and organizational aspects that regulate the generation of medical representations. The next five sections present empirical studies of how radiological vision is produced and employed in collaborative medicine, and the final section reflects on the consequences of these studies for ways of thinking about the organization of medical work in hospitals.

Diseases, representations and distributed cognition

Doctors rarely regard medical problems from the perspective of the patient as a person anchored in his or her natural or social environment. Instead, the disease, like the patient's body, is generally attended to as a set of signs or representations. This is similar to how laboratory researchers work (Knorr Cetina, 1992). The medical problem is discursively generated in the clinic and converted to the requirements of the medical institution and its activity systems by professional practitioners and their use of representations and expert systems, and the problem develops according to the orientation and the schedule of the clinic. This represents to some extent what Berg (1992) has described as the construction of 'medical disposals'.

Indeed, X-ray pictures represent patients and their health problems. They are artificial products, but in many clinical situations they are privileged over the patient. X-rays are characterized by an 'ontological ambiguity': nature does not reveal itself in an X-ray in a 'natural and necessary' fashion. Rather, it is the radiologist's task to replace ambiguity with certainty and to generate a shared and objective radiological vision among the users of X-rays. To do this, the radiologist needs lexical knowledge about pathological images and anatomical structures, and procedural knowledge about how to describe X-rays and how the actual production of an X-ray may affect the resulting image. According to doctors in the ward several systems exist for describing X-ray pictures, so one and the same picture might in principle be described differently by different radiologists. The visual image of an X-ray thorax also depends on whether the patient follows the breathing instructions from the radiology assistant when the X-ray is taken. A process of distributed cognition takes place before an institutionally approved radiological vision of the disease or the patient's bodily condition is established.

Using Latour's (1986) wording, the 'it' of the disease is often like the 'it' of a nation's economy: it has to be made visible by artificial means. Activity systems, not isolated individuals, transform biological processes into signs that make diseases or bodily conditions visible for the clinical practitioners.

'Ideas', 'things' and 'marks' were mentioned by Hacking (1992) as cultural resources that characterize scientific research. Such resources also characterized the problem-solving situations in the thoracic ward. In general, theories or knowledge ('ideas') about diseases did not alone generate diagnoses, neither did bodies or biological conditions ('things'). Diagnoses were not arrived at by equipment, technology or doctors ('things'), nor by representations, discursive forms or other signs ('marks'). Instead, medical problems were solved through the collaborative integration of these resources. They formed a kind of 'prefiguration' (Schatzki, 2002) that guided evolving activities. Each single resource might open many directions for the problem-solving process. An important part of the problem-solving process is to make the resources work as restraining factors in relation to each other and to guide the distributed processes to medically acceptable conclusions. In this perspective, radiological vision is generated and made useful within a system of interactive relations with other institutional resources. During this process, however, some resources might gain privilege over others.

Annemarie Mol (2002) has shown that within medicine one and the same bodily condition may attract multiple and differently enacted meanings. The same generic disease is not the same object of practice for radiologists, pathologists, surgeons, oncologists, or specialists in thoracic medicine. Typical of the specialized expertises that constitute the 'discourse of medicine' (Mishler, 1984), a specialist in thoracic medicine has a conception of a specific disease grounded in his or her practice in the ward related to a specific patient. This practice-based conception is specific to thoracic medicine and informs its approach to medical problem solving. The radiologist has a different conception of disease based on his or her practice of producing radiological representations and descriptions. The pathologist, who focuses on tiny samples of tissue or fluids from the patient's body, has an even more narrowly defined relationship with the patient. Similarly, the conceptions of disease among surgeons are related to surgical practice, which consists of direct body work, mobilizing specific resources (staff, theatre time), and managing organizational constraints. When these different medical experts collaborate, they have to coordinate their diverse practical conceptions into a sufficiently shared understanding of the problem at hand to be able to render their medical interventions adequate, if not effective as well as efficient.

X-ray diagnosing and social interaction

To produce a radiological description a radiologist needs more information than is provided by the X-ray itself. At the conference meeting, each requisition for an X-ray is followed by a short description of the patient's problem. This information guides the radiologist's descriptive work. In one case at the thoracic meeting the radiologist's description was responded to by the audience with comments that it was imprecise and of little practical value. When the radiologist was informed that the patient had received a diagnosis from a previous examination, he said in a loud voice that he had not been informed about that, and had he known the pathological results he would have given a completely different description. This bears out the radiologist's sensitivity to information not contained in the X-ray, and the collaborative nature of its interpretation.

Indeed, collaboration around the interpretation of X-rays may be described in terms of 'dialogicality' at different levels. First, the requisition to the radiology department provides information about the patient's problems which is vital for the kind of description that is made. After that, a dialogue takes place between the radiologist's use of declarative knowledge about anatomy and pathology and the specific X-ray, and sometimes colleagues are involved in this process. The radiologist also expects to receive information about results from other examinations if relevant. In the meetings with doctors outside the radiology department, a third dialogue takes place about the patterns on the X-ray made visibly relevant by the description. In this meeting questions may be raised which sometimes constitute problems for the radiologist and sometimes lead to new understandings of the X-ray.

For the radiologist the X-ray is made practically useful when it is described and can be presented to an audience. However, the radiologist's function does not stop with the X-ray description. S/he also has to demonstrate the X-ray to other doctors. The description of an X-ray requires verbal and non-verbal expressions, and these expressions require some kind of response to provide the presentation with meaning. So an interaction takes place between an institutionally appointed expert and an audience with mixed and different professional qualifications and approaches to the X-rays. The aim of the radiologist's presentation is to make the audience share his or her vision, to make the other doctors see and accept what the radiologist considers relevant and important and to ignore the rest. This is attempted partly by the radiologist's use of the X-ray to document the validity or plausibility of his or her own description, while the formulated description makes the X-ray into a valid documentation of biological conditions. This is similar to a basic principle of common-sense thinking termed 'the documentary method of interpretation' by Harold Garfinkel (1967). Used in relation to representations, the documentary method of interpretation helps reproduce the medical order as transparently representative of the bodily order.

Institutionally, the radiological description represented the expert's voice. Doctors I talked to emphasized that it was important that a radiologist present the X-ray descriptions. But a significant issue was also who participated in the conference and could respond to the radiological presentation. Doctors in the audience would make comments on the X-rays presented and the radiological descriptions; they asked questions and sometimes they even challenged the radiologist. They might disagree with the description or criticize the presentation for not detailing the description well enough. In such meetings between medical experts, ceremonial rules of ordinary deference and demeanour were not always at work; personally and professionally this might be experienced as face threatening by participants (Måseide, 2003).

On one occasion the radiologist who demonstrated CT pictures of a lung tumour informed the meeting that, according to the radiological description, enlarged lymph glands were spotted in the lungs. This was significant information, because if a lung cancer is to be treated by surgery, there must be no sign of expansion of the disease. Enlarged lymph glands in the lungs or the mediastinum indicate that the disease has spread. To make the X-ray into useful evidence for a decision for or against surgery in this case, the radiologist had to make the enlarged lymphatic glands described visible to the audience. The radiologist who presented the pictures was not the same radiologist who had described them in the accompanying report. The former examined the pictures carefully but could not find enlarged glands. This raised the problem of what kind of validity the visually unverified but institutionally authorized description could have. Should the participants rely more on the authority of a professional expert's statements than on what appeared visible to the presenting radiologist? A surgeon asked who had written the report and was told by the radiologist that it was made by an experienced colleague. The surgeon then asked if this colleague was more or less experienced than the radiologist who presented the pictures. By this approach, a context for problem solving, more practical than institutional, was formulated. The radiologist answered that the writer was a senior radiologist and locally recognized for his professional skills. This referral to professionals with local prestige and authority, what Cook-Gumperz and Messerman (1999) have called 'local identities', invested the description with more authority.

The fact that the radiological evidence could not be observed by the team of problem solvers, however, broke with a major principle of clinical medicine: the authority of the doctor's own perception (Freidson, 1970). The meaning of this principle has of course changed within the practice of hospital medicine; many doctors work with signs from patients they have never seen and will never see. But here the principle of authoritative knowing transfers from seeing patients' bodies to interpreting others' statements about those bodies. After some discussion it was decided to ask if it was possible to have another expert description from the radiology department. Later one of the consultants said that, if the present description was verified by a new radiological description, it would be accepted. A proposition about visual evidence would then be accepted on the basis of an institutionally authorized description, even if it was not observed in other settings by other observers.

As the above account suggests, to reach a shared agreement about what is seen on an X-ray picture and its clinical consequences is often the result of micro-political processes. One of the consultants once emphasized the value of such conferences as the thoracic meeting. The different participants had different qualifications and no single doctor had all the total competence needed to find adequate and acceptable solutions to the most common problems. It was important, he said, to be corrected by others and hear the voices of different perspectives and opinions. This was also the case with regard to the practice of providing practical meanings for X-rays.

The process of generating radiological images[1]

Our account thus far confirms that 'radiological vision' is a version of what Goodwin (1994) termed 'professional vision'. In ward conferences it is produced by the radiologist's combination of talk and pointing when presenting X-rays. Paul Atkinson (1995) has argued in favour of regarding talk as a means to engendering medical vision. The discourse of X-ray watching consists of a mixture of pointing, professional terminology and ordinary language. In this way, radiological discourse makes a distinction between what should be seen and what should be ignored in an X-ray. Hence, radiological discourse conducts what Goodwin (1994) called 'highlighting' and makes radiological objects visible for the audience.

Extract 1

1. Radiologist: (uses a pen to point to and mark the form of the
2. figures he wants to show on the X-ray) Yes well (.) first we look
3. at the coronary side (.) that it is located on the side of uh (. . .)
4. hmm hmm (inaudible) an (.) extended uh like in clavicular direction
5. a uh tumor (a 'yes' from the audience). Can see it there. And
6. (.) on the picture right in front (.) we see that it lies in toward (inaudible)
7. and on the picture right behind (.) we can see that it gives a bit
8. impression in vena cava superior (. . .) Then a film was taken that I will
9. show to you finally.

In extract 1 the radiologist starts the process by presenting several X-rays that show a radiological density from different directions. He verbally describes the location of what may be a tumour as he simultaneously moves a pointer to show the form and direction of it. This is verbal and interactive visualization, and an image gradually emerges as the talking, pointing and seeing unfold. The radiologist uses the plural pronoun 'we' when referring to radiological perception. In this setting the plural pronoun has a double meaning. On one hand, it refers to the institutionally authorized radiological vision, which is a collective phenomenon. On the other hand, 'we' is used to include the audience in the radiologist's perceptive acts and to formulate a collective vision. The authorized and the collective vision become one. At this stage the audience gives no other verbal response than the 'yes' in line 5. But the lack of verbal response is significant and backchannels a collective acceptance of the radiologist's presentation. The radiologist's seeking for something that emerges through seeing and pointing in lines 3–4 indicates that his performance takes its lead from the verbally realized regime of framing radiological meaning. It is important to him to show the audience that the tumour does not grow into vena cava superior. This part of the presentation not only establishes the location of a tumour within recognized anatomical structures; it is also an implicit but significant message to the surgeons that this tumour may be operable.

In extract 2 the radiologist makes further comments about the X-rays before showing an MR film.

Extract 2

10. Radiologist: The film I will show you in (inaudible) here where one then can see
11. (..) uh (. . . . .) uh the tumor yes (..) vena cava superior at the back (.) and uh
12. the tumor here in front and this here I think has to be right (. . .) down toward
13. right atrium then (.) and (inaudible) partly toward (inaudible) but mostly
14. right atrium (inaudible) and uh (..) it lies toward frontal thoracic wall uh so
15. he has taken the usual (inaudible) which also show how this here lies
16. toward (..) uh frontal thoracic wall without affection from it (.) one senses
17. a small clearing stripe of (air) there and that may well be (.) caused by a
18. bit fat tissue I presume (. . .) uh now there is no capsule that I can see and
19. I cannot see any sign of capsule (. . . .) (inaudible) down down toward (. . .)
20. this here I think must be (inaudible) level then it is visible that pericardium
21. is marked because there is a clear black line there (.) which then uh shows
22. that the tumor is disconnected actually (pause). These pictures did not give
23. any particular information about density and uh (inaudible) (.) but it
24. shows I think (inaudible) that this here might be the tumor.

This continuing monologue develops further evidence for the localization of the tumour. By mentioning the anatomical structures while he points to them, the radiologist creates a visual object on the X-ray and an anatomically located image grounded in the professional practitioners' stock medical knowledge. Many participants make small sketches of the lungs on their pads where they locate the tumour according to the radiologist's presentation. In this way the information is distributed and stored in their memory and rendered portable from the conference as a fact for further activities. The presentation also prepares and guides the audience for viewing the magnetic-resonance imaging (MRI) film that the radiologist will get to next. A major point of the radiologist's talk is that the tumour he makes visible has no contact with the thoracic wall, even if it is close. In lines 22–24 the radiologist mentions some flaws in the X-ray, but he concludes that in his opinion what he has demonstrated is the tumour they expect to find in one of the patient's lungs. He even refers to what he makes visible as 'the tumor'. Then the MRI film is shown without much accompanying talk (extract 3).

Extract 3

25. Radiologist: Yes it shows the same then you see that (.) vena cava (.) superior
26. looks as if it moves in relation to the tumor which is fixed toward frontal
27. thoracic wall. And it is here we see then that (..) it looks nice you know (.)
28. I don't know the value of something like this pre-surgically I really don't
29. (. . . .) it might have no value at all.

While the film is shown, the radiologist's talk is visibly directed to the surgeons. The film is used to confirm what the radiologist has already has said about the tumour. A strong case of medical evidence is thus built up by the use of different X-rays, by the use of a radiological description, by showing a film, by verbally establishing a system of anatomical reference, and by visualizing a lung tumour through talk and pointing. Collectively, this can be said to constitute distributed perception.

At the end of extract 3, the radiologist states that he is not saying anything about the practical consequences of the X-rays and the MRI film. After the film, the surgeon asks for more precise information about the location of the tumour (extract 4).

Extract 4

32. Radiologist: Yes (.) it lies (..) in the rear and to the right=yes lies like
33. at the rim of right (name of anatomical structure). We can actually see
34. that better on the CT pictures (..) because (inaudible because of several
35. and simultaneous voices)

36. Surgeon: Could it possibly be something else than cancer?
37. Chief physician: Could it be a (thyerogen) Ole?
38. Radiologist: I have to think about that (pause). No.

The questions of location and what kind of phenomenon is observed on the X-ray require several turns of talk and involve several speakers. At this stage, the surgeon and the chief physician take part in this dialogic process. After the radiologist's attempt to make the location visible in more precise terms, the surgeon asks if this might be something other than cancer and the chief physician follows up by asking if this might be a rare kind of tumour. After a pause, the radiologist dismisses both suggestions. Implicitly it is thus concluded that from a radiological point of view the image made visible on the X-ray represents a malign lung tumour.

Radiological vision as socially distributed activity

The purpose of the detailed presentations of X-rays in the thoracic meeting or other ward conferences is to establish a shared medical vision of the X-ray. Treatment conferences attended by medical specialists from diverse organizational units constitute interfaces between different 'communities of practice', to borrow a term from Lave and Wenger (1991). When a radiological vision of the X-ray is accepted by the group of collaborating practitioners, the X-ray becomes an object with power to guide and apply force on the problem-solving process.

In many cases a detailed radiological description is not enough. As suggested above, the description often requires an exchange of talk between different participants before it is accepted. Extract 5 refers to a radiological presentation of a suspected tumour discovered in the patient's mediastinum.

Extract 5

1. Resident physician: He has normal bronchoscopy and no lung symptoms
2. (.) no common symptoms (pause) And normal pulmonary function.
3. Chief physician: Yes maybe we should have a look at the CT pictures
4. Radiologist: Yes (finds the pictures and put the first on the overhead.

5. He points to where the tumor is located) Also swelling at aorta pulmonal
6. window over against (inaudible)
7. Surgeon: That white there?
8. Radiologist: That white there (.) well that (.) it is (.) it is uh vena cava superior
9. Surgeon: Okay
10. Radiologist: And then it is aorta which (stretches) out there
11. Surgeon: Yes
12. Radiologist: That swelling there
13. Surgeon: Mmm. What does the next picture show down there?
14. Radiologist: Next picture shows (says something about carina)
15. Surgeon: (Asks about something he perceives in mediastinum)
16. Radiologist: Yes (.) in front of uh (.) in front of carina (..) and (inaudible)
17. Surgeon: (Asks if the localization in relation to aorta is as he sees it)
18. Radiologist: Yes
19. Surgeon: So it is far up?
20. Resident physician (also asks about the localization)
21. Radiologist: Yes it is above carina
22. Resident physician: Yes (.) so it lies (.) it lies approximately at carina?
23. Surgeon: Yes and what is this?
24. Resident physician: I don't know (. . .). It is a man (.) without lung symptoms
25. (.) accidentally discovered in a check up because of a (..) general dermatitis
26. Surgeon: There isn't a tumor other places then?
27. Resident physician: Nothing is found. There is nothing in the prostate gland
28. (.) nothing in testes (inaudible). What we want to know is if this is indication
29. for mediastinoscopy.

When the resident physician ends the final part of his case presentation (lines 1–2), the chief physician asks for the CT pictures to be presented. The radiologist takes over and starts pointing to where the suspected tumour is located. He also mentions a swelling near the aorta pulmonal window. As he ends his description, the surgeon asks about a white shadow that is visible on the picture (line 7). He is informed that this is normal anatomical structure. As the surgeon responds with short comments to signify acceptance or understanding, the radiologist goes further in engendering the radiological vision. Lines 13–19 constitute a short verbal exchange sequence that is vital for the establishment of a vision shared by the radiologist and the surgeon; in this sequence the radiologist's description is led by the surgeon's questions. In line 20 the resident joins the sequence with another question about location. He gets a positive answer and asks for more precise information (line 22). However, it is the surgeon who takes the floor (line 23), turns to the resident and asks about what kind of medical problem this is. To make a surgical evaluation of the CT pictures possible, the problem needs to be more clearly framed. The surgeon's question refers directly to the radiological image presented. But the X-ray is transformed into something different from the representation by the resident's answer (lines 24–25). With his answer, they encounter a patient as well as a medical problem. The problem at hand is expanded beyond the original representation and the radiological description. The surgeon now wants to know what kind of problem this is and if tumours are found in other places in the patient's body. This leads to the final lines (27–29), which indicate further proceedings. The resident informs participants that they need the surgeon's help to determine if this is a case for mediastinoscopy, a surgical examination of the patient's mediastinum.

In effect, the exchange sequence captured in extract 5 can be regarded as embodying an activity system. It includes a resident physician, a chief physician, a radiologist, a surgeon, and representations or signs in the form of CT pictures, talk and pointing. This distributed process produces a shared, co-negotiated radiological vision of what the X-ray shows, and it makes the radiological information relevant from a surgical point of view.

Initially, the X-rays are different for different participants. To the doctors from the thoracic ward, the CT pictures referred to above may represent a kind of enigma, a question about what they can see on the X-ray that demands an answer. To the radiologist, the challenge is to give an accurate and convincing description. The surgeon wants to know the purpose of the X-ray and to see if surgery makes practical sense according to the X-ray. The surgeon has a more practical approach than the radiologist and the thoracic specialists. In the thoracic meeting the X-rays have these different meanings. Part of the collaborative problem-solving process is to turn the X-ray into an object with an agreed or settled visual meaning, made relevant and acceptable for medical purposes interventions.

X-ray presentations and the interaction order

X-ray descriptions are usually part of the case constructions in ward conferences, and the doctor who presents the case usually knows the radiological description. However, in the thoracic meeting the X-ray is normally presented by a radiologist. The exchange of talk between various participants that usually follows is to some extent regulated by the doctor who presents the case or the chief physician who chairs the conference. But to a large extent the discursive process develops without much top-down regulation. Each verbal move responds to a previous move and opens up for or lays restrictions on the next move. To draw on an insight developed by Duranti (1997), the distributed process in which the X-ray takes place consists of utterances or other expressive moves produced by different participants 'who are attuned to when to speak and about what and careful at fitting what they will say with what has just been said'. This discursive process has an emergent character. In extract 6, the doctor who presents the case starts talking about radiological data. This verbal move is recipient-designed and implicitly addresses the radiologist, who is thus invited to take the floor. Much of the distribution of this medical talk takes place effortlessly. In this sequence of talk the chief physician also participates by responding to the consultant's referral to what is seen on pictures from computer tomography.

Extract 6

1. Consultant: He has normal bronchoscopy (.) uh has normal
2. spirometry (. . . .) but on CT we again find this (inaudible) find
3. something else that has uh (..)
4. Chief physician: Yes
5. Consultant: We put a small question mark if it is only this or
6. if it is something more
7. Radiologist: (puts the CT pictures on the overhead) It is correct
8. that something more is seen (inaudible). Then he has a process
9. in his liver and both ultra sound and uh and CT (.) it is completely
10. consistent with (inaudible)

In extract 6 the radiologist takes the floor after the consultant first mentions what is seen on the CT pictures and asks if there is more to be seen on the screen. Then the radiologist takes over. This effortless integration of adequate talk from different agents without naming the next speaker is quite common when medical cases are presented and discussed. Successful exchange demonstrates that the participants take part and are involved in a common activity. Since the radiologist is normally not explicitly asked to take the floor, he or she has to be attuned to the talk of the case presentation to make adequate moves. In this case the radiologist confirms the message stated by the consultant and makes it conform to the radiological description. This short sequence also represents a small activity system at work. It creates a collective understanding of the problem at hand, it connects the radiological description with other forms of medical information about the case to form a consistent picture of the problem, and it indicates a form of social solidarity, which is necessary for the collaborative problem-solving system to work effortlessly.

There is also a ritual element to this kind of work. As the doctor who presents the case is informed about the radiological description, he or she might present the description on his or her own. On one occasion, the resident started to refer to the radiological description. The chief physician quickly interrupted and said, 'we will leave that to the radiologist'. A radiological description 'belongs' to the radiologist and the radiology department in such situations. It is important to show necessary deference and demeanour, to use Goffman's (1956) terms, acknowledging the roles and rights of the participants in the problem-solving system who represent other specialties and other parts of the medical organization, in order to make the problem-solving system work.

The presentation of X-rays is a performance with other professionals as audience and this audience affects how the presentation is performed. The radiological performance might include elements of what have been referred to as the 'poetic functions of speech' (Burke, 1973; Jakobson, 1960). These elements are expressive forms that communicate more than the propositional content and guide the generation of a shared radiological vision. In extract 7 the radiologist presents a radiological picture showing lung tumours.

Extract 7

1. Radiologist: There are of course glandular tumors in hilii (.) at both sides
2. (.) uh (.) and (.) in addition (.) considerable lymphatic tumor <u>under</u> (.) uh
3. under carina (.) with bulging at the rear and medial (inaudible) to main

4. bronchus (while talking the radiologist points to what he mentions) and
5. also (.) large (.) lymphatic glands centrally in mediastinum (.) between
6. trachea and uh vena cava superior (.) and similarly (inaudible) for the
7. aorta pulmonal window. Uh (.) it is one uh (.) yes in the lung tissue (.)
8. so it is (takes the picture up from the overhead and looks at it against
9. the light) it was completely normal conditions (.) it is no more (..) here
10. are several drawings but they are quite normal (these are bold vessel
11. drawings). Uh so it might be (inaudible) lung (inaudible) tumor (.) and
12. uh (.) like radiologically it might of course be sarcoidosis then (.) but
13. we cannot rule out that it may be a lymphoma of course. But it should
14. be even more cavernous.

The processual and emergent character of the presentation is indicated by the many pauses, hesitations and the picking up of CT pictures for closer examination (extract 7). The presentation is what Hymes (1981) called 'situationally creative': it follows the script of the radiological description, but it is situationally realized. The presentation is achieved by the radiologist at a specific time, in a specific site, which includes a specific audience, and it applies a pre-established script to a specific X-ray. For the presentation the radiologist uses convincing terms like 'of course' (lines 2 and 12); he uses qualifiers like 'considerable', 'completely', 'quite' (lines 2, 9 and 10); he emphasizes words (lines 2 and 5); he uses the pointer to underscore his talk; and he holds up the CT picture and looks at it against the light source from the overhead equipment. This close examination is a visible act integrated into the presentation. It also makes the radiologist visible, not as a ventriloquist for the radiology department, but as a professionally competent and active participant in the creation of radiological vision. Together this constitutes a system of signs for the situation that occur in addition to the verbal propositions. This implies that, as medical discourse, radiological presentations often include poetic elements. Poetic elements of the radiological presentation may also be used for role distancing and other identity work.

The radiological description is the script that directs the radiological presentation. The notion of 'radiological description' indicates an objective and professional product. It is an institutional product of the X-ray department delivered in an objectivist speech genre. This objectivist genre is another version of the poetics of radiological discourse. That is, as a text it is formulated in a style that has a performative function. The following written description of an X-ray from the X-ray department is an example:

> In mid field of right lung is seen a one centimeter large obscurely bounded density. It is difficult to find again in lateral plane, but it can be located completely in front. Supplementing examinations with diagonal pictures and transillumination have to be conducted in order to . . .

This verbal quote refers to the authorized, unhesitating and convincing voice of the radiology department. This ritualized, formalized and performative style belongs to the medical institution; it represents an instrument of power and may oblige the participants to follow established paths. In collaborative medicine, however, such forces may be challenged or rejected through various micro-political processes on the practical clinical level. And as seen, collaborative medical problem solving in hospitals mobilizes different kinds of tactics and strategies.

The practical use of X-rays

A middle-aged male patient had been diagnosed with an inoperable lung cancer and was treated with cell cures. The patient was presented at one of the thoracic meetings after he had finished two cures. The question was whether a third cure should be started. The discomforts from the first two cures had been minimal and the patient was reported to be prepared for a third. The resident started by attaching to a light box the first X-ray taken before the first cell cure. He then demonstrated multiple abnormal and clearly visible spots and shades located on the images of both lungs. After that, the X-ray taken after the first cure was compared with the first. On the second X-ray the spots were almost gone and the shades had become distinctly thinner. The visual difference between the first two X-rays was declared to show significant improvement. The second X-ray was then compared with the most recent one. Once the third X-ray was attached to the light box a consultant declared that in his opinion the shades looked even thinner on the last X-ray. A significant visual difference was thus formulated. Some other doctors remarked that they could not see any difference. They exchanged opinions about this for a while. When the exchange paused, one of the most experienced consultants said in a low voice that in his opinion the latest X-ray was a unanimous indication for a third cure. By this assertion he too formulated a visual difference between the images of two X-rays. The chief physician was ambivalent and said he was not sure if the new X-ray really could count as an indicator of improvement. Immediately, another consultant declared in a firm voice that in his opinion the latest X-ray should pass as evidence of remission. No opposition to this statement was verbalized and the chief physician contributed by adding that this was also a patient who wanted to fight: 'He is a robust person' the chief physician concluded.

So far the validity of the radiological evidence presented was established not so much on the basis of visual scrutiny as on talk. A collaborative process developed a collective vision of radiological evidence and the process unfolded through discourse. The doctors from the unit to which the patient belonged were sympathetic to him and wanted to give him whatever chances there might be. Prolonged chemotherapy was the only hope they could offer, and they obviously wanted to offer something, especially since the patient was assigned good moral qualities. The assignment of moral qualities in patients is a common exercise in collaborative medical problem solving (Måseide, 2003). But they needed radiological evidence to produce an institutionally legitimate account of their decision about a third cell cure. Visual radiological evidence had to be discursively transformed to conform not only to a medical order, but also to a moral order. However, the talk about the case continued. When a shared understanding of the radiological evidence had been reached, a resident informed the meeting that a 'suspect change' in the patient's left hip had just been found. This new information might have changed the established professional vision of the X-rays. The thin shades, still to be seen, which now served as evidence for remission, might by the remark about the ultrasound examination be transformed into indicators of a disease that has spread even to the patient's skeleton. Under such circumstances a new cell cure would be out of the question. A short but inconclusive discussion followed about whether the 'change in the hip' might be metastases. But then the chief physician closed the case with the following comment about the new information: '*We will say that it has not progressed.*' By this statement he made the information about new visual evidence irrelevant for the moment.

In a situation of uncertainty, a problem was thus discursively generated that conformed to what became the preferred medical and moral solution. In this process the voices of local clinical authorities were privileged, and they were made institutionally accountable.

An epilogue on organization

Ward conferences may count as what Levinson (1979) called 'speech activities'. As problem-solving systems, they are totally dependent on talk and conversation. The participants in these activities take part through sets of diverse participation statuses. This also means that as medical problem solvers, they participate in different kinds of discursive 'games', albeit games with life and death effects. An important insight from the analyses above is that significant parts of collaborative medical problem solving in hospitals are discursively organized to deal with signs and sign systems. Moreover, these signs and sign systems become participants in, and resources for, the doctors' problem-solving processes. This analysis of the doctors' activity systems highlights their collaborative unfolding and provides insight into the organization of medical work in hospitals.

Collaborative medical problem solving refers on one hand to processes that may be distributed over relatively long periods of time and between different expert organizations and spatial locations. On the other hand, while still socially distributed, collaborative medicine is also situational; an example is ward conferences. They have many of the characteristics of face-to-face interaction or social encounters: they are to a large extent regulated by an interaction order and they are oriented to, and regulated by, signs and sign systems. Even if these conferences follow an institutional schedule, they have an emergent character and are constituted by an overlapping chain of more or less self-organized and unfolding activity systems with diverse and changing participants. These activity systems produce appropriate medical cases, generate shared radiological visions and determine their application as evidence in decision-making.

By restricting the distributed perspective to local activity systems, attention focuses on fundamental organizational aspects of collaborative problem solving in hospital medicine. The activity systems, with their emergent character, are discursively constituted and regulated. Even if such activity systems are institutionally and professionally directed, the specifics and concreteness of problem-solving work mean that these activity systems are regularly invaded by discursive forms and social and moral considerations or practices from the life world. In this sense the work of medical problem solving is situationally organized from the bottom up. Since the professional and institutional principles and demands of medical practice also have a symbolic character similar to medical signs and sign systems, they do not in principle change the bottom-up character of how collaborative problem solving is organized. They become integrated in the activity systems at the level of collaborative clinical practice. As such it is at the local level that they have to be made useful, relevant or irrelevant for the management of the problem at hand. In many cases medical and professional discourses are used to transfer social and moral principles from the life world into the practical context of medical problem solving to replace professional and institutional principles and to make medical solutions institutionally accountable.

Note

1 Transcription conventions: (.) short pause; (..) each additional dot indicates a longer pause; (pause) long pause.

References

Atkinson, P. (1995) *Medical Talk and Medical Work* (London: Sage).

Atkinson, P. (1997) *The Clinical Experience: the Construction and Reconstruction of Medical Reality* (2nd edn) (Aldershot: Ashgate).

Berg, M. (1992) 'The Construction of Medical Disposals: Medical Sociology and Medical Problem Solving in Clinical Practice', *Sociology of Health and Illness*, 14, pp. 151–80.

Berg, M. (1995) *Rationalizing Medical Work* (Cambridge, Mass.: The MIT Press).

Burke, K. (1973) *The Philosophy of Literary Form: Studies in Symbolic Action* (Berkeley: University of California Press).

Cicourel, A. V. (1990) 'The Integration of Distributed Knowledge in Collaborative Medical Diagnosis', in J. Galegher, R.E. Kraut and C. Egido (eds) *Intellectual Teamwork: Sociological and Technological Foundations of Cooperative Work*, pp. 221–42 (Erlbaum, NJ: Hillsdale).

Cook-Gumperz, J. and Messerman, L. (1999) 'Local Identities and Institutional Practice: Constructing the Record of Professional Collaboration', in S. Sarangi and C. Roberts (eds) *Talk, Work and Institutional Order*, pp. 145–81 (Berlin: Mouton de Gruyter).

Duranti, A. (1997) *Linguistic Anthropology* (Cambridge: Cambridge University Press).

Engeström, Y., Engeström, R. and Kerosuo, H. (2003) 'The Discursive Construction of Collaborative Care', *Applied Linguistics*, 24, pp. 286–315.

Freidson, E. (1970) *Profession of Medicine* (New York: Harper and Row).

Garfinkel, H. (1967) *Studies in Ethnomethodology* (Englewood Cliffs, NJ: Prentice-Hall).
Goffman, E. (1956) 'The Nature of Deference and Demeanor', *American Anthropologist*, 58, pp. 473–502.
Goffman, E. (1961) *Encounters: Two Studies in the Sociology of Interaction* (New York: Bobbs-Merrill).
Goffman, E. (1983) 'The Interaction Order', *American Sociological Review*, 48, pp. 1–17.
Goodwin, C. (1994) 'Professional Vision', *American Anthropologist*, 96, pp. 606–33.
Gray, A. and Harrison, S. (eds) (2004) *Governing Medicine: Theory and Practice* (Maidenhead: Open University Press).
Hacking, I. (1992) 'The Self-vindication of the Laboratory Sciences', in A. Pickering (ed.) *Science as Practice and Culture*, pp. 29–64 (Chicago: The University of Chicago Press).
Hutchins, E. (1995) *Cognition in the Wild* (Cambridge, Mass.: The MIT Press).
Hymes, D. (1981) *'In Vain I Tried to Tell You': Essays in Native American Ethnopoetics* (Philadelphia: University of Pennsylvania Press).
Jakobson, R. (1960) 'Closing Statement: Linguistics and Poetics', in T. Sebeok (ed.) *Style in Language*, pp. 350–77 (Cambridge, Mass.: The MIT Press).
Knorr Cetina, K. (1992) 'The Couch, the Cathedral, and the Laboratory: On the Relationship between Experiment and Laboratory in Science', in A. Pickering (ed.) *Science as Practice and Culture*, pp. 113–38 (Chicago: The University of Chicago Press).
Knorr Cetina, K. (1999) *Epistemic Cultures. How the Sciences Make Knowledge* (Cambridge, Mass.: Harvard University Press).
Latour, B. (1986) 'Visualization and Cognition: Thinking with Eyes and Hands', *Knowledge and Society*, 6, pp. 1–40.
Lave, J. and Wenger, E. (1991) *Situated Learning: Legitimate Peripheral Participation* (Cambridge: Cambridge University Press).
Levinson, S. C. (1979) 'Activity Types and Language', *Linguistics*, 17, pp. 356–99.
Måseide, P. (2003) 'Medical Talk and Moral Order: Social Interaction and Collaborative Clinical Work', *TEXT*, 23, pp. 369–403.
Mishler, E. G. (1984) *The Discourse of Medicine: Dialectics of Medical Interviews* (Norwood, NJ: Ablex).
Mol, A. (2002) *The Body Multiple: Ontology in Medical Practice* (Durham: Duke University Press).
Resnick, M. (1994) *Turtles, Termites, and Traffic Jams* (Cambridge, Mass.: The MIT Press).
Schatzki, T. R. (2002) *The Site of the Social* (University Park, Pa: The Pennsylvania State University Press).
Suchman, L. (1987) *Plans and Situated Actions* (Cambridge: Cambridge University Press).
Timmermans, S. and Berg, M. (2003) *The Gold Standard: the Challenge of Evidence Based Medicine and Standardization in Health Care* (Philadelphia: Temple University Press).

11

Why Do Doctors Not Engage with the System?

Christine Jorm, Jo Travaglia and Rick Iedema

Introduction

In the last decade, determination of the extent of medical errors in health care systems (Baker and Norton, 2004; Brennan *et al.*, 1991; Davis *et al.*, 2002; Eysenbach *et al.*, 1999; Institute of Medicine, 2000; Wilson *et al.*, 1995), coupled with public inquiries into major breaches of patient safety (Department of Health, 2001; Douglas *et al.*, 2001; Health Services Commissioner, 2002; Redfern *et al.*, 2001; Sinclair, 1994) and active media interest (Anonymous, 2000; Cowan *et al.*, 2002; Swan, 1997) has led to a worldwide patient safety movement (Secretariat, WHO, 2002). One of the basic tenets of this movement is the premise that in order to address the problem of medical errors, attention should be focused on diagnosing weaknesses in, and building improvements to, the current health care system (Amalberti *et al.*, 2005; Leape and Berwick, 2005; Reason, 2000).

Accordingly, Leape argues that 'human beings make mistakes because the systems, tasks and processes they work in are poorly designed' (Department of Health and Design Council, 2003, p. 3). The location of causal factors within the system, or structure, and outside of the individual agency is further reflected in statements on adverse events. An example from a National Health Service (NHS) manual reads: 'The root cause of this turn of events, and of the majority of mistakes taking place in medical environments is the system itself – a system whose flaws eventually lead to what is called a "human error"' (Department of Health and Design Council, 2003, p. 17). The most influential report on patient safety, *To Err is Human,* has as subtitle 'Building a safer health system'. It is this report which has represented a strong force towards getting clinicians, managers and policy makers to accept the importance of a 'no-blame' approach to patient safety (Institute of Medicine, 2000): when things go wrong, we should not in the first instance target individuals, but the systems within which they work. Frequently, in this work the system is described as 'highly pressured', 'flawed', 'complex', and system redesign is advocated to 'provide the basis for designing flaws out of the system before they result in such needless tragedies' (Department of Health and Design Council, 2003, p. 17). In this literature, 'the system' is construed as central to the most 'wicked' problems affecting health care (van Bueren *et al.*, 2003).

Physicians are being called on to contribute to fixing 'the system' in two major ways: as part of voluntary teams, which use a variety of methods to identify the causes of particular incidents (Bagian *et al.*, 2002; Iedema *et al.*, 2006; Wald and Shojania, 2001), and as leaders and participants in quality and safety improvement strategies designed to redress these factors (Gollop *et al.*, 2004; Ham, 2003). Yet the literature shows that many physicians resist engaging in such strategies, even while they espouse a clear commitment to providing the best care for their patients (Cornbleet *et al.*, 2002; Shekelle, 2002). Difficulty in gaining physician engagement is frequently identified as a factor in the failure of quality improvement initiatives as a whole (Brennan, 2002; Classen and Kilbridge, 2002; Goode *et al.*, 2002; Gustafson *et al.*, 2003; Ham *et al.*, 2003; Irvine Doran *et al.*, 2002; Jorm and Kam, 2004; Kizer, 2001; Locock, 2003; McLoughlin and Smallwood, 2002; Shekelle, 2002; Wiener, 2000). There is therefore a tension between the role and positioning of individuals and the focus on the overall system for work process improvement.

In this chapter discourse analysis is used to explore physicians' statements about 'the system' that delivers health care. In particular we are concerned with how physicians position themselves in relation to 'the system', their attribution of causes for the current design or function of the system and the degree of objectification they use to determine their engagement with the system. Our analysis seeks to clarify, then, how 'the system' is conceptualized in doctors' talk, and how and why their engagement with 'the system' is an issue. To this end, the chapter is structured as follows. First we provide some background on the use of the term 'health care system'. We then turn to describing our method and presenting our data. In our discussion we step back from this empirical detail to reflect on the implications of how doctors position themselves discursively in talk for the success of the clinical safety and quality agenda.

The 'health care system'

Contemporary health policy is increasingly concerned to engender awareness on the part of clinicians that they are not isolated operators, but that they are enmeshed in a complex health care system comprised of interrelated teams, services, practices and processes (Plsek, 2001). The term 'system' is used in policy documentation to reference a variety of facets of health services organization: the logic of work practices, the cooperative orientation of cross-disciplinary relationships, the interdependence of many health services and their 'products', and the centrality to clinical quality and safety of the organizational management of clinical work. For clinicians who have been trained into individualizing modes of working (Degeling *et al.*, 2003), these notions are rather alien. This is producing a tension with the concerns of policy makers who are increasingly feeling the heat of rising public concern about the apparently low standards of safety and quality in our health services (Brennan *et al.*, 1991; Wilson *et al.*, 1995). With regard to addressing those concerns, the term 'system' is becoming central to constructions of clinical work organization, practice improvement and hospital reform (Kohn *et al.*, 1999). Without attention to the 'system' within which the clinician works, it is hard if not impossible to provide acceptable service in a publicly accountable way.

But 'system' plays an additional important role in health policy making. Besides using the term 'system' to draw clinicians' attention away from the specifics of clinical–scientific techniques and towards the nature of their collaborations with colleagues, policy makers also use 'system' to ameliorate concern on the part of clinicians about the increasing visibility of their own practices – whether as a result of clinical service outcomes data that are being published, clinical pathway information that is made available to clinicians and patients, personalized league tables that advertise comparative achievements among clinicians, or root cause analysis investigations that lay bare hospital-caused ('iatrogenic') injury, illness or death. The general ethos that underpins contemporary health policy is that only full visibility of all aspects of practice can lead to an adequately managed and constantly enhanced service and practice. By maintaining that this visibility remain framed within a systems perspective, policy makers in effect seek to obviate clinicians having to fear or experience personalized blame (Runciman *et al.*, 2003).

These two ways in which 'the system' suits the health policy reform agenda notwithstanding, the term is of course far from unproblematic.

A deconstruction of how the term 'system' was used to refer to organizations was published some decades ago by David Silverman (1968). In a seminal article, Silverman writes: 'The problems involved in viewing an organization as a system [are that] an organization is thought to have a goal which is something more than the sum of the goals of its members [and it] has certain "needs" which must be met... "to survive" ' (1968, p. 222). By attributing goals and needs to 'organization' in this way, Silverman argues, this discourse anthropomorphizes the organization: 'by treating the "goals" and "needs" of organizations as givens, it seems to us that we are attributing apparently human motivations to inanimate objects: in other words, we are reifying the organization' (Silverman, 1968, p. 223). For Silverman, 'reifying the organization' comes down to creating the illusion of a harmonious and unified workforce, rendering the discourse and actions of individuals invisible and unproblematic. But in fact, Silverman argues, 'our "system"... is only the present outcome of the ends sought by different groups and the actions which they have chosen to pursue in the light of the means available to them' (1968, p. 234).

While Silverman was concerned to question general use of the term 'system' to describe single organizations, our focus in this chapter is on a much larger entity: 'the health system', which includes health organizations, individual practitioners, the (health) bureaucracy and government, in addition to all the processes of care. Nevertheless, Silverman's deconstruction of the term 'system' is of interest to the concerns of the present chapter for two reasons. First, this deconstruction provides insight into one dimension of what health policy reform is concerned to achieve: a harmonious and well-oiled 'system' where clinicians happily cooperate and co-organize their practices and services. Second, Silverman's argument can now be deployed not just to understand contemporary policy making, but also to clarify how *doctors* position themselves in these discourses, whether and how they take them up, and what this means for their enactments of medical identity and clinical quality and safety. These latter issues are of importance, because doctors in particular are professionals for whom the systems concerns of policy makers tend to have been less prominent than their professional medical autonomy (Freidson, 1970), with important consequences for how doctors view the clinical quality and safety agenda and its exhortations to achieve lifelong learning, continuous improvement and accountable practice.

In what follows, we analyse interview data derived from in-depth discussions with medical doctors around questions of clinical quality and safety. We analyse these data with an eye to how the doctors position themselves in relation to 'the system'. Thus, our analysis is motivated by the following questions: do the doctors position themselves autonomously and as having no power to intervene in the system, or do they position themselves as capable agents who can intervene and help reshape the system?

An important reason for us to illuminate how doctors position themselves in relation to the health system is that 'professional reflexivity requires that practitioners begin listening more carefully to themselves, attending to their own rhetorics of persuasion . . . that is, listening with a critical ear to their own sense making and knowledge making practices' (Hall and White, 2005, p. 388). To achieve that reflexivity, the analysis presented here operates on the Meadean principle that '. . . the structural properties of mental organization of individual members of a society reflect the relational properties of social organization characteristic of the society within which that individual acquires its capacities for thought and action' (Mühlhäusler and Harre, 1990a, p. 90). Thus, a speaker often displays these relational properties in their talk, including those of moral responsibility and commitment (Mühlhäusler and Harre, 1990a). Our study pinpoints how doctors frame their moral commitment to improving health care, and challenges the common outcome of doctors' scientific training which is 'that people [they themselves included] have fixed attributes, beliefs and capacities which are somewhere inside . . . and [that these] can be identified in designated sites or methods' (Hall and White, 2005, p. 388, see also Taylor and White, 2000). Our study reveals doctors' positionings and identities as social constructions produced by 'people's on-going engagement with one another in talk, text and interaction' (Hall and White, 2005, p. 385).

Method and analysis

A major Sydney tertiary referral hospital was the site of fieldwork for a study on the interaction of specialty medical culture with patient safety and quality issues. It had been the workplace of the interviewer (the principal author) for 11 years as a senior doctor, the last two with cross-hospital organizational responsibilities. As part of the fieldwork, permission was sought for interview from a random sample of the 243 senior medical staff attached to the hospital. Of the 66 selected, eight were excluded due to peripheral association with the hospital (e.g. semi-retired), two were excluded due to participation in another section of the fieldwork, four were on prolonged leave and there were 11 refusals. The final data set consisted of 41 interviews. Specialties interviewed were: 15 physicians, 13 surgeons/obstetricians, 11 emergency physicians, intensivists or anaesthetists, and two psychiatrists.

A semi-structured interview design was used to elicit participants' viewpoints and feelings while allowing for the possibility of obtaining a range or set of comparable data with concrete statements being made by subjects about at least some issues (Flick, 2002, p. 93). The interview script contained 18 questions which were a combination of open, hypothesis-driven and confrontational design. The questions were designed to help 'describe and interpret the cultural behaviour of a group' (Cresswell, 1998, p. 95), and particularly physicians' behaviour towards patient safety and quality issues.

While it has been said that 'one-shot interviewing lends itself to a partial, sanitized view of experience, cleaned up for public discourse' (Charmaz, 2000, p. 525), here most interviews were in the context of the interviewer's (Jorm) sustained involvement with the research participants (only 6/41 were met for the first time at the interview). This interpersonal contact proved important to ensuring the open and honest nature of the interviews that were conducted, and allowed the interviewer to place responses in a rich context of shared knowledge. Full informed consent was obtained, and interviews were recorded then transcribed. Most (39) interviews took place in the subject's consulting rooms or hospital offices.

The interview data are derived from participants' answers to the following questions:

1 It has been said by others: 'I give good care, but the system often lets patients down.'
2 How do you feel about this? Is this true in your case?
3 Would you like to be more involved in improvements to the system?
4 What are the barriers to this?

Constructing the relationship between doctors and the system

Let us begin with exemplifying the main tensions that affect how doctors construct their role in relation to the organization and safety of patient care. In the following extract, a doctor articulates his ambivalent attitude towards the organizational context in which he is working. In this discourse, the doctor constructs clinicians initially as powerless, but then explains that there is no option but to go on attempting to improve the system (extract 1).

Extract 1

S11 I think that's true, I think there's only so much that you can do as an individual to ensure the care of the patient. I think every anaesthetist in particular could do more as an individual. Again it gets back to the idea of giving some sort of perfect sexy anaesthetic and then leaving the patient to the mercy of the system where you know junior people are left to look after them. You can't be here 24/7 looking after the patient. The system has to take care of them to some extent but you could do more and so I think that's partly true. There's a limit to what you can do as an individual and you have to rely on others in, in any system and the system does sometimes fail. Fail the patients particularly and it probably fails the professionals as well sometimes, and you know we just have to keep working to improve it.

In this extract, the slip from *I* to *you* to *we* is a shift 'along a gradient of self-involvement responsibility' (Mühlhäusler and Harre, 1990b, p. 200). The use of the word *individual,* reinforced by repetition, evokes a lack of agentive ability on the part of the single medical practitioner, while at the same time reinforcing their uniqueness. At the same time, the system moves through various embodiments in the subject's talk. First it is described as an identity with volition ('it takes care'), it then becomes the object and outcome of workers' agency ('you have to keep working'), and finally it is construed as a dynamic: 'you have to rely on others in any system and systems sometimes fail'. Within the space of a few sentences, the talk shifts across different constructions of the relationship between self and system, setting out a large spectrum of stances that also reappears in the rest of the interview data.

One important analytical strategy we adopt is to focus on doctors' construction of 'we' to understand whether they see themselves as being isolated from 'the system' or whether they see themselves as being an integral part of the system. Admittedly, the analysis of 'we' is complex (Mühlhäusler and Harre, 1990b). There are two common types of usage, one referencing 'the dyadic face-to-face group of intimates' and the other referencing 'larger social groups in absentia of the act of speaking' (Mühlhäusler and Harre, 1990b, p. 199). The way 'we' is mobilized in the talk of these doctors is significant for the following reason. In cases where 'we' references only individual doctors, an opposition is created between the autonomous professional and 'the system', justifying the doctor's disengagement from attempts to engage with questions of clinical quality and safety beyond their own narrow specialist domain. In other cases, 'we' is used to point to a more inclusive conceptualization. Here it can encompass doctors, nurses, other health care workers and even hospital managers and administrators and health bureaucrats. This construction, of course, points to the possibility of communicating with these other professionals about the nature of the work, and potentially addressing its shortcomings. In what follows we provide examples of a spectrum of different articulations. This prepares us for the subsequent discussion section, where we flesh out our argument that the degree of inclusiveness invested in the pronoun 'we' is inversely proportionate to the degree of reification of 'the system'.

Denying personal responsibility and medical–organizational agency

At one end of the spectrum, then, interviewees construe the system as so complex as to be not just outside the control of individual doctors, but also beyond the scope of their responsibility. In extract 2, for example, S37 explains that the system is not just 'a disaster' but also intimates that this system provides a brake on the good work done by local hospital administrators and doctors. For this interviewee, the system equates with a Department of Health that has little knowledge of local practice and yet makes decisions that affect people at the front line.

Extract 2

S37 Oh, I think the system is a disaster. I think it's got a public service mentality. A lot of people there work very hard but the system is, right from the top, right from the very top, the Department of Health, not from the very top . . . but there is a structure in there that's basically completely alienated from the local people. They don't seem to ever come out and know what is really going on at the local level. Therefore, the structures they set up and the demands they make on the local administration are often unrealistic and bound to fail . . . the local administrators . . . work quite hard . . .

In effect, this interviewee speaks about the system in two ways. Those at its head are seen as distant from the practitioners, lacking the volition or desire to engage in a process of persuasion or relationship. The method of management is structural, in other words regulatory.

The result is described graphically in the talk that follows on from the previous extract:

Extract 3

S37 . . . it's like having a football team, where nobody knows exactly who is in the team and what they're supposed to do. You can work hard every week, and get beaten 80–0 every week, and I think that is what sort of happens.

Another interviewee created a similar force field in her discourse. Her complaint about the system operates from the reference point of the patient, setting the system up again as unforgiving fact:

Extract 4

S10 People with mental illness have needs that go from education to housing to general health to family intervention . . . generally I think people work as hard as they can within the systems that are there for them.

For yet another interviewee, the dominant control mechanism is financial. In this response, the elderly are construed as the site of system problems, because they are a drain on its resources. Here, finance undergirds the speaker's conceptualization of the system:

Extract 5

S17 I would say that the system is trying to cope with a whole lot of people growing older and older . . . I think that's what we're really struggling with these old, old people. And I think that is where the system, these people cost a lot of money to look after and a lot of money to get home and maybe that's where the system is you know.

Another way in which the system is reified and put at a distance is by constructing it as an external, facilitative structure. In extract 6, the interviewee portrays his relationship with the system as one of basic, static support: 'the system is slipping out from under us'.

Extract 6

S5 I don't see we necessarily need improvements to the system, I see the system was fine before and it's slipping out from under us. You know what I mean . . . I'm here to provide a standard of care that we used to have . . . I think a lot of the camaraderie and colleagueship of the public hospital system is destroyed. We don't have a plastic surgery ward anymore . . . I introduce myself to the resident every week or 2nd week (laughing). That's if we have one. So you sort of feel the system is slipping out from under you and you don't feel... nurses are providing the same expert care... it goes back to the system which a standard of care which was fine previously and may not have been perfect but was certainly able to reliably and consistently produce what is perceived by most people as better outcomes: more reliably more constantly. So, I don't think we need improvements, I just think we need to stop the slide. Perhaps we need to go back up the slippery dip a bit.

Here too the doctor constructs the system as having it own momentum, leaving them with a complete lack of control; that is, an inability to exert agency against the force of the system. This view of the system as enabling background resource reappears in interviewee S19's response, who uses a story to illustrate a system problem:

Extract 7

S19 ... the other day I was in the operating theatre and thinking how silly it was that the phone was above where the sterile gowns and the scrub sister were. I just laughed at it. It's so stupid. If I go near the phone I might de-sterilize the gowns. And I thought we've been building modern hospitals for 40–50 years surely some one could have designed an operating theatre that was shaped the right shape, and the phone was in the right spot... every time we build an operating theatre we make it up and parts of it don't work. We shouldn't have different systems everywhere in all hospitals... So there should be some effort to try and do that, so a system that had all those things in it and then I would plug into it in the appropriate spots.

The system problem of course is not just the flawed theatre layout, but the lack of learning on the part of those considered responsible for the layout. To some extent, the speaker construes personal and professional involvement: *'we've been building hospitals, we just keep building them'* does concede a degree of responsibility for the system.

Some interviewees, such as S2 below, were clear that greater engagement by individual clinicians was essential, but still construed 'the system' as an independent and largely static entity (extract 8).

Extract 8

S2 It's okay. No it's not the system. It's the people. It's not the system. People blame the system but people they lose sight of the fact that they do not put in the work. That's the problem. People clock on and clock off and they . . . they don't come in and see sick patients and patients are sicker and sicker and sicker and it's the same system and . . . that despite a system that is terrible we should be able to rise above it but no one will rise above it because the ethos is that this is the way it's done. For an operating list you can't get a guy operated on because of the number admitted. It's all into minutes and stuff like that. I think that people just kind of disappear and night residents don't hand over and there are no rounds and stuff like that, I think that they need to have a good look at the way that they practice and I don't think it's fair to blame the system . . . it's still the individuals who should be able to rise above it so it's not really the system, I think individuals can do it.

The speaker appears confused about how to conceptualize his personal role in relation to 'the system'. He states *that despite a system that is terrible we should be able to rise above it but no one will rise above it*. The use of the word *we* here includes the speaker, but the phrase *no one* distances the speaker from the imperative to act. Again, in the sentence, *it's still the individuals who should be able to rise above it so it's not really the system I think individuals can do it*, a tension arises between the idea that individual clinicians can rise above the system and take charge of it, and the idea that very few individuals in fact do so. The upshot of this construal, we suggest, is that the interviewee positions the system as an ambiguous force: it is an immutable mass that is either in control of what individuals do, or it is entirely malleable.

This either/or construal of the power of the system to influence or be influenced reappears in a good number of interviews. In extract 9, a doctor describes their painfully evolved ability to manipulate the system.

Extract 9

S26 I've . . . figured ways of getting round the system now . . . like waiting lists . . . . I give the patients a date and then I know what's going on . . . if my list is cancelled I know exactly who is on that list and I decide where to put them. Similarly, every way in which I can see that the system is going to possibly fail, I just work my way round it.

I It must be exhausting?

S Yea, I mean it's, in a way you have to but otherwise it spoils your professional reputation. I am not prepared to say that I am not, I couldn't work out the system enough to protect my patients from it, I'm not prepared to say that. I won't do that, I've worked a way round a lot of the things that have holes in the floor that people sort of slip through and I just plug them up.

In the subsection that follows, we consider responses that were more ambivalent about the status of the system, and less categorical about the nature of the clinician–system relationship.

Construing 'system' as a set of practices

In shifting away from construing the system as an inert entity that exercises its blind force over what clinicians do, we begin to engage with interviewees for whom the system was to some extent implicated in – if still dominant over – their own practices. Typical of these construals is that speakers begin to extend their vocabulary from 'the system' (as derogatory notion) to include terms like 'procedure', 'management' and 'standards' (extract 10).

Extract 10

S15 Yes, I think that is true. I think myself and my colleagues we do our very best to make sure we do a good procedure, instruct in the postoperative management things and we get let down sometimes by others . . . you can't do everything yourself . . . nursing staff – can completely negate all the positive input that we have . . . it's not looked after properly if they don't have the same professional standards as us.

This doctor's engagement with the clinical work at the level of organizational coordination by using terms such as the ones just listed is somewhat defeated by their use of *we* as referring only to senior medical practitioners. The others – outside of this 'we' – are judged to at times adopt less proper professional standards, negating the doctors' attempt at systematizing their work (*we do a good procedure*).

In extract 11, the interviewee is willing to acknowledge they have the ability to engage with the system, but denies they have the resources to do so adequately. As in the previous extract, the doctor's capacity to act 'on the system' is made impossible by 'external factors', such as the availability of time.

Extract 11

I What about barriers to you doing more to improve the system?

S13 I think the biggest barrier is resources and time. The only way, by and large, systems improve . . . [is because] there is someone who takes it upon themselves to drive the process... my colleagues are actually too busy. They don't have the time to do it. It's not because they don't have the inclination to do it, but they just can't do it. They physically don't have the time. So I think it is a big resource issue in terms of actually improving system processes and at an individual level there is a resource issue too because you know, to, to basically keep yourself up to date with current treatments, current issues, current management all these sorts of things, you know for me it's a lot of work to do that. You know, we have no time to do that.

In the next extract we hear a doctor who openly struggles with how to balance their responsibility for their clinical patient cohort and their engagement with the system in order to improve it (extract 12).

Extract 12

S3 ... we're probably deluding ourselves if we don't think that part of giving good care is trying to improve the system. I think we insulate ourselves from the difficulties in the system by saying 'well all I can is what I am doing right now because I can't control those other things'. I think you're still not giving good care if you don't try and address the system problems that result in the total care not being good. And I find that a really hard conflict... I can't, I can't do everything. I can't stand by the patient's bed until they leave the hospital. I have to leave and I have to give responsibility to other people... I think you've got to start to try to work towards [improvements]. The difficulty is then you just stress out because there is just too much to do and you can't do it all. So it's trying to get the balance and I think that each person works out what they think is the right balance for them to cope. It's all about coping and being happy with your life really.

This interviewee feels that *we doctors need to be involved in improving the system*. However, the speaker softens his opinion with the use of *probably*, and *trying* suggests the system might be unalterable. He introduces the views of colleagues with the sentence: *I think we insulate ourselves from the difficulties in the system by saying 'well all I can is what I am doing right now because I can't control those other things'*. This projection is then further developed into a broader excuse for inaction, with *you* employed perhaps to create distance between the speaker and this uncomfortable admission: *The difficulty is then you just stress out because there is just too much to do and you can't do it all... It's all about coping and being happy with your life really.*

The next subsection turns to interview responses that construed a radically different relationship between the speaker and facets that previous speakers projected onto the immutable entity, 'the system'. Thus, we move from discourses that construct a zero-sum relationship between individual (doctor) agency and the power of the system, towards a complex blurring and interweaving of identities, roles, responsibilities and resources.

Constructing personal responsibility and medical–organizational agency

Further towards the other end of the spectrum, then, respondents construe the individual doctor not just as being better able to affect the system (and with that clinical outcomes for patients), but they also introduce a more complex relationship between personal agency and organizational-level phenomena.

Extract 13

S13 So at a system level it is a health system and it's a complex system and so despite individual people being very good at their particular jobs there are often just straight-out system problems which is not anyone's particular fault which contribute to a bad outcome [but] we need to work to improve it and make it work in the patient's best interests.

In this extract, no blame is directed at either the system or people in the system: problems arise from an inevitable complexity seen as being inherent in clinical work. Moreover, the speaker invokes a collective medical responsibility for improvement: *we need to work to improve it and make it work in the patient's best interests.*

In extract 14, the interviewee expresses acceptance of responsibility for the patient in the face of system problems. The way this is realized in the talk is by introducing an equating between 'potential problems in the system' and 'what I do'.

Extract 14

S8 I guess the bottom line from my point of view is that the main person responsible for the care of my patients is me, so if there are potential problems in the system for providing care for the patients I just need to be here more frequently. That's the way I deal with it.

Yet another doctor construes full responsibility for what the system is and does by placing himself at its centre. The equation between individual and context is complete by asserting that 'we are the system' (extract 15).

Extract 15

S30 As a geriatrician we are the system. Okay. Good care is systemic. It's longitudinal, so if I make a good diagnosis I don't pat myself on the back and walk away . . . I've got to then do the next step and that's treatment and the next step . . . so, we are the system and in the context . . . giving good care has to involve the system. Now there may be difficulties with other people handing over . . . but it's something we have to work with, which is still, still me as a person, me as a person delivering care. I have a concern at the moment with [community services] . . . we're separated structurally and because of that there are breaks in continuity. So I could say, 'look I'm delivering good care but because they're letting me down . . . is not my problem' . . . But, in fact, it is my problem and so I'm whingeing and whining . . . [Instead I need] to engage, to fix up the problem because I feel, it is my responsibility, this is my field and my patients.

In this discourse, the system is reconfigured from entity (noun) into attribute (adjective): 'systemic'. This attribute now becomes a descriptor of the doctor's practice, building a direct link between what doctors do and judgements that external stakeholders may have about its degree of systematization. This shift may also be illustrated with what another interviewee (S38) said: *You know, you can run a hospital from any kind of building or tent . . . it's not so much the facilities as the staff morale and people working together and feeling valued.* What is implied is that doctors have responsibility for staff morale and therefore for engaging with and supporting fellow workers, not just doctors. The two doctors just heard, rather than maintaining a categorical dichotomy between individual agency and the system's agency, construe medical practice as needing to be more holistic or 'systemic'. For them, medicine needs to move away from operating in isolation from the processes and practices that contextualize, facilitate and support doctoring.

Discussion

Our analysis above presented three ways in which our interviewees construed their relationship with the others in the health care system: a categorical dichotomy between doctors' practices and the system; a cross-over category that contained a more ambivalent discourse, and a category that contained forms of discourse that created a radical continuity between doctors' practices, identities and the broader facets of the organization of health services. No doubt, had we applied a more delicate kind of grammatical analysis we might have been able to diversify our analytical depiction. Rather than aiming for linguistic specificity, however, our purpose is to sketch out a broad spectrum of stances evident from the interviews. It is in that sense that our analysis above provides us with the necessary tools to begin to address the implications of how doctors construe their relationship with 'external entities and/or processes' for how they approach the challenge of enacting practices that realize clinical quality and safety.

In a nutshell, our argument is composed of three moves. First, we do not approach our interviewees' statements as 'natural and necessary'; that is, we regard their statements as not just descriptive of particular circumstances, but also as constitutive of their own identities and positionings. Put differently, their discourse embodies both statements about the world and enactments or performances of a particular medical self. This, in turn, has implications for how we hear their responses. Rather than regarding what doctors say as immutable and as reflecting 'a real world out there', we prefer to regard their responses as bringing (performing) particular realities into being and as perpetuating these through their talk. Further, if these realities are performed and perpetuated by what the doctors say, it becomes possible to raise questions about their preferred discourse(s), and propose alternative ones.

Second, our argument centres on the view that clinical quality and safety cannot be sequestered as issues that pertain to how an external system is structured. Some of the responses heard above projected the problem as being contextualizing factors, leaving doctoring free of the responsibility to address potential shortcomings. Ironically, these responses construe 'the system' much in the way that the policy makers and health services managers construe it, and that David Silverman (1968) deconstructed as constituting a reification of peopled processes and practices. In that sense, then, the doctors who externalize the system from their own work objectify the system as an entity that should support, facilitate and resource their own practices. This 'tool' view of the system reduces everything that contextualizes doctoring (nursing, allied health, management, policy making) to mere supportive mechanisms, and increasingly malfunctioning ones at that, all conspiring to undo medicine's good works.

Third, this argument would not be complete without capitalizing on the insights of those doctors heard subsequently for whom their own and others' practices and processes are intimately and mutually implicated. For these interviewees, doctoring is a dynamic whose substance needs to be negotiated and is accomplished not just with peers but also with other professionals (nurses, allied health professionals, managers and policy makers). These processes and practices can to a greater or lesser extent be 'systemic' – that is, coordinated with the work, the concerns and the interests of others.

In sum, the quality and safety agenda, as it arose from a rising concern about iatrogenic error (Brennan *et al.*, 1991; Wilson *et al.*, 1995), requires a radically different discourse from that which reifies and objectifies 'the system'. As the geriatrician put this in the last extract seen above, *I could say, 'look I'm delivering good care but because they're letting me down . . . is not my problem' . . . But, in fact, it is my problem and so I'm whingeing and whining . . . [Instead I need] to engage, to fix up the problem because I feel, it is my responsibility, this is my field and my patients.* This doctor puts paid to the opposition created between an externality – what others do or have done – and his own work, by pointing to the interrelatedness of what people across health care do. In this talk, clinical quality and safety inhere in the acknowledgement that what the clinician does and says has implications for the systematicity – the relatedness and coherence – of health care services.

Conclusion

Our argument above has centred on showing that a new discursive stance may connect the concerns at the heart of the safety and quality agenda to what specific clinicians do and say. In putting this argument, we are conscious of the problematic nature of doctor engagement and discontent due to loss of autonomy and the rapid rate of health organizational change (Edwards *et al.*, 2002; Graham, 2006). Other reasons for doctors' unhappiness included inadequate support, drops in salary, falling status and rising levels of accountability (*British Medical Journal*, 2001; Smith, 2001). As was evident from some of the earlier extracts in this chapter, physicians feel increasingly dislocated by changes in health care structures, and are increasingly conscious of mismatches in expectation between themselves, their patients and the health service (Kassier, 1998; Kerr *et al.*, 2002; Taylor, 2002).

A common interpretation is that it is not the nature of the clinical work that makes physicians unhappy, but rather '. . . the aspects of the professional's role that detract from working with patients' (Graham, 2006, p. 45). In a review of efforts over the last five years to reduce medical errors, Leape and Berwick (2005) argue that among the major barriers to improvements to patient safety were the complexity of the health system, professional autonomy and professional fragmentation, and the imposition of authority structures. 'The normal human resistance to change', they argue, 'was amplified by fear of loss of autonomy, antipathy toward attempts by others outside the profession to improve practice, and skepticism about the new concept that systems failures are the underlying cause of most human errors' (Leape and Berwick, 2005, p. 2387). To compensate for these feelings of marginalization, doctors should be more involved in incremental, iterative and bottom-up change strategies (Ham, 2003).

Put in terms of our analysis, when doctors become marginalized from changes in 'the system', they may espouse discourse that reinforces the dichotomy between their identity and personal medical work on the one hand, and the looming system encroaching on their practice, on the other. The incremental strategies recommended by Chris Ham are therefore doubly important: they may obviate the need for doctors to create a categorical rift between what they do and what others do, and it may create greater continuity in both discourse and practice between medicine, nursing, management and policy making. Ultimately, we would hope that our analysis contributes to people being able to reflect better on the positions that they have chosen to espouse, and on the consequences of those espousals for others. More importantly still perhaps, we regard discursive deconstructions such as the ones presented above as integral to people being enabled and empowered to reconfigure their identity. It is only on the basis of such identity shift on the part of all clinicians in the health care system that we may begin to see the aims of the clinical quality and safety agenda to be realized.

References

Amalberti, R., Auroy, Y., Berwick, D. and Barach, P. (2005) 'Five System Barriers to Achieving Ultrasafe Health Care', *Annals of Internal Medicine*, 142(9), pp. 756–64.

Anonymous (2000) 'Medical Errors Must be Minimised', *The Australian* (8 November).

Bagian, J. P., Gosbee, J., Lee, C. Z., Williams, L., McKnight, S. D. and Mannos, D. M. (2002) 'The Veterans Affairs Root Cause Analysis in Action', *Journal on Quality Improvement*, 28(10), pp. 531–45.

Baker, G. R. and Norton, G. P. (2004) 'Adverse Events and Patient Safety in Canadian Health Care', *Canadian Medical Association Journal*, 170(3), pp. 353–4.

Brennan, T. A. (2002) 'Physicians' Professional Responsibility to Improve the Quality of Care', *Academic Medicine*, 77(10), pp. 973–80.

Brennan, T. A., Leape, L. L., Laird, M. M., Nan, M., Hebert, L., Localio, A. R., Lawthers, A. G., Newhouse, J., P., Weiler, P. C. and Hiatt, H. H. (1991) 'Incidence of Adverse Events and Negligence in Hospitalized Patients: Results of the Harvard Medical Practice Study', *New England Journal of Medicine*, 324, pp. 370–6.

British Medical Journal (2001) 'Survey: Why are Doctors So Unhappy?', *British Medical Journal*, 322 (7294). http://bmj.bmjjournals.com/cgi/content/full/31/322/7294/DC3/ (accessed 4 May 2006).

Charmaz, K. (2000) 'Grounded Theory: Objectivist and Constructionist Methods', in N. K. Denzin and Y. S. Lincoln (eds) *Handbook of Qualitative Research*, pp. 509–35 (London: Sage).

Classen, D. C. and Kilbridge, P. M. (2002) 'The Roles and Responsibility of Physicians to Improve Patient Safety within Health Care Delivery Systems', *Academic Medicine*, 77(10), pp. 963–72.

Cornbleet, M. A., Campbell, P., Murray, S., Stevenson, M., Bond, S. and Joint Working Party of the Scottish Partnership Agency for Palliative and Cancer Care and National Council for Hospice and Specialist Palliative Care Services (2002) 'Patient-held Records in Cancer and Palliative Care: a Randomized, Prospective Trial', *Palliative Medicine*, 16(3), pp. 205–12.

Cowan, J. A. J., Dimick, J. B., Stanley, J. C. and Upchurch, G. R. J. D. (2002) 'Surgeon Volume as an Indicator of Outcomes after Carotid Endarterectomy: an Effect Independent of Specialty Practice and Hospital Volume', *Journal of the American College of Surgeons*, 195(6), pp. 814–21.

Cresswell, J. (1998) *Qualitative Inquiry and Research Design: Choosing among Five Traditions* (Thousand Oaks/New Delhi/London: Sage).

Davis, P., Lay-Yee, R., Briant, R., Ali, W., Scott, A. and Schug, S. (2002) 'Adverse Events in New Zealand Public Hospitals I: Occurrence and Impact', *New Zealand Medical Journal*, 115(1167), pp. U271.

Degeling, P., Maxwell, S., Kennedy, J. and Coyle, B. (2003) 'Medicine, Management and Modernisation: a "Danse Macabre"?', *British Medical Journal*, 326, pp. 649–52.

Department of Health (2001) *The Report of the Public Inquiry into Children's Heart Surgery at the Bristol Royal Infirmary 1984–1995: Learning from Bristol* (London: Stationery Office).

Department of Health and Design Council (2003) *Design for Patient Safety* (London: Department of Health).

Douglas, N., Robinson, J. and Fahy, K. (2001) *Inquiry into Obstetric and Gynaecological Services at King Edward Memorial Hospital 1990–2000* (Perth: Health Department of Western Australia).

Edwards, N., Kornacki, M. J. and Silversin, J. (2002) 'Unhappy Doctors: What are the Causes and What can be Done?', *British Medical Journal*, 324(7341), pp. 835–8.

Eysenbach, G., Thomas, L. and Diepgen, L. (1999) 'Patients Looking for Information on the Internet and Seeking Teleadvice', *Archives of Dermatology*, 135, pp. 151–6.

Flick, U. (2002) *An Introduction to Qualitative Research* (Thousand Oaks/New Delhi/London: Sage Publications).
Freidson, E. (1970) *The Professon of Medicine* (New York: Harper and Row).
Gollop, R., Whitby, E., Buchanan, D. and Ketley, D. (2004) 'Influencing Sceptical Staff to Become Supporters of Service Improvement: a Qualitative Study of Doctors' and Managers' Views', *Quality and Safety in Health Care*, 13, pp. 108–14.
Goode, L. D., Clancy, C. M., Kimball, H. R., Meyer, G. and Eisenberg, J. M. (2002) 'When is "Good Enough"? The Role and Responsibility of Physicians to Improve Patient Safety', *Academic Medicine*, 77(10), pp. 947–52.
Graham, R. (2006) 'Lacking Compassion: Sociological Analyses of the Medical Profession', *Social Theory and Health*, 4, pp. 43–63.
Gustafson, D. H., Sainfort, F., Eichler, M., Adams, L., Bisognano, M. and Steudel, H. (2003) 'Developing and Testing a Model to Predict Outcomes of Organizational Change', *Health Services Research*, 38(2), pp. 751–76.
Hall, C. and White, S. (2005) 'Looking inside Professional Practice: Discourse Narrative and Ethnographic Approaches to Social Work and Counselling', *Qualitative Social Work*, 4(4), pp. 379–90.
Ham, C. (2003) 'Improving the Performance of Health Services: the Role of Clinical Leadership', *The Lancet*, 361(9737), pp. 1978–80.
Ham, C., Kipping, R. and McLeod, H. (2003) 'Redesigning Work Processes in Health Care: Lessons from the National Health Service', *The Milbank Quarterly*, 81(3), pp. 415–39.
Health Services Commissioner (2002) *Royal Melbourne Hospital Inquiry Report* (Melbourne: Health Services Commissioner).
Iedema, R., Jorm, C. M., Long, D., Braithwaite, J., Travaglia, J. and Westbrook, M. (2006) 'Turning the Medical Gaze in upon Itself: Root Cause Analysis and the Investigation of Clinical Error', *Social Science and Medicine*, 62(7), pp. 1605–15.
Institute of Medicine (2000) *To Err is Human: Building a Safer Health System* (Washington, DC: National Academy Press).
Irvine Doran, D. M., Baker, G. R., Murray, M., Bohnen, J., Zahn, C., Sidani, S. and Carryer, J. (2002) 'Achieving Clinical Improvement: an Interdisciplinary Intervention', *Health Care Management Review*, 27(4), pp. 42–56.
Jorm, C. and Kam, P. (2004) 'Does Medical Culture Limit Doctors' Adoption of Quality Improvement? Lessons from Camelot', *Journal of Health Services and Research Policy*, 9(4), pp. 248–51.
Kassier, J. (1998) 'Doctor Discontent', *New England Journal of Medicine*, 339, pp. 1543–5.
Kerr, D., Bevan, H., Gowland, B., Penny, J. and Berwick, D. (2002) 'Redesigning Cancer Care', *British Medical Journal*, 324, pp. 164–6.
Kizer, K. W. (2001) 'Establishing Health Care Performance Standards in an Era of Consumerism', *Journal of the American Medical Association*, 286(10), pp. 1213–17.
Kohn, L. T., Corrigan, J. and Donaldson, M. E. (1999) *To Err is Human: Building A Safer Health System* (Washington, DC: National Academy Press).
Leape, L. L. and Berwick, D. (2005) 'Five years after *To Err is Human*: What have We Learned?', *Journal of the American Medical Association*, 293(19), pp. 2384–90.

Locock, L. (2003) 'Healthcare Redesign: Meaning, Origins and Application', *Quality and Safety in Health Care*, 12, pp. 53–8.

McLoughlin, V. and Smallwood, R. (2002) 'Clinical Support Systems Program: Why do We Need Clinical Practice Improvement? A Government Perspective', *Internal Medicine Journal*, 32(5–6), pp. 233–6.

Mühlhäusler, P. and Harre, R. (1990a) '*I*: Indexicalities of Responsibility and Place', in P. Mühlhäusler and R. Harre (eds) *Pronouns and People: the Linguistic Construction of Social and Personal Identity*, pp. 87–130 (Oxford: Basil Blackwell).

Mühlhäusler, P. and Harre, R. (1990b) '*We*: Speaking for More than One', in P. Mühlhäusler and R. Harre (eds) *Pronouns and People: the Linguistic Construction of Social and Personal Identity*, pp. 168–206 (Oxford: Basil Blackwell).

Plsek, P. E. (2001) 'Redesigning Health Care with Insights from the Science of Complex Adaptive Systems', in Institute of Medicine, US (ed.) *Crossing the Quality Chasm: a New Health System for the 21st Century*, pp. 309–22 (Washington, DC: National Academy Press).

Reason, J. (2000) 'Human Error: Models and Management', *British Medical Journal*, 320(7237), pp. 768–70.

Redfern, M., Keeling, J. and Powell, E. (2001) *The Royal Liverpool Children's Inquiry* (London: The House of Commons).

Runciman, W. B., Merry, A. F. and Tito, F. (2003) 'Error, Blame and the Law in Health Care: an Antipodean Perspective', *Annals of Internal Medicine*, 138, pp. 974–9.

Secretariat, WHO (2002) 'Quality of Care: Patient Safety', Fifty-fifth World Health Assembly, provisional agenda item 13.9, A55/13 (23rd March).

Shekelle, P. G. (2002) 'Why Don't Physicians Enthusiastically Support Quality Improvement Programmes?', *Quality and Safety in Health Care*, 11(1), p. 6.

Silverman, D. (1968) 'Formal Organizations or Industrial Sociology: Towards a Social Action Analysis of Organizations', *Sociology*, 2 (May), pp. 221–38.

Sinclair, C. M. (1994) *Report of the Manitoba Pediatric Cardiac Surgery Inquest* (Winnipeg: Manitoba Provincial Court).

Smith, R. (2001) 'Why are Doctors So Unhappy?', *British Medical Journal*, 322, pp. 1073–4.

Swan, N., (1997) 'Medical Scandal at One of the Most Respected UK Hospitals: the Health Report', Radio National Transcript (May 12).

Taylor, C. and White, S. (2000) *Practising Reflexivity in Health and Welfare: Making Knowledge* (Buckingham: Open University Press).

Taylor, I. (2002) 'At Least Some of the Unhappiness is Due to Excessive Accountability', *British Medical Journal*, 324, p. 1452.

van Bueren, E. M., Klijn, E. H. and Koppenjan, J. F. M. (2003) 'Dealing with Wicked Problems in Networks: Analyzing an Environmental Debate from a Network Perspective', *Journal of Public Administration Research and Theory*, 13(2), pp. 193–212.

Wald, H. and Shojania, K. G. (2001) 'Root Cause Analysis', in K. G. Shojania, B. W. Duncan, K. M. McDonald, R. W. Wachter and A. J. Markowitz (eds) *Making Health Care Safer: a Critical Analysis of Patient Safety Practices* (Evidence Report/Technology Assessment: Number 43), pp. 51–6 (Rockville, Md: Agency for Healthcare Research and Quality).

Wiener, C. (2000) *The Elusive Quest: Accountability in Hospitals* (New York: Aldine de Gruyter).

Wilson, R., Runciman, W. B., Gibberd, R. W., Harrison, B., Newby, L. and Hamilton, J. (1995) 'The Quality in Australian Health Care Study', *The Medical Journal of Australia*, 163(9), pp. 458–71.

12

Nursing through Time and Space: Some Challenges to the Construct of Community of Practice

Sally Candlin and Christopher N. Candlin

Introduction

This chapter addresses a number of issues which relate to the construction over time and space of professional discourses within the practice of nursing. Discussion of these issues draws on the now well-established construct of *communities of practice,* first developed by Jean Lave and Etienne Wenger (Lave and Wenger, 1991; Wenger, 1998) and now extensively adopted across a range of social, educational, human and management disciplines. One objective of the chapter is to draw on the discussion of nursing practice to offer a critical perspective on this construct.

A focus on nursing through time and space emphasizes what is a relatively under-researched diachronic perspective on the communication practices of nursing. Such a focus can also be applied to highlight how synchronic analyses of the discourse of nursing practice, based as they frequently are on samples of text typically drawn from nurse–patient encounters, require historically informed professional and institutional grounding. This is particularly true if these texts are to be used as evidence of how changes in practice over time are reflected in particular choices of talk and action. Changes in discursive practice derive from other professional, organizational and institutional changes taking place within the health care sector in general, and in the nursing profession in particular. One consequence of the latter changes is a mixed and sometimes confused perception by the general public of what in fact constitutes nursing practice. Among these changes are, for example, the institutional reorganization of the health care services in the UK with the advent of National Health Service Trusts, and the professional changes brought about by the emergence of multidisciplinary teams, even though the existence of such teams is not entirely novel as the narratives in this chapter indicate. Other more recent developments include the advent and provision of telemedicine with its utilization of nurses in a new role and a new modality, changes in nurse education, and the development of an expanded role for nurses as nurse consultants and nurse specialists. For example, although online access for the general public to health care related information has delivered responses to the specialist queries of many, it has also had the effect of changing professional–client relationships, creating anxieties in relation to professional role on the part of both consumers of services and of health care workers and would-be nurses.

Our objective in this chapter is to draw on narratives of experience and practice from a range of nursing professionals to reflect on these and other changes. We do so to provide some empirical discursive grounding to these changes. By refracting our data through the construct of community of practice, we seek to achieve two objectives: to illuminate these narratives as evidence of changes in professional membership, and to use that evidence to offer some critique of the community of practice construct itself.

Communities of practice

The construct of community of practice has since its invention been centrally linked to three sets of defining concepts: the domain of interest and domain-related competence; membership, relationship and community; and activity, practice, and shared repertoires of experience. Members are said to be 'mutually engaged', their engagement is located in a 'joint enterprise', and the pursuance of this enterprise over extensive periods of time and within recognizable routines in established space is seen to develop among them a 'shared repertoire' of recognized and mutually intelligible performances and interpretations, including, we may assume – although Lave and Wenger do not single this out especially – common discourses. Performance and interpretation signal the twin cognitive and social bases of the construct. The emphasis on participation and reification of these membership practices points to the alacrity with which it has been adopted in a range of professional fields, latterly in the context of education and training. Indeed, Wenger, either singly or with colleagues, continues to be active in promoting the construct and its application in diverse sectors of government, business organizations, education, professional and local associations, even in philanthropy, and either face to face or Internet-mediated, also in the context of international development (Wenger *et al.*, 2002; Wenger and Snyder, 2000; Wenger, 2004a, b).

Furthermore, these concepts and their epistemological bases have continually informed the writings of other scholars, attracted by its focus on *membership* with its implications for enhancing collective learning, fostering of commitment to community, defining of mutual expertise, and the encouragement of shared interaction and practice. Writing from a sociolinguistic perspective, for example, Eckert and McConnell-Ginet (1992) highlight membership as a typically sociolinguistic concept, but see the construct of community of practice as linking membership to the concept of mutuality of engagement in a practice, and – of importance for the focus of this chapter – to the construct of identity:

> . . . an aggregate of people who come together around mutual engagement in an endeavour. Ways of doing things, ways of talking, beliefs, values, power relations – in short practices – emerge in the course of this mutual endeavour. As a social construct, a community of practice is different from the traditional community, primarily because it is defined simultaneously by its membership and by the practice in which that membership engages. (Eckert and McConnell-Ginet, 1992, p. 464)

We note the emphasis here on three defining characteristics of the construct: agency, historicity and mutuality. It is these three characteristics that Eckert and McConnell-Ginet regard as circumscribing the foci of research into the nature of communities of practice. To this we may add the goal orientation of the membership, as Scollon (1998) emphasizes from a discourse analytical and ethnographic perspective: 'A community of practice is a group of people who over a period of time share some set of social practices geared towards some common purpose . . . Everyone is multiply membered in various communities of practice' (Scollon, 1998, p. 13). Significantly for this chapter, however, is his emphasis, in this same definition, on the dimension of time: '. . . that such a community of practice would develop a history over time of novices entering, moving through into expertise, and retirement from the community' (Scollon, 1998, p. 13). Wenger (1998) himself connects with this concept of locally shared history and members' biographies when he states: 'Learning and the negotiation of meaning are ongoing within various localities of engagement, and this process continually creates locally shared histories' (Wenger, 1998, p. 125).

As Corder and Meyerhoff (in press) identify in a recent paper drawing on the construct of community of practice to explore intercultural communication, there is a clear connection made between the construct and social constructionism more broadly with its emphasis on identities being created through cultural performances, a connection exemplified in the work of Holmes and Stubbe (2003) on communication patterns in workplace communities of practice. The potential for the construct to provide an overarching explanatory metaphor for patterns of performance and interpretation in communication is central to Holmes and Meyerhoff's (1999) paper on the construct in the context of research into gender. Here, they argue, 'belonging', and identity affirmation through belonging, enable members to entertain and exploit mutualities in awareness of interactional routines, modes of communicating and interpersonal styles, facilitating, they argue, rapidities in information flow, swift understandings of agendas, appreciation of member contributions and, to a degree, shared understandings of the world.

Along with Wenger himself and commentators like Scollon (1998) and Holmes and Meyerhoff (1999), the emphasis on the social practices of a community of practice suggests some clear linkages to parallel discursive practices (see Fairclough, 1992; Chouliaraki and Fairclough, 1999), but not just to particular uses of the forms of language, but to practices such as: involving acknowledging and claiming identities in interactions; representing in appropriate genres what is accepted and conventional knowledge; signalling membership by a range of semiotic and sociolinguistic performances; managing inter- and intra-community relationships by acknowledgement of rights, duties and roles; and enabling and achieving outcomes for agreed and determined tasks in which processes of resourceful and appropriate deployment of communication competency are clearly at a premium.

Two further conditions on the nature of the construct seem to be necessary. First, by defining the community of practice in terms of its members being multiply-membershipped across communities, there is a potential for the community to be enriched by the various other-community experiences of individual members. Of course, the exercise of such potential can produce tensions as issues of competing priorities and agendas influence the dynamics of the community. Second, there has to be some sense of order within the orders of discourse of a community of practice. Some sense of governance and regulation needs to enable the community's development and effectiveness. That this governance and regulation is realized and assured through the shared discourse(s) of members is a point made by Sarangi and Roberts (1999), when they propose: 'The institutional order [of a community of practice (SC and CNC)] is held together not by particular forms of social organization but by regulating discourses' (Sarangi and Roberts, 1999, p. 16).

Nursing within the context of communities of practice: some critical issues and some questions

The foregoing has established some of the features of the construct of community of practice to locate the discussion with a particular and specific community of practice, that of nursing – a community several times adopted by Wenger (1998) as a key exemplar for the construct itself.

Prior discussion has indirectly suggested some critical points at issue in relation to the construct. We identify some of these more explicitly here, and in relation to our nursing focus. Interestingly, they parallel some of those discernible in a recent publication (Barton and Tusting, 2005), and from papers delivered at a recent conference (from which that book in part derives) on the theme of *Beyond communities of practice: language, power and social context* (ISCAR Conference, Seville, September 2005; Jackson, personal communication).

- Who constitutes the 'membership' of the community of practice, and what are some of the characteristic community practices of nursing?
- What is the extent of the 'mutuality of engagement' among members?
- How are 'joint enterprise' and 'mutuality of goal' to be defined in nursing and among nurses?
- How are the constraints imposed by changes over time accommodated, and how do these impact on nurses?
- What is the effect on 'mutuality' of differences in professional space, and in territoriality, among nurses?
- How is agreement reached among members over the 'shared repertoire of joint resources for negotiating meaning'?

To address these questions we have been informed by the general nursing literature and by the discourses of particular nurses we have interviewed. Each nurse occupies a professional space within a particular specialty of nursing, and while nursing itself may be seen as a community of practice in the terms outlined so far, and is explicitly referred to as such by Wenger, it is, like all communities, one which has developed its own culture. Here culture is defined, not in terms of ethnicity/nationality, but, in the manner of Corder and Meyerhoff's (in press) study, and more generally, as a group of people who share common interests, ideals, values, beliefs and behaviours. Importantly for our argument, so too do these specialty areas of nursing develop their own cultural beliefs, values and behaviours.

Such particularization immediately opens up the question: who and what constitutes the community of practice within nursing? The question is significant, since sharing this 'specialty' space there are likely to be other nurses, other professionals such as nurse practitioners (nurses who have begun to adopt practices traditionally controlled and enacted by doctors), and patients and their significant others, bringing into question the constitution of membership of a community of practice and the extent of 'mutuality' of engagement of its members. Do different professions, for example, within the same site of engagement share goals? How indeed are 'joint enterprise' and 'mutuality of goal' identified when members bring with them, for example, their own cultural values, experiences, knowledge bases, needs and expectations?

Exploring the constructs: nursing through time and space

To investigate the issues raised by the overall question relating to changes in nursing practice over time and through space,[1] we spoke with a range of nursing colleagues, each of whom occupies a particular professional space and is working and/or may have worked in a variety of specialty areas. The nature of the study was explained and permission to participate was given willingly. The methodology was informed by the discussion in Sarangi and Candlin (2001) on the matter of what they term 'motivational relevancies'; that is, what motivates researchers to regard particular processes of research and data as 'relevant', in this case, the decision to deliberately seek to engage participants in a cooperative and hermeneutic exploration of issues both they and the researcher/analyst raised. (For arguments in favour of such a methodology in the health care context, see Candlin and Candlin, 2003.) The professional experiences of participants spanned time frames between 20 and 40 years, and represented a number of areas, such as nursing research, academia, administration and clinical education. Practice experiences of those participating included: midwifery, child and family health, aged care, mental health, cardiology, intensive care and nuclear medicine. The two researchers were both familiar with the profession of nursing, the first author as a nurse academic, after first working extensively in the areas of midwifery, health visiting and aged care as the specialist health visitor in a high retirement area outside

Australia, and the second author as a researcher into health communication more generally.

Participants were keen to reminisce and to narrate their experiences. In that we wished to encourage the disclosure of appropriate information, participants were allowed to digress and discuss issues freely with the researcher, enabling hitherto unprepared for questions to arise. Because the first author had been engaged in nursing practice for many years, we regarded the research as an ethnographic study where examples from her own experiences and practice could be legitimated. Participants were aware that each was met at a specific point on their professional and life trajectory and in a specific space, by a researcher who was similarly located on her own trajectory and occupying her own professional space. The meeting of participant and researcher/participant meant that at that point in time, their trajectories converged in the sharing of the professional space they occupied.

Referring to the discussion above on the construct of community of practice, we outline here as an introductory summary a number of issues that were raised which relate to the constitution of membership of such communities, and with specific reference to nursing. Other issues that arose related closely to the question of the extent to which 'members' can be held to enjoy 'mutuality of engagement'. Such issues connect with the changes in nursing practices over time that we identified at the outset of this chapter, and the impacts these changes have had on nurses, invoking the extent to which they may be said to be involved in a 'joint enterprise' and to share 'mutuality of goal'. Among the significant results of changes in practice which participants identified were increases in patient autonomy, power and self-determination. Others referred to the innovatory emphasis on research and evidence-based practice as both necessary and important, but an emphasis likely, again, to raise questions of mutuality within the 'community'. Of concern to at least one participant were the changes in management structures, practices and styles. A recurring theme, often initiated by the participant/researcher, was the impact which health organizational change had had on nursing discourse(s).

The constitution of the 'membership' and some characteristic practices of nursing

In its most straightforward sense, membership of the community of nursing practice, by definition, must include those who are registered as such by the authorizing body of that country or state, having first successfully undertaken a three-year programme of training or education, either in hospital (prior to 1986 in New South Wales) or within the tertiary education sector. A summary description of the participants – cited in relation to their narratives in what follows – indicates some of the many areas of health care in which they are key figures, and thus the professional spaces which they occupy. Some of the spaces occupied by non-participants include paediatrics, oncology, palliative care and community nursing, but such a list as this does not identify the general characteristic practices of nursing. In this regard, one participant when discussing the characteristic practices of the nurse said:

> . . . what you're really asking related to professionalism. . . . at least in Australia nurse education is now in the tertiary sector of education and takes its place alongside other health professions such as medicine, physiotherapy, occupational therapy, and so on. It means that nursing practice is not just a matter of 'doing' and 'doing as we are told' but 'doing' with understanding and thoughtfulness. It means being critical and reflective about what we do, analyzing what we have done, and working out how we can improve practice, pushing back the frontiers of knowledge and thus improving patient care. This means understanding what other professional colleagues do which then also helps us to be effective members of a multidisciplinary team. Thankfully, health care is more team-based these days both in terms of nursing teams and multidisciplinary teams – and as someone who has worked in a multidisciplinary team I know how enriching the experience can be. (Nurse academic)

Another nurse, now working in an intensive care unit, spoke about one of the nursing characteristics – being assertive – seeming to link this with the hospital-based training which she had experienced:

> Nursing has become more assertive. We work more in teams now, then there were fewer RNs. We had to perform tasks and worked our way up from the pan room. Everything was defined. Now there aren't enough places in nursing homes, so we are left with the difficult patients. The attitude is the 'nurses can do'. (Intensive care (ICU) nurse)

Another talked about the ideals of the training school and the reality of the practice on the wards:

> We were encouraged in our training to be conscious of the emotional psychological needs of patients, but found on the wards that I was

> criticized for spending time with needy patients re their emotional needs....

She then compared this with the experiences of being a registered nurse.

> Each trained nurse was given responsibility for eight patients, all their care, developing a much more intimate and informed relationship. There was more direct exchange with doctors. We were responsible for writing reports on patients and giving them to the next shift. (A midwife who later in her career became a counsellor)

These narratives connect with the findings of other research studies; for example, Taylor *et al.*'s (1999) study on nurses' models of work-based stress; Crawford *et al.*'s (2001) study into the value placed on community health nurses in primary care teams; and Nolan and Crawford's (1997) research into the meanings of spirituality in mental health care.

The extent of 'mutuality of engagement'

Within each area of nursing practice there must be a degree of teamwork for successful outcomes to be achieved. One nurse who had trained at a large teaching hospital overseas felt that there was no longer the same degree of teamwork as she had experienced earlier in her training:

> There was hierarchy and I don't think that this is a bad idea as you learnt from nurses who had nursed longer than you. There was also respect. There was much more sharing of information and care for each other than there is now. Today I feel nurses are rushed. It's like working in a huge corporation where you churn out your results on a conveyor belt. I was taught to regulate my energy. In other words, two nurses made the beds together... two nurses did a bed bath...

She then discussed how later things had changed:

> I have had to wait for another nurse to come and help me roll a patient and to change sheets... Today the nurses have no time to get to know the patient. Nurses are tired out and when I would come as a casual I would be given the heavy patients. Fair enough but not a good use of resources if you did not know the patients.

These experiences are in sharp contrast to those described by J, an intensive care nurse. Her narrative referred to working together with colleagues. In that sense, her experiences are reminiscent of the situation described by Hak (1999) who, when observing nurses in an intensive care unit (ICU), noted that while two nurses were each caring for their patients, one, without either party saying anything, stopped what she was doing and went to the aid of her colleague. This is not unusual in situations where nurses work together in the same specialty area. As this nurse in ICU remarked when told of this situation: 'Well of course, we're doing it all the time.' She implied by this remark that situations that ICU nurses are confronted with every day involved the accomplishment of tasks of which a lay person would be totally unaware. It may also be the case that nurse–patient communication is taken by lay persons as 'conversational' and everyday, misinterpreting the therapeutic communication achievable in that 'casual' mode (see Fenwick *et al.*, 2001 and Candlin, 2000). In the ICU nurse's context of practice, such situations are mutually understood and resources are utilized appropriately, thus reinforcing one of the tenets of Wenger's definition of a community of practice, while at the same time emphasizing its increasing multidisciplinarity. Our nurse spoke relevantly to this issue, not only about her working with nursing colleagues, but about the advent of multidisciplinary teams:

> We also work within a multidisciplinary team, and value the contributions of social workers and other allied health professionals. (ICU nurse)

Discussion of such multidisciplinarity serves to expand the construct of community of practice and to reinforce how members of distinct communities now routinely work together to address situations and problems. Such communities are not isolated units but work together in a situation of mutual concern, their practices overlapping (see Figure 12.1 below) but engaged in a common interdisciplinary and intercommunity goal. Such expanded and complex communities within nursing offer potential for the enhancement of health outcomes and personal professional growth as the spaces occupied by individuals overlap with those occupied by members of other communities in what is now an expanded community of practice.

Such a sharing of professional space by multidisciplinary, semi-autonomous or autonomous teams working within what has been called the new work order (Gee *et al.*, 1996) can be challenging and also unsettling, as Iedema and Scheeres (2003) note:

> First, they affect most workplace participants, leaving few untouched: members of management, workers and professionals. Second, the ways in which individuals respond to these changes vary. For some,

> building new relationships, learning new practices, changing allegiances, and shifting work focus can be unsettling and even debilitating: for others it can be empowering and offer opportunities. (Iedema and Scheeres, 2003, p. 319)

The effects of this 'empowering and offering of opportunities' as a result of working within multidisciplinary teams can also be rewarding and positive, as has been the experience of a nurse, P, who trained in the 1970s, now working in the area of nuclear medicine. She feels valued as the nurse in the team and is often consulted on issues related to nursing:

> As the only nurse on the team, I am often approached for my opinion. I feel valued.

She remarked that this confirmed her previous experiences working in aged care in the early 1990s, as it confirmed the experience of the nurse who had been the specialist health visitor in geriatrics in the early 1980s. While her experience of the latter was positive, and even empowering, it only became so after an indifferent beginning demanding considerable attention to relationship building through the strategic use of discursive practices designed to encourage mutuality. As an example, the overlapping of the communities serving aged care is demonstrated in Figure 12.1, underpinning how each community of practice redefines each other in the focused context of specific goal-oriented interaction.

Nurses, however not only engage with other nurses and health professionals but also with the patient, now increasingly being seen as an equal partner in care (Candlin, 1997). Such a partnership represents a change from the disease focus of health care earlier in the twentieth century, and from the dominance of the medical model. It was not until the

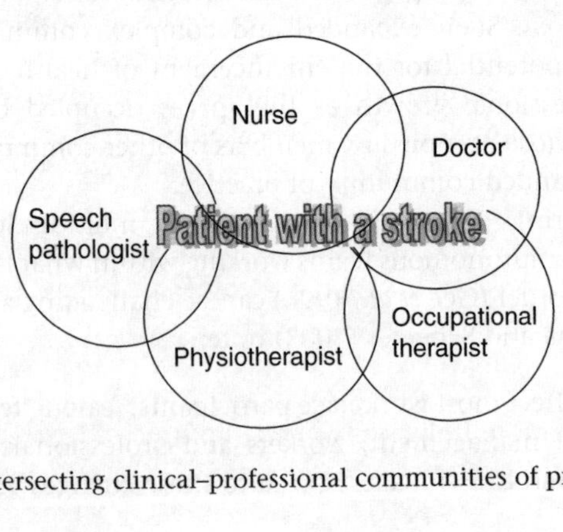

Figure 12.1 Intersecting clinical–professional communities of practice

Declaration of Alma Ata in 1978 that health was defined not simply as the absence of disease but 'a state of complete physical mental and social well-being'. While many consider this more recent statement to still be an inadequate definition of health, it does capture a change in health care practices and funding arrangements. (See the emphasis on refocusing on the patient 'body' in McDonald and McIntyre, 2001.) With this, medical dominance, where health care workers were subservient to doctors, and where patients were expected to comply unquestioningly with doctors' instructions, was called into question. Collectively, social and institutional changes occasioned greater awareness by health professionals of power relations within the workplace. At the same time, issues of professional deskilling of nurses continue to be raised in what is a contested professional environment (see Herdman, 1992, 2000). The relevance here of changes in the social and institutional order to changes in the meanings that are being made in the community of practice, and to changes in the distribution of roles and practices within that community, offers important challenges to the scope and orientation of Wenger's original construct, as Tusting (2005) argues in her chapter on language and power in communities of practice in Barton and Tusting (2005):

> I have argued that since Wenger's model of the community of practice places the negotiation of meaning at the heart of his understanding of practice, it is an omission not to consider in more depth the role of language and other forms of semiosis within this, and the relationships between processes of meaning making and other social dynamics. (Tusting, 2005, pp. 52–3)

The above-mentioned changes and their new discourses, in turn, have had effects on nursing education and training programmes. The consciousness of students has been raised, not only to the matter of enhanced patient autonomy (Candlin, 2002), and to a concomitant increasing autonomy for nurses, but also to the necessary and appropriate use by all members of interpersonally appropriate discursive choices. This includes a sharper awareness of the effects of such choices on professional–client relationships and an appreciation of the potential of such relationships for affecting health outcomes. This potential is exemplified by J, a nurse in ICU, describing her current practice in the context of spirituality:

> Nurses look more holistically at the person. Last week I was able to pray for a lady who was obviously worried. Then she said 'I'm not

just worried about the operation. I'm worried about afterwards.' So then we prayed for that too. We can approach the spiritual needs and look more holistically at the person. (Intensive care nurse)

What is interesting in this narrative is that the nurse was able to address spiritual matters and the patient was able to articulate her needs and not lie in bed as a passive recipient of care. Given the nature of their contact, this was undoubtedly conditional on the nurse first engaging with the patient and building up a trusting relationship with her.

Societal changes, the growth of multicultural, migratory and pluralist societies, together with changes in professional ideologies, have been accompanied by advances in medical science. All these factors have contributed to changes in professional training and education programmes. Nurse education in a number of Western countries is now university based, no longer following the hospital-based apprenticeship system, and provides almost a classic counterpoint to that focus on 'apprenticeship' as a central characteristic of Lave and Wenger's (1991) original formulation of the construct of community of practice.

D, a nurse educator in aged care, addresses the consequences of these educational changes and the empowering effects she sees they have had on the profession, the roles and practices of members in the multidisciplinary team, and, crucially, the impact they have had on patient care:

> The big change has been a political one and refers to the change in nurse education – from a hospital-based training and apprenticeship system to education in the tertiary sector. This has had an empowering effect on nurses. Prior to these changes in education, doctors were regarded as God. With the changes, doctors are now part of the team. There is more equality and there is meaningful dialogue over patient care. (Nurse educator, aged care)

'Joint enterprise' and 'mutuality of goal'

These changes to the institutional and social order within nursing, especially the advent of the multidisciplinary team, foregrounds the importance of taking a diachronic perspective on the construct of community of practice. We have seen earlier in this chapter how *time* plays a central role in accounting for the construct. How in terms of time and time change are the defining concepts of 'joint enterprise' and 'mutuality of goal' then to be appraised? How can we ensure that given the changes over time to the practices of nursing, agreement can be reached and maintained in relation to the concept of the 'shared repertoire of joint resources for negotiating meaning'?

A number of participants highlighted different approaches to nursing care over time. Such changes are undoubtedly in part related to societal changes, to improved standards of living, and to rapidly changing demographic patterns, which in turn impact on patterns of disease. In the words of more than one participant: 'they go home quicker and sicker' – a reference made explicitly by one interviewee to the demands consequently placed on the family and also on community services. Another referred to the demands placed on the ward nurses, in particular, who not only had to care for sicker patients, but also had to cope with more technical equipment, which in turn took up more time, leaving less time to talk with patients.

Such observations were supported by the participant who said:

> Patients no longer come into hospital for ten days when they give birth. Sometimes they go home the next day, frequently within three days. Conditions which once required major surgery and/or lengthy stays now require only day surgery. One also often hears that 'people are being discharged quicker and sicker'... this puts a burden on community care. In this sense there have been some fundamental changes in community nursing... other changes relate to the high tech nature of some treatments. Are we seeing nurses who must communicate with machines rather than/as well as with people? (Nurse academic)

Participants also speak of the changes in attitudes to authority on the part of both nurses and patients. Another nurse academic, C (trained in the 1960s) talks here about the effects on nurse preparation programmes in an apprenticeship system. Her response, when compared with that of the nurse academic (J) cited above, is a reminder of the time trajectory through which the profession itself has travelled:

> What we learned really was how the hospital ran its wards. The language was very medical. We followed the orders given by the sister and she got her orders from the doctor... The language was medical language... We didn't talk to doctors. Only the Sister talked to the doctor. We were taught that doctors were addressed as 'sir' and we stood with our hands behind our backs when we talked to them... we couldn't have relationships with doctors or porters. There was a hierarchy of behaviours. We could joke with a porter, and an Honorary could joke with a nurse but not vice versa... We

> had to keep our distance from patients. We had to be objective and impersonal. We were there for a reason. We could be kindly but not involved. We couldn't show emotion. We had to leave our personal life at the front door. We couldn't call patients by their given names. (C, nurse academic)

The nursing practices which accompanied such training were less subject to the availability of financial resources than they are now, as is highlighted here by J, an ICU nurse:

> Money never seemed to be a problem. We never thought about budgets – 'the hospital' always paid. It was all low-tech. There were no CAT scans then. But everything was also more rigid... We came on duty early and left late.

There was an expectation also that work that was not finished by the end of a shift would not be left for others. While financial resources appeared to be available, there is a hint that these were not necessarily translated into human resources. There was a concern that the patient should experience continuity of care and a concern that colleagues would not be overburdened. Goals which had been mutually set were mutually achieved through nurses giving self-sacrificially of their time. The concept of teamwork, even across shifts, was obviously present but unspoken, and not explicitly identified.

The ICU nurse, J, talked further about the changes which have occurred since her earlier nursing days – changes which she welcomed and embraced: advances in technology; availability of increased financial resources; enhanced autonomy for nurses; awareness of shifts in professional role and in power distribution, to the point where nurses handle situations which were once the domain of doctors.

> Technology is great and in ICU we enjoy a one-to-one relationship with patients. There are now more trained staff and we work more cohesively. Communication is good between staff members, it even spills out into off-duty activities. We go out for meals together, and we have interest groups. And that helps us understand people better, we know the people we work with as people (not just nurses) and that spills over into our relationships with patients and relatives. We appreciate that they have lives not defined by illness. We have family conferences – the doctor is the leader, but that's alright because he has an overall view and he has more authority. But nurses are now more autonomous. They say more. Patients and relatives ask more

> questions of nurses now and they recognize their experience and expertise. (J, ICU nurse)

A parallel experience is recorded by a participant working in a cardiology unit:

> I remember calling doctors for lots of things in the past that I now handle. This might be different in our area because we have a fair amount of ability to treat medical events because we have a range of standing orders for patients. Also because nurses can now refer to paramedical services such as social workers, physio and the like – this also means that we ask more pointed questions to assess patients about such need. (Cardiology unit nurse)

Not all such changes in nursing practices were regarded positively, illustrating the point we made earlier in relation to contested ideologies and practices within complex communities of practice. As one participant remarked:

> The aseptic technique of dressings I believe was much better then than now. I have always felt it is harder to manipulate plastic forceps than metal ones. To me there is an art in doing a dressing . . . we were taught strict barrier nursing techniques which ensured the patient as well as the nurses and other patients . . . the hospitals are dirtier today than when I trained and I think there is more infection than before . . . I believe there is an art in cleaning the wards. You not only had cleaning staff who did a proper job but the nursing staff ensured that trolleys, resusc trolleys etc were cleaned properly . . . Nurses used to give out the meals to patients and were able to ensure that patients were fed properly as well as drinking properly. Now kitchen staff dump the meals on the bed trolley and leave them there. I have seen elderly patients miss out on a meal because the nurse did not get around to seeing the patient and it was taken away again by the kitchen staff. No accountability and where does it leave the patient. I feel the pride and love have gone. Gently caring and feeding a patient increases the patient's ability to heal himself.

Exploring contested positions is important in weighing up mutuality within a community of practice. Views need to be triangulated, and deeper causes for apparent discontinuities explored. (See Wigens, 1997 for a discussion concerning contested positions on management in surgical nursing.) Some are the consequences of shift of role and status over time of participants in the community. Such an example is the current emphasis on research and evidence-based practice. The need for such fundamental change in practice is highlighted by a nurse academic:

> As a midwife I faced a situation where I felt that we had an unacceptably high rate of infections in the ward. We all had our own ideas about causative factors, but at the same time none of us had the skills to begin investigating in a methodical and scientific manner... we were the products of training. We weren't educated. (Nurse academic)

Now students and postgraduate nurses are exposed to and influenced by the 'hard' sciences, by epidemiological studies, and by work in social sciences more broadly. They are trained in research methods. There exists numerous high quality journals such as *The Journal of Nursing Research,* which encourage the use of many and varied research paradigms and provide a platform for the publication of nursing research. Increasingly too, textbooks are authored by nurses. No longer are the textbooks written by doctors for nurses (for example Pilley, 1884; Sears, 1958). There is an acknowledgement that the medical and nursing professions are related but different. Neither group can work in isolation – nurses are not doctors' handmaidens, nor junior doctors, but professionals in their own right. Such independent professionalism would seem to reinforce a key concept within the construct of community of practice, albeit now much more complex, multidisciplinary and contested in nature.

Impact of change on nursing discourses

If negotiation of meaning is a central concept in the construct of community of practice, then, as we have indicated earlier, the description, interpretation and explanation of language and discourse in key domains and sites within that community have to be identified as central practices for the researcher/analyst. We focus here briefly on two such areas of discourse: managing interdiscursivity within a complex community of practice, and topic selection in an expanded repertoire of nursing communication.

Those socio-institutional changes addressed by the participants in the narratives so far in this chapter have undoubtedly impacted upon the discourses of both health professionals and patients. (For one example from the context of a hospital emergency department, see Heslop, 1998.) Such changes were the theme of a seminar discussion some years ago among a group of nurse academics addressing the question: 'What is a nurse?' In the manner suggested by the definitions of goal and purpose associated with the construct of community of practice, participants looked at what they as nurses were expected to do – the functions that they had to undertake in their clinical role. They identified the functions (*inter alia*) of *healer/carer, advocate, counsellor, educator, researcher, manager, technician*. No doubt there are many more functions that might have been identified, but their range and diversity, and their frequent overlapping and associated practices, not only further complexifies the construct of community of practice, but suggests that the associated interdiscursivity linked to such interdisciplinarity makes the analysis of such hybrid discourse a key methodology for exploring the construct itself. The discourse of the nurse as healer/carer is also the discourse of the nurse as counsellor or as educator, as by the same token are the discourses of the nurse as manager and as researcher.

Figure 12.2 displays this interdiscursivity, where the functions are not seen as occupying closed spaces, but spaces which are open and which can connect with any other space.

As the nurse academic, C, suggests earlier when talking about attitudes which existed at the time of her training, what were once held to be 'impermissible' topics of nurse–patient talk have now become permissible if not common. This has become a liberating experience for some nurses who feel that they can now legitimately deploy more fully their knowledge and experience acquired through years of clinical practice, reading and research. One participant, working in cardiology and engaged in nursing research, discussed this issue and the effects it has had on her current practice. Her narrative is of interest not just for how it marks the passage of time in nursing, but also in relation to our

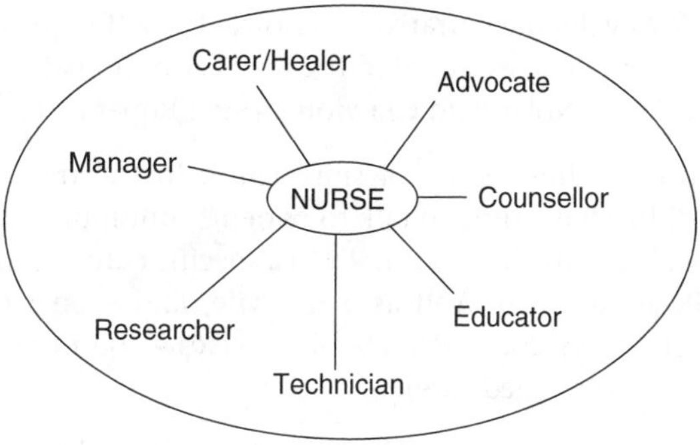

Figure 12.2 The different roles in nursing (from Candlin, 1992)

more theoretical interest: the ways in which language has been defined within the construct of community of practice. Note how she refers to both the strategic use of discourse in relation to medical issues at hand, as well as the need to accommodate (linguistically and interpersonally) patients from varied social and cultural backgrounds, and from different age groups:

> Nurses now talk to patients about their medical treatment, past and future, and answer a lot of questions doctors used to handle. Nurses' assessments seem a lot more involved. I think I ask more questions about medical symptoms to assess patients about such needs. Interestingly I don't know if it's the same way doctors do. By that I mean I think we approach this in a more casual/informal way conversationally and perhaps the patients see it as chat.... As I move from bed to bed at times I feel a bit like an actor. I'm aware that my language and some actions change as I moved from the 75 year old doctor's mother to the tribal Aboriginal from around Alice to a farmer to a... I've never had a problem with that although in the article below [referring to Aranda and Street, 1999] it seems that some nurses have. In fact I quite enjoy being 'different people'. It's part of my attraction to patient care, I think. My life has always been filled with a wide range of people from different backgrounds and classes. I enjoy it. How can you relate to others if you are always the 'formal nurse'? Whatever that is. (Cardiology unit nurse)

Changes over time within particular communities of practice affect not only modes of interaction and professional stance, but, as we note, also changes in the permissibilities of theme and discourse topic which professional practitioners can introduce – as here in therapeutic communication in nursing. The nurse cited below who works in the aged care sector provides a valuable narrative, acknowledging the spiritual dimension of the individual as essential in the delivery of holistic nursing care (see Candlin, 1996; Nolan and Crawford, 1997; Roper *et al.*, 1996):

> We can now address issues of spirituality. In the training system, students didn't have time to talk to patients, not much of one's own life entered into care. In 1983 an RN in a specific cultural environment could talk about faith. And as a midwife, and even working in a secular system, we could talk about miracles – the miracle of birth. (Nurse educator in aged care)

However welcome this change may be by this nurse educator, it represents yet another challenge to that mutuality of experience seen as characteristic of the construct of community of practice. (Makoni and Grainger's (2002) work on what they refer to as 'comparative geronto-linguistics' is also informative here.) Where lies the mutuality among nurses who may not share or be quite unfamiliar with the many beliefs and practices present in a multicultural and pluralistic society? What challenges does this present to the inner resources and discursive expertise of the nurse (see Candlin, 1995)?

While the potential for considerable demands on the professional resources of the nurse is ever present in all areas of nursing, the reality is that the spiritual and emotional needs of patients are likely to be greater within the professional space occupied by aged care and palliative care nursing. Here patients meet nurses as their time trajectory through life approaches its final moment. It is at the meeting of the trajectories of nurse and patient within this space that demands become acute. Not only are the physical needs of the patient more complex within situations of physiological multi-system breakdown, but so patients' social and emotional needs become more demanding as they seek 'to put one's house in order', and closure and resolution are sought for personal and family issues which may be complex and demanding. It is in such critical moments that the construct of community of practice is under greatest stress and requires further differentiation and further flexibility. Mutuality of experience and sharedness of goals among members cannot be equally counted upon and may need to be proactively constructed at all stages and moments of their professional practice, and in respect of all encounters with which they are professionally engaged.

Some implications for practice

The narrative data that we have adduced here demonstrate that among professional and practising nurses there are varied perceptions of the health care system and the delivery of health care. There is every indication that the construct of a community of practice of nursing, however useful as a point of focus for discussion and research, cannot be regarded as a homogeneous entity. Indeed, to cite one index, the spaces occupied by different specialties within nursing impose demands which have resulted in unequal distribution of variable resources. One such example is the imbalance of resource allocation often claimed between high technology areas such as hospital-based clinical nursing, in comparison with more low technology areas, such as preventive health/health promotion and aged care.

But discussions of membership and 'belonging' go further than inequalities in resource allocation. Further questions need to be raised, all of which stem from the discussion of the construct of community of practice with which we began this chapter. One of these relates to the increasing specialization within the profession, such that nurses from one specialization find that they have little in common with colleagues working in a different specialization, and have more in common with the work-located members of a multidisciplinary team – whether such a team is formally constructed within the institution, or more informally developed by relationship building with other health professionals in the specialty area. If this were the case, then not only does it raise issues of conflicting loyalties inimical to the cooperative nature of a community, but challenges the very notion of the community of practice consisting of members of a profession. It would imply that a community of practice is bound together not by people (i.e. by professional membership) but by the institution (i.e. the medical specialty).

One solution would be to reinforce Scollon's (1998) emphasis on multiple memberships of communities of practice – initiated originally by Wenger. It may be, further, that the very concept of membership needs to be replaced by one of subscription. Not meaning by this some form of payment, but rather a highly dynamic practice of subscribing to a range of communities, while retaining a personal centre – albeit one accommodating multiple and changing identities. When this idea of multiple membership (subscription) was put to a person working within a multidisciplinary team she at first disagreed but on further thoughtful discussion the notion of belonging to more than a single community of practice was proposed. This was not considered to be problematic, since multiplicity did not carry with it for her either the connotation of divided loyalty or conflict of interest.

From our narrative data it would appear that given professional training and expertise, and enabled by enhanced interpersonal communication skills, practitioners can manage this multiplicity through negotiation and consensus building. In the case of nursing it may be that multiple memberships or subscriptions can be managed so as to permit participation both within a speciality and in a multidisciplinary community. This is so, we feel, because the communities are bound, individually and together, not by the institutions of medicine, nursing, or by bureaucracy, but by altruistic caring, and the desire to meet human needs. This meeting of need is mediated by the compassionate caring of health professionals and by developing and engaging in a high level of discourse competence. Given this, joint resources can be deployed to negotiate mutualities of meaning in situations which may initially be difficult to understand or indeed to accept. This might breach the apparent defining conditions of the construct of community of practice. Holmes and Meyerhoff's (1999) overarching sense of an enabling 'belonging', facilitating such negotiation, takes on a greater significance in such moments, not only as a definer of membership but as a challenge for would-be members, and their professional educators, to achieve.

Note

1 Ethics clearance was obtained from the academic institution in which we are based (Macquarie University, Sydney, Australia).

References

Aranda, S. K. and Street, A. F. (1999) 'Being Authentic and being a Chameleon: Nurse–Patient Interaction Revisited', *Nursing Inquiry*, 6(2), pp. 75–82.

Barton, D. and Tusting, K. (eds) (2005) *Beyond Communities of Practice: Language, Power and Social Context* (Cambridge: Cambridge University Press).

Candlin, C. N. (2002) *The Cardiff Lecture, 2000; New Discourses of the Clinic: Rediscovering the Patient in Healthcare* (March) (Cardiff: Cardiff University). Available on http://www.cf.ac.uk/encap/hcrc/publications.

Candlin, C. N. and Candlin, S. (2003) 'Healthcare Communication: a Problematic Site for Applied Linguistics Research?', *Annual Review of Applied Linguistics*, 23, pp. 134–54.

Candlin, S. (1992) 'Communication for Nurses: Implications for Nurse Education', *Nurse Education Today*, 12, pp. 445–51.

Candlin, S. (1995) 'Transcultural Issues in Nurse Patient Communication', *Geriaction*, 13(7), pp. 28–33.

Candlin, S. (1996) 'Spirituality in Nursing Practice: From Chaos to Transcendence', *Geriaction*, 14(4), pp. 8–13.

Candlin, S. (1997) 'Towards Excellence in Nursing: an Analysis of the Discourse of Nurses and Patients in the Context of Health Assessment', doctoral dissertation (Department of Linguistics, University of Lancaster, UK).

Candlin, S. (2000) 'New Dynamics in the Nurse–Patient Relationship?', in S. Sarangi and M. Coulthard (eds) *Discourse and Social Life*, pp. 230–45 (London: Longman).

Chouliaraki, L. and Fairclough, N. L. (1999) *Discourse in Late Modernity: Rethinking Critical Discourse Analysis* (Edinburgh: Edinburgh University Press).

Corder, S. and Meyerhoff, M. (in press) 'Communities of Practice in the Analysis of Intercultural Communication', in H. Kotthoff and H. Spencer-Oatey (eds) *Handbook of Applied Linguistics:* Vol. 7, *Intercultural Communication* (Berlin: Mouton de Gruyter).

Crawford, P., Carr, J., Knight, A., Chambers, K. and Nolan, P. (2001) 'The Value of Community Health Nurses based in Primary Care Teams: "Switching the Light on in a Cellar"', *Journal of Psychiatric and Mental Health Nursing*, 8 (3), pp. 213–330.

Eckert, P. and McConnell-Ginet, S. (1992) 'Think Practically and Look Locally: Language and Gender as Community-based Practice', *Annual Review of Anthropology*, 21, pp. 461–90.

Fairclough, N. L. (1992) *Discourse and Social Change* (Cambridge: Polity Press).

Fenwick, J., Barclay, L. and Schmied, V. (2001) ' "Chatting": an Important Tool in Facilitating Mothering in Neonatal Nurseries', *Journal of Advanced Nursing*, 33(5), pp. 589–93.

Gee, J., Hull, P. and Lankshear, C. (1996) *The New Work Order: Behind the Language of the New Capitalism* (Sydney: Allen and Unwin).

Hak, T. (1999) ' "Text" and "Con-text": Talk Bias in Studies of Healthcare Work', in S. Sarangi and C. Roberts (eds) *Talk, Work and Institutional Order: Discourse in Medical, Mediation and Management Settings*, pp. 427–52 (Berlin: Mouton de Gruyter).

Herdman, E. A. (1992) 'The Deskilling of Registered Nurses: the Social Transformation of Nursing Work in a New South Wales Hospital, 1970–1990', doctoral dissertation (University of Wollongong, Australia).

Herdman, E. A. (2000) 'Challenging the Discourses of Nursing Ageism', *International Journal of Nursing Studies*, 39(1), pp. 105–14.

Heslop, L. (1998) 'A Discursive Exploration of Nursing Work in the Hospital Emergency Setting', *Nursing Inquiry*, 5(2), pp. 87–95.

Holmes, J. and Meyerhoff, M. (1999) 'The Community of Practice: Theories and Methodologies in Language and Gender Research', *Language in Society*, 28(2), pp. 173–85.

Holmes, J. and Stubbe, M. (2003) *Power and Politeness in the Workplace* (London: Longman).

Iedema, R. and Scheeres, H. (2003) 'From Doing Work to Talking Work: Renegotiating Knowing, Doing and Identity', *Applied Linguistics*, 24(3), pp. 316–37.

Lave, J. and Wenger, E. (1991) *Situated Learning: Legitimate Peripheral Participation* (Cambridge: Cambridge University Press).

McDonald, C. and McIntyre, M. (2001) 'Reinstating the Marginalized Body in Nursing Science: Epistemological Privilege and the Lived Life', *Nursing Philosophy*, 2(2), pp. 234–39.

Makoni, S. and Grainger, K. (2002) 'Comparative Gerontolinguistics: Characterising Discourses in Caring Institutions in South Africa and the United Kingdom', *Journal of Social Issues*, 58(4), pp. 805–24.

Nolan, P. and Crawford, P. (1997) 'Towards a Rhetoric of Spirituality in Mental Health Care', *Journal of Advanced Nursing*, 26(2), pp. 289–94.

Pilley, J. J. (1884). *Elementary Physiology: an Introduction to the Study of Hygiene* (London: Geo. Gill and Son).

Roper, N., Logan, W. W., and Tierney, A. J. (1996) *The Elements of Nursing: a Model of Nursing based on a Model of Living* (4th edn) (New York and Edinburgh: Churchill Livingstone).

Sarangi, S. and Candlin, C. N. (2001) ' "Motivational Relevancies": Some Methodological Reflections on Sociolinguistic Practice', in N. Coupland, S. Sarangi and C. N. Candlin (eds) *Sociolinguistics and Social Theory*, pp. 350–88 (London: Longman).

Sarangi, S. and Roberts, C. (1999) *Talk, Work and Institutional Order: Discourse in Medical, Mediation and Management Settings* (Berlin: Mouton de Gruyter).

Scollon, R. (1998) *Mediated Discourse as Social Interaction: a Study of News Discourse* (London: Longman).

Sears, W. G. (1958) *Anatomy and Physiology for Nurses* (3rd edn) (London: Edward Arnold Ltd).

Taylor, S. White, B. and Muncer, S. (1999) 'Nurses' Cognitive Structural Models of Work-based Stress', *Journal of Advanced Nursing*, 29(4), pp. 974–83.

Tusting, K. (2005) 'Language and Power in Communities of Practice', in D. Barton and K. Tusting (eds) *Beyond Communities of Practice: Language, Power and Social Context*, pp. 36–54 (Cambridge: Cambridge University Press).

Wenger, E. (1998) *Communities of Practice: Learning, Meaning, and Identity* (Cambridge: Cambridge University Press).

Wenger, E. (2004a) 'Knowledge Management is a Doughnut: Shaping Your Knowledge Strategy with Communities of Practice', *Ivey Business Journal* (January). Available at http://www.iveybusinessjournal.com.

Wenger. E. (2004b) 'Learning for the Small Planet: a Research Agenda'. Available at http://www.ewenger.com/research.

Wenger, E. and Snyder, W. (2000) 'Communities of Practice: the Organizational Frontier', *Harvard Business Review*, January–February, pp. 139–45.

Wenger, E., McDermott, R. and Snyder, W. (2002) *Cultivating Communities of Practice: a Guide to Managing Knowledge* (Cambridge, Mass.: Harvard Business School Press).

Wigens, L. (1997) 'The Conflict between "New Nursing" and "Scientific Management" as Perceived by Surgical Nurses', *Journal of Advanced Nursing*, 25(6), pp. 1116–22.

Index